THE EDGE OF WORDS

THE EDGE OF WORDS

God and the Habits of Language

Rowan Williams

B L O O M S B U R Y
LONDON • NEW DELHI • NEW YORK • SYDNEY

First published in Great Britain 2014

Copyright © Rowan Williams, 2014

The moral right of the author has been asserted

A Continuum book

Bloomsbury Publishing Plc
50 Bedford Square
London WC1B 3DP

www.bloomsbury.com

Bloomsbury is a registered trademark of Bloomsbury Publishing Plc

Bloomsbury Publishing, London, New Delhi, New York and Sydney

A CIP record for this book is available from the British Library.

ISBN 978-1-4729-1043-1

10 9 8 7 6 5 4 3 2 1

Typeset by Fakenham Prepress Solutions, Fakenham, Norfolk NR21 8NN
Printed and bound in Great Britain by CPI Group (UK) Ltd, Croydon CR0 4YY

MIX
Paper from
responsible sources
FSC® C020471

CONTENTS

PREFACE

M y first duty is to acknowledge with enormous gratitude the generous invitation from the electors of Lord Gifford's foundation to deliver a series of Gifford Lectures in the University of Edinburgh in November 2013. This provided a necessary stimulus to begin gathering together an assortment of questions and reflections jotted down over a number of years and to give them something of a shape. Some of the ideas outlined here have their remote origins in another series of lectures given at Edinburgh, the Gunning Lectures of 1993, which I never had an opportunity of revising for publication. In retrospect, this was a blessing: I have been able to revisit those earlier explorations with the benefit of longer consideration and in the light of more recent published discussion of some of their themes, and my judgement on several issues has changed a good deal. Some of the ideas here, especially those in Chapter 5, have had an airing in one or two academic contexts, notably the D Society in Cambridge, where in the autumn of 2010, at the kind invitation of Professor Sarah Coakley, I engaged in a discussion with Professor Simon Blackburn on the philosophy of language; my thanks to both of them for the conversation on that occasion and others from which I have profited. More recently, in the spring of 2013, the members of Professor David Ford's graduate seminar in Cambridge engaged in a spirited and acute discussion of a preliminary text of the lectures; their comments and suggestions were of the greatest help in clarifying and extending the arguments.

The lectures were delivered over a two-week period, during which my Edinburgh colleagues were unstintingly warm in their hospitality and generous with their responses; I am deeply grateful to all of them, from the Vice-Chancellor through to the students who asked questions in both formal and informal settings, and also to Lynn Hyams for looking after the practical arrangements. Particular thanks to Dr David Grumett, who organized a session in which six graduate students presented responses to the lectures which have done a good deal to sharpen and improve what is here. I'm grateful to Russell Almon, Andrew Blaski, Evan Graber, Sangduck Kim, David Robinson and J. T. Turner for their insights on that occasion.

Ongoing exchanges with numerous friends have enriched the material presented in all sorts of ways. Oliver Davies, Stanley Hauerwas, Douglas Hedley, Fergus Kerr, Richard Sennett, George Steiner and Graham Ward will recognize themes we have talked around in various contexts; and various members of the Trialogue Conference have, over more than a decade, enormously enriched my thinking about language and interpretation. I continue to be stretched and stimulated by John Milbank, whose penetrating review of an earlier book of mine has prompted much fresh thought. Catherine Pickstock's theological reflections on language have long been a major gift to my own thinking. Philip Shepherd's bold meditations on 'recovering our senses' helped to consolidate some of the thoughts in Chapter 4, and his friendly encouragement has meant a great deal. To Andrew Shanks I owe a very great debt for very many things, including his outstanding and continuing re-evaluation of Hegel; but not least among them is an introduction to the work of Iain McGilchrist, whose impact on this book will be very clear. Recent interdisciplinary colloquia in Cambridge, on the body and on the theological significance of the philosophy of Merleau-Ponty, have provided a welcome opportunity further to test out some of the material contained in this book, and the invitation to deliver the second Edward Schillbeeckx Memorial Lecture at the University of Nijmegen in December 2013 allowed me to re-work and (I hope) clarify some of the argument of the first chapter. And examining a Dublin PhD thesis by Anne Thurston while finalizing the text of the lectures proved a deeply enriching experience, both confirming and extending a number of points; my thanks to her for her insights.

Chapter 6 in particular owes more than I can say to what I have learned over many years from Ruth Furneaux, Sara Maitland and Martha Reeves.

The late John Crook gave me, in instruction and example, such understanding as I have of the use of the koan in meditation.

To my colleagues in Cambridge, especially at Magdalene College, my thanks for all their friendship and support. Later in the book, I note – echoing the late and lamented Dewi Phillips – that saying 'I can't tell you how grateful I am' is precisely the way we tell someone how grateful we are; and that is what, as always, I want to say to Jane and the family.

Rowan Williams
Cambridge, Feast of the Epiphany, 2014

INTRODUCTION

Does the way we talk as human beings tell us anything about God? This may sound a slightly odd question: on the whole, when Christian philosophers and theologians have tried to understand what if anything the world tells us about God, they have concentrated on what you might call formal features of the universe, ideas about cause and order and so on. But perhaps the very way we speak and think can be heard as raising a question about the kind of universe this is, and thus about where and how language about God comes in.

The lectures on which this book is based arise from a conviction that thinking about how we talk does indeed raise questions like that. They assume that the fact of language is a good deal more puzzling than we usually recognize, and the bulk of this book deals with the different areas in which we ought to be puzzled. If, for example, it is true that language is not *just* like other physical processes, it can't be thought about *just* in terms of stimulus and response, material causes and material results. And then again, it is one of the features of our language that what is said can always be answered; despite the way we sometimes use the phrase, there really are no 'last words' in discussions or arguments. Even when we come to a fixed agreement about some disputed question – a problem in physics, say, or a disputed date in history – that is simply the platform on which more, and more interesting, questions can be pursued. In the realm of creative art, above all, there are no 'conclusions', only points at which to pause in a continuing and developing practice. Yet language *is* unmistakeably a material process, something that bodies do; so thinking harder about the oddities of language may help us see new things about bodies, indeed about 'matter' in general; it may open up for us some thoughts about how the material world carries or embodies messages, how matter and meaning do not necessarily belong in different universes. And the sheer diversity of the ways in which meaning is embodied and communicated should leave us with some puzzles over the way in which speech generates such a huge amount of apparently superfluous untidiness and eccentricity. Instead of moving calmly towards a maximally clear and economical depiction of the environment, our language produces wild and strange symbolisms, formal and ritual ways of talking (not just in religion), a passion for exploring new perspectives through metaphor and so on. Unsurprisingly, it also learns how to use gaps in its flow, moments either of frustration or of overwhelmingly full significance, moments when we are brought to silence, as part of its continuing search for an adequate response to what it is 'given', the search for ways of 'making sense'.

Making sense involves sharing and exploring the significance of perceptions, a capacity to question our clarity or truthfulness in the light of communications from others or renewed engagement with what's in front of us; to make mistakes and to deal satisfactorily with them; even to suspend judgement at certain points because we are aware of not having the conceptual or linguistic equipment to enable decisions. It is a good deal more than finding a simple depiction of 'what's out there'. And the not-so-simple aspects of making sense are, I want to suggest, where we might begin to see some of the ways in which talking about God is not a marginal eccentricity in human language but something congruent with the more familiar and less noticed oddities of how we speak. We might also begin to see how claims to be speaking truthfully about God can still be made even if we take it for granted that we cannot produce definitions of God or detailed descriptions of 'what it is like to be divine'.

Our language claims, implicitly and explicitly, to present to us the patterns and rhythms of our environment – including the 'inner environment' of our own history or psychology – in a new form. It claims to *represent*. In the pages that follow, I shall be using the word 'representation' a good deal. I'm conscious of the wide variety of ways in which it can be and has been deployed by philosophers, but my own use of it is meant to draw attention to the interesting fact that we can claim to be speaking truthfully about many aspects of our environment without actually trying on every occasion to *reproduce* or *imitate* it. To say that a form of words or images 'represents' reality is to leave ourselves free to recognize that language may be truthful even when it is not descriptive in the strict sense.

And if this is an accurate account of how we talk, we can say a little more about what's going on in and around our speaking. We speak in the trust that what we say 'answers' to something more than what we find familiar or convenient. But we also assume that what it is answerable *to* is going to need a very wide range of linguistic reserves to be appropriately or defensibly identified in what we say. If a statement may be truthful even when it doesn't consist simply of a catalogue of agreed and observable components of what we experience, then this suggests not only that we live in a world of intelligible communication but that this communication works quite diversely. It is as if the 'patterns and rhythms' of the environment constituted a shape or set of shapes which could reappear in more than one specific embodiment; as if there were indeed a distinction of the kind classical and mediaeval philosophy expressed as the tension between form and matter. If such a distinction can be prised away from the crude dualism with which it is so often thought to be allied (pure structure versus mindless stuff), we may get a little further forward. In a nutshell, what we need is a metaphysics that thinks of matter itself as invariably and necessarily communicative – not as a sheer passivity moulded by our minds into intelligible structure. Matter itself becomes a specific 'situation' of intelligible form, no more and no less; and the mythology of a 'naturally' meaningless or random materiality, a sort of residue of impenetrable physical stuff, becomes impossible to sustain.

What I am proposing in this study is that the more we reflect on speech and its claims to represent an environment – in the widest sense of the word 'represent' – the more our universe looks like a network of communication. Intelligence is not an afterthought; that a material evolutionary process should eventually come up with a material organism which sees and imagines itself, and makes certain material noises and gestures in the confidence that it is actively modifying its environment by sharing intelligible patterns with other organisms, suggests that the material process in question (and thus the entire material environment that generates it) is intrinsically capable of producing the actions we call understanding. This is a universe in which the exchange of 'information' is basic; so much any serious scientist has to begin with. But thinking about language pushes us a bit further. This is a universe in which this metaphor (for such it is) of 'information' exchange has more implications than we initially might think; a universe in which something like conscious relation is the focus towards which material process moves – in which conscious relation is what is 'basic', in a slightly different sense. The recognition that we may be telling the truth about our world through unusual habits of speech – metaphors, gestures, fictions, silences – is a recognition of the diversity of ways in which information comes to us and is absorbed and embodied afresh. But to see this is also to see how we might formulate the idea of an abundant or 'excessive' reality engulfing our mental activities so that our language does strange things under its pressure; and this is where connections with theology most strongly suggest themselves.

These are broadly sketched proposals and will need filling out in what follows. They are also dependent on what I acknowledge to be an eclectic philosophical hinterland. But they are obviously congruent with some of the structures and models tentatively offered by certain scientists of the brain and the neural system and by some philosophers of language. I hope that this eclecticism will not divert attention from the relative simplicity of the central question: does the way we speak tell us anything about the universe we are in? And if it does suggest that this universe is (to borrow the annoying phrase beloved of continental philosophers) 'always already' language-saturated and language-bound, if it suggests that active communication and relation are the fundamental agency of things, does this in turn suggest anything about what it is that provides both context and support for every event or entity in the universe? A philosophical or phenomenological reflection can do little more than raise – but raise insistently – the question; a religious philosopher will want to add that developing these insights brings us to a point where claims about the action and 'character' of what believers call God at least appear to belong in the same world of discussion as our general investigations of consciousness and speech. Speaking about the God of traditional religious belief – routinely described as intelligent, loving, free to communicate with creation – is not, in this perspective, an incomprehensible aberration in intellectual life, a colossal misapplication of terms, but recognizably related to these issues about what it is to be a linguistic being in a universe whose currency is intelligence and intelligibility.

So this book will not be attempting to offer that unlikely product, a new and knockdown 'argument for the existence of God'. But it will be seeking to place our talk about God in the context of what we think we are doing when we communicate at all, when we aim to 'represent' our environment, when we press our words and images to breaking point in the strange conviction that we shall end up seeing and understanding more as a result. If this book persuades some readers to be more puzzled than before over the ways we use language, it will have done part of its work; if it persuades them to listen afresh to how and where the language of faith in a communicating God comes in to our habitual speaking, it will have done what I most hope for.

My title indicates something of this. As will be clear, I hope to bring into focus some of the frontier territories where our speech shows itself to be a wilder and odder thing than we usually notice (whether we are doing philosophy or just talking). But to recognize this puts various sorts of imaginative and intellectual challenges before us: there is an 'edge' to the question, and it is that edge also that I hope may come into view in these pages.

1

A FUTURE FOR 'NATURAL THEOLOGY'?

'Natural theology' once meant the kind of discourse about God that you could develop without appealing to the unreliable authority of claimed revelation; it was, in intention, a democratizing move, a demystifying move. But it has had implications that still leave a certain sense of anxiety for theologians of another kind; and prominent among these is a deep ambivalence about the effect of a 'natural theology' on the very idea of a God who acts. If we bypass revelation, we bracket any notion that God actively interrupts our perceptions or thought processes, that God 'gives' the divine self to be known in any very direct way. We may conclude at the end of the argument that there is an all-pervasive divine presence in things, or else perhaps we may develop intuitions about some reality reflected in that uniquely problematic not-quite-thing that is human subjectivity. A God discovered in that kind of way is a God who *waits* to be discovered; who can perhaps be spoken of figuratively in devotional language as 'patient', 'self-abnegating', even in some sense powerless, if you want to use terms that have some sort of personally evocative resonance. But for the purposes of *this* kind of discourse, philosophical discourse, this is a God who has to be thought of as essentially silent, passively there to be uncovered by our enquiries.

Perhaps we might arrive at a way of speaking about God at the end of the argument; perhaps the evidences of God's character that have emerged in reflection on the presence that we have attempted to track will allow us scope to work out what are the 'Relations which men and the whole universe bear to Him', to quote the words of Lord Gifford's bequest.[1] But in such a framework we are basically moving from consideration of what is more clear to what is less clear, from the contemplation of inner climate and outer environment (moral laws and starry heavens) to reverent supposition, to what we might call evocation as opposed to invocation. Language about God comes to look like a more or less plausible or defensible supplement to some more standard kind of discourse, summoned up with due caution and reserve; a supplement that both picks up a scatter of unresolved questions and lends a certain emotional colouring – 'reverence', perhaps – to our response to our environment: God as a background to the clearer and more brightly coloured world we routinely inhabit.

Now it has become something of a tradition for Gifford Lecturers periodically to kick over the traces and protest at this framework. From Karl Barth to Stanley Hauerwas, we have heard a succession of formidable assaults on a scheme that assumes the inadmissibility of revelation and the irrelevance of sacred narrative and community practice in exploring the roots of our talk about God. Hauerwas, a few years ago, began by explaining why he could not begin from a starting point that effectively ruled out the identification of the God being spoken about in these lectures with the Trinitarian God of Christian faith.[2] And I admit to sharing this unease. But when all this has been said, the story is not quite over for 'natural theology'; we are still left with a question which I believe to be not only interesting but vital for the health of talk about God. We might put it like this: the old-style longing to get behind authority and tradition and revelatory claims was in some degree an effort to find ways of speaking about God that were not vulnerable to *history* – to the contingencies of politics and power and social imagination that had shaped the doctrine of believing communities, but simply to counter

1   See Stanley Jaki, *Lord Gifford and His Lectures: A Centenary Retrospect* (Macon, GA: Mercer University Press, 1986), p. 73.
2   Stanley Hauerwas, *With the Grain of the Universe: The Church's Witness and Natural Theology* (London: SCM Press, 2002), pp. 15–17.

this with the insistence that we can *only* begin from tradition and community doesn't necessarily help. Indeed, it threatens to land us in exactly the same problem by suggesting, seductively, that we don't have to worry about tracing the history of this or that mode of speech, how and where people learn to speak like this – which is always a focal issue when we are trying fully to understand what is being said. Appealing to tradition and community without some reflection on history can be a way of avoiding uncomfortable critical questions about legitimate authority – just as appealing to timeless metaphysical argument can be a way of avoiding the specifics of human practice and habit. What I should like to examine here is whether there is a form of natural theology that is not about avoidance – so as to guard against the avoidance that unqualified rejection of natural theology can lure us into (a risk to which someone like Hauerwas is fully sensitive). There is indeed at the heart of all Christian theology, as Wittgenstein said about the Gospels,[3] a story with an imperative attached. But the question is, what makes us able to learn to recognize such an imperative, let alone respond to it? Hauerwas refers[4] to the seminal and condensed work of the Dominican theologian Cornelius Ernst in order to nudge us in the direction of that question. Ernst wrote that the point of Aquinas's 'proofs' of God's existence 'was to show how one might *go on* speaking of "God" in the ordinary world',[5] in the context of our ordinary ways of making sense of things. But this does not mean reducing the oddity of what we say about God, making God one of the things we make sense of. It is more to do with showing what it is like for 'everyday' speaking to be interpenetrated and made puzzling by other sorts of speech – discovering that 'ordinary' language is a lot less ordinary than we usually suppose, much more liable to rupture and strangeness (more on this in later chapters). We learn at least something by mapping the points where things become interestingly difficult, where the ordinary comes under pressure.

Wittgenstein was – famously – prompted to rethink his philosophy of language by the challenge to describe what was the 'logical form' of a

---

3 Ludwig Wittgenstein, *Culture and Value*, ed. G. H. von Wright in collaboration with Heikki Nyman, trans. Peter Winch (Oxford: Blackwell, 1980), pp. 31–2.

4 Hauerwas, op. cit., pp. 27 and 164.

5 Cornelius Ernst, *Multiple Echo: Explorations in Theology*, Fergus Kerr OP and Timothy Radcliffe OP (eds) (London: Darton, Longman and Todd, 1979), p. 74.

particular Italian gesture of abuse.[6] Analysing what was going on in such a
context required more than a view that treated propositions as picturing
the logical shape of a state of affairs: ordinary language, stripped to its
bare descriptive skeleton, turns out to be only a part of a far larger and
more variegated pattern of activity. In similar vein, the brilliant Australian
cartoonist, Michael Leunig, writes about how he learned the use of the
word 'God'. 'I have come to regard God', he writes, 'as a one-word poem –
probably a folk poem. I learnt it from my parents when I was a child, as they
wandered about the backyard or in the house. My father might say rather
despairingly "Where in God's name is the bloody hammer?" and my mother
might answer "God only knows".'[7] 'God' is, for a child like this, a 'useful
word', says Leunig, for a 'vague and mysterious' allusion to what profoundly
matters, as inescapable as 'the taste of honey, the shape of the moon'.[8] But
I don't believe – despite his word 'vague' – that Leunig is encouraging us
not to *think* about how we use the word: on the contrary, he is urging us to
notice, and think about, the fact that the way the word enters the everyday
is to do with what is not resolved or controlled. He goes on to say that the
way in which he was subsequently introduced to propositions about God
in a catechesis rather more formal than that available in the backyard made
little sense against the background of this initial 'folk poetry' learning. He
does not put it quite like this, but the implication is that the propositions,
as he learned them, reduced God to an (admittedly unusual) inhabitant of
the universe, whose acts and opinions and – usually adverse – judgements
could be predicted and who was endowed with a monopoly of sanction and
control. This is to portray God and God's dealings with the world as simply
another 'department' of description: here is an agent with these properties
and habits, to be added to the list of other agents with properties and habits.
God 'comes in' as an extra item in our routine description of what is the
case. Somehow, beginning purely and simply with narrative and tradition

6   Norman Malcolm, *Ludwig Wittgenstein: A Memoir* (Oxford: Oxford University Press, 1958), pp. 58–9.
7   Michael Leunig, *The Lot: In Words*, (Camberwell, VI: Penguin Group (Australia), 2008), p. 234.
8   Ibid., p. 235.

may risk obscuring what is distinctive in talking of God, the 'grammar' Leunig learns from his parents.

Ironically, the anti-revelationist rhetoric of Lord Gifford's natural theology on the one hand, with its aspirations for a rational clarity independent of churchly superstition, and the ambitious and detailed descriptions of a revealed God that so frustrated Michael Leunig on the other hand can become opposites that unite to frustrate an adequate account of such a grammar. The former is shy of saying anything about how God acts because we ought to be reticent about any contingently based claims to identify an extra agent in the universe. The latter tells us not to be shy because we can rightly have confidence about such an extra agent. And both equally sidestep the question of 'going on speaking of God' *if* it is true that speaking of God is characteristically or primitively something quite other than identifying another agent in the universe. As I hope we shall see later on, and as many recent writers have repeated,[9] caution about descriptions of God's action is not a back door for anti-realism, denying that words about God have any reference at all in anything like the usual sense. But if we are to defend that point, we need a mapping exercise that will clarify two things. First, we have to explore the sort of moments in our familiar perception and discourse where familiar description fails – not because we have identified a problem that for the time being we don't have the resources to solve, but because something is apparently demanded of us – in order to make an adequate linguistic response to our situation – which is not just another attempt to describe agencies negotiating with each other or combining to effect a specific outcome. It is not only that answers fail to come – we have to think again about the questions. Second, we need to explain why a response to this 'something demanded of us' is not properly understood as an *arbitrary* move, drawing us away from precision, labour or indeed truthfulness. As Cornelius Ernst suggests in the essay already quoted,[10] this may entail looking very critically at the usual way in which we

9   For a very intelligent discussion, see Andrew Moore, *Realism and Christian Faith: God, Grammar, and Meaning* (Cambridge: Cambridge University Press, 2003); also the essays in Colin Crowder (ed.), *God and Reality: Essays on Christian Non-Realism* (London: Mowbray, 1997), and Michael Scott, *Religious Language* (Basingstoke: Palgrave Macmillan, 2013), especially chapters 11–14.

10 Ernst, op. cit., pp. 73–5.

distinguish 'literal' and 'metaphorical' language: to think of language about God as 'metaphorical' is not to abandon truth claims nor to suggest that such language is the cosmetic elaboration of a simpler and more 'secular' literal truth. It is more like putting the question, 'What sort of truth can be told only by abandoning most of our norms of routine description?'

Ernst's approach is a (typically) complex one, but worth unpicking just a little further. Habitually, he says, we take certain ways of talking about 'God' as relatively unproblematic – as literal utterances, simple noun-and-verb references to things God has done, is doing and will do: the sort of utterance we meet in the Bible all the time. But, Ernst argues, what is going on in biblical speech is more complicated. There is an underlay of language taken for granted, a world in which people talk about 'God', but precisely this language is being disrupted and transformed because of certain events that give that word a new and difficult content. Here 'God' comes to work like a metaphor, in fact: a word whose territory we think we know is invited to play away from home in order to capture something that more familiar usage can't cope with. When Hebrew Scripture says that YHWH (the enigmatic and unpronounceable designation of Israel's Lord and Saviour) is God, *elohim*, or that YHWH *elohim* does or says this or that, there is a presupposition that we already know something of what *elohim* means. We are saying that the one we identify as the YHWH who does or says this or that is appropriately called *elohim*. An implicit grammar is at work: what the Hebrew texts are saying might be rendered as 'the agent in this situation – the agent we suppose to be at work if this situation is not just a matter of pure historical contingency, the agency, say, that calls the Hebrew people out of slavery – is an agent in whom we can see the contours of what we mean by "God"' – even if recognizing this stretches the application of the word.

Try approaching Thomas Aquinas's Five Ways with this in mind. Aquinas's argument can be read as saying something like this. When we start looking at or listening to the ways in which we make sense of our environment, there will be features in it that will not let us rest content with the unexamined continuation of the language we have got used to. What we live out in our 'ordinary' experience of the world appears under a certain kind of light as profoundly puzzling. The puzzles may be, as Aquinas enumerates them, to do with how we grasp the interconnectedness of the processes in the middle of and in virtue of which we exist; but Ernst is suggesting that, in an intellectual climate less sure of how to articulate that sort of puzzle, the key moments may be more like what we read about in the Bible – moments when we have to think through afresh what the ultimate and most radical possibilities of our humanity might be. If Aquinas can say that the interpretative context that holds together the entire realm of causality and dependence is what is generally meant by 'God', so, Ernst implies, the interpretative context that holds together the history of exodus and covenant, the record of liberation and committedly available forgiveness and renewal, is what is generally meant by *elohim*, however little we had thought so to start with.

What we mean by 'God' is in any case, says Ernst, specified less by a set of philosophical protocols than by a bundle of activities, linguistic and symbolic practices ('prayer, ritual, even swearing'; shades of Leunig) that characteristically interrupt or unsettle the course of 'ordinary' speech, the speech of straightforward description. Against this background of argument, *neither* the language of Scripture *nor* the language of metaphysics is 'literal' in the sense of being unproblematically descriptive: it would be better to say (I am paraphrasing Ernst's argument freely here) that there are moments when our speech is jolted into a register different from its normal one, and more specifically a register that is generative of fresh meaning. Ernst defines 'meaning' as 'the process or praxis by which the world to which man [*sic*] belongs becomes the world which belongs to man';[11] so a generative shift of register is an event in which we become more fully cognizant of our location in the world and at the same time more resourceful in plotting our way in it and casting it in coherent shape so as to be more free in its regard (it is worth noting that a more recent study of *Metaphysics and Transcendence* by Arthur Gibson[12] offers an exceptionally sophisticated account of the significance of the 'counter-intuitive' in philosophical argument and a wide-ranging discussion of what metaphor means when applied to God, all of this echoing a good deal of what Ernst has to

11 Ibid., p. 75.
12 Arthur Gibson, *Metaphysics and Transcendence* (London: Routledge, 2003), especially chapters 3 and 8. The latter, like Ernst's essay, looks at how the Hebrew *elohim* for 'god' (qua supernatural agent in a general sense) can function as a metaphorical marker of the presence of 'the' God, the one God of Israel named by the tetragrammaton YHWH.

say). Ernst has further things to say about the particular way in which this illuminates the generation of actual doctrine, not simply the prolegomena of theology, but we shall come back later to this.

A defensible natural theology, then, in the light of some such understanding, would be a discourse that attempted to spot where routine description failed to exhaust what 'needed to be said' (however exactly we spell out the content of this phrase). This is emphatically not about spotting explanatory gaps in the usual sense (this would be to look only for extra descriptive resources that happen not to be available as yet). It is more like the recognition that a faithful description of the world we inhabit involves taking account of whatever pressures move us to respond to our environment by gesturing towards a *context* for the description we have been engaged in – not as a further explanatory level, but as a cluster of models and idioms and practices working quite differently from the discourse we have so far been operating, without which our 'normal' repertoire of practice would not finally make sense. Such a picture has something in common (though with essential qualifications) with the startling approach to natural theology of another maverick Thomist interpreter of the mid-to-late twentieth century, Victor Preller. He proposed that 'the program of natural theology [was] to lead the intellect through a series of judgments which hopefully will result in a negative insight productive of the further judgment that the intellect has encountered a non-intelligible level of experience incapable of formulation in a conceptually meaningful question. The conclusion of natural theology is then the paradox that the human intellect is ordered to a reality it cannot know.'[13] Put less provocatively – and the flat assertion that the reality of God is something we cannot 'know' damagingly ignores just the complexities of what *knowledge* may mean – the process we are seeking to characterize is one in which we are brought to a point where to *go on speaking* at all requires a shift of expectation, away from the assumption that there will be a point of descriptive closure, some expression or formulation

13 Victor Preller, *Divine Science and the Science of God: A Reformulation of Thomas Aquinas* (Princeton, NJ: Princeton University Press, 1967), pp. 179–80. See also the essays by Stanley Hauerwas and Fergus Kerr in the volume dedicated to Preller's memory, Jeffrey Stout and Robert McSwain (eds), *Grammar and Grace: Reformulations of Aquinas and Wittgenstein* (London: SCM Press, 2004).

that is definitively adequate to what is in view. This happens when a descriptive account which is correct or sustainable as far as it goes leaves out of consideration what we most want to talk about: to carry on a conversation or exploration, we have to jettison the mode of discourse we have so far taken for granted. What is lacking is not more evidence, more facts, more knowledge in the usual sense of the word. Stanley Cavell's celebrated essay on Shakespeare's *Othello* ends with the observation that Othello's problem in the play was not that he lacked knowledge but that 'he could not yield to what he knew'.[14] We shall be hearing more from Cavell, but his phrase is a pregnant if paradoxical one for the present discussion. When we acknowledge the impulse to continue when 'ordinary' description is done with, we are not looking for extra material to work on but accepting that what confronts us is still 'interrogating' us: to seek a register for speaking in this situation might indeed be described as a 'yielding to what we know', accepting the limits of certainty but looking for a discourse that can be *acknowledged* between speakers (to borrow one of Cavell's key terms).

Applying this to Aquinas's 'five ways', we might say that he is, for example, inviting us to develop the discourse of causality to the point where we sense the need to change gear: everything we encounter is involved in relations of dependence; if dependence is built in to how we make sense of anything at all, are we bound to find ourselves looking for a language to express some sort of global dependence? It has been strongly argued[15] that there is a logical flaw in the way Aquinas puts this: to say that for *every* phenomenon there is a cause is not to say that *all* phenomena must therefore have a (single) cause. But that is not quite the thrust of Aquinas's overall point, which could be better expressed by saying that if it is part of the definition of every particular intelligible phenomenon we encounter that it is contingent, i.e. the result of a process of some sort, we can reasonably say that it is part of the definition of finite and intelligible being that it is invariably involved

---

14 Stanley Cavell, *The Claim of Reason: Wittgenstein, Skepticism, Morality and Tragedy* (Oxford and New York: Oxford University Press, 1979), p. 496. The essay appears as 'Othello and the Stake of the Other' in Cavell, *Disowning Knowledge in Seven Plays of Shakespeare*, 2nd edn (Cambridge: Cambridge University Press, 2003), pp. 125–42 (quotation from p. 141).

15 Classically and elegantly by Anthony Kenny, *The Five Ways: St Thomas Aquinas' Proofs of God's Existence* (London: Routledge and Kegan Paul, 1969), chapter 4.

in processes of causation, and thus marked by dependence. All energy we
encounter is involved in energy exchanges; but are we not then pushed
to ask about the character of energy as such (pure act, in an older terminology), energy that is simply what or as it is, not as the result of a process
of exchange? If we move in that direction, then in order to make sense of all
specific cases of talking about energy or action we do not seek for another
object to explore. It cannot be another *instance* of anything, as if the global
dependence of finite being were a case of dependence in general; nor can we
see this as some absolute first link in a causal chain (which would be to deny
the premise that everything in the universe is dependent, since one thing,
the first of the series, would then not be dependent). Something is required
which is expressible only in connection with the language of dependence
yet cannot be formulated within the normal frame of reference that we use
to deal with causal relations. If dependence is built in to the structure of all
possible experience and understanding, we are saying that to *be* anything
intelligible at all is to be caused; we could leave it at that, but this would
be to ignore the question about whether and how we 'frame' this comprehensive statement. And the frame proposed is the proposal that finite being
as such and in sum is marked by dependence: to *exist as a discrete subject of
predication* is to depend. So that which is depended *on* is evoked or gestured
to; but, to paraphrase Preller, we can't formulate a sensible question as to
what sort of thing it is that doesn't depend because, by definition, we have
now moved away from asking about *sorts* of things, and the questions we
started with no longer move us forwards.

2

A natural theology that started from something like this model would
(does) look very different from a process of accumulating features of the
world that can be explained only by supposing a creative agent. We do not
move towards a probable conclusion from a survey of the evidence.[16] And

---

16 Richard Swinburne has developed a very sophisticated argument for the existence
of God based on probability (see *The Existence of God*, 2nd edn (Oxford: Oxford
University Press, 2004); however it is (probably) unfair to characterize him as arguing
that the existence of God is itself no more than a probable conclusion.

it is worth pausing for a little to look at how this relates to the first great modern essay in complicating and undercutting some kinds of 'natural theology'. Kant is, on the one hand, hostile to arguments that deploy appeals to causality or dependence; but on the other sees language about God precisely as a 'framing' exercise for making sense of our intelligible experience of the world. His First Critique famously mounts an assault on the idea of arguing from contingent to necessary being, on a number of grounds.[17] He has already seen off the ontological argument, which he reads as an attempt to deduce an existent reality solely from its idea, an attempt that separates ideal and real existence as if ideal existence were a defective version of real existence, the latter being distinguished by the presence of an essential property (the 'property' of really-being-there). We cannot argue that something *has* to exist just because it is that sort of thing – so that if we tried to think of it as non-existent, we shouldn't really be thinking of it at all but of a deficient version of it, lacking an essential feature.[18] But when we turn to the argument from contingent being to necessary being, Kant claims that this just takes us back to the unsatisfactoriness of the ontological argument by another route. The argument 'If there is anything contingent there must be something necessary' smuggles into what looks like an argument from experience, a definitional sleight of hand: a contingent reality is determined by causes in the world; a necessary reality is determined only by its own concept, and this concept is that of an *ens realissimum*, a supremely real entity. But we have seen that it is impossible to argue that anything *has* to be really there just because it is that sort of thing; so we have to abandon this as an argument for a really existing 'necessary being' and conclude that an argument from contingency cannot be sustained. Since the idea of causality only works within the field of sense experience anyway,[19] there can be no move outside the series of material and contingent causes to an extra-worldly first cause starting off the series of material causes. Hence Kant's move in the Second Critique to another way of positing the reality of something on which everything in the world

---

17 Immanuel Kant, *Critique of Pure Reason*, trans. Norman Kemp Smith, 2nd impression (London and New York: Macmillan, 1933), pp. 507–14.

18 Ibid., pp. 503ff.

19 Ibid., p. 511.

depends.[20] Rational existence, existence as a thinking and morally free subject, presupposes that there is a unity in our experience, such that moral action is not some sort of revolt or struggle against the nature of things. To imagine the opposite would be to suggest that our mind is instinctively at odds with the stuff of its perceiving and reflecting. We must presuppose a final fit between our moral aspirations and dispositions and the world – a fit that we could call 'happiness': 'the condition of a rational being in the world, in whose whole existence everything goes according to wish and will',[21] the condition of an agent who never meets with frustration. But I as an agent am not the cause of nature: I am a dependent element within it, and so cannot bring about this 'fit'. On what can the idea of such a fit be grounded? Only on the supposition of a cause of the natural order in which happiness and right willing coincide.

So where exactly does what we outlined earlier agree with and where does it depart from Kant? Is it vulnerable to his criticism of arguments from contingency to necessity? Or is it a version of the Second Critique argument which posits a formal coincidence of happiness and goodwill, a moral context for the natural order, while denying absolutely that we could have knowledge of such a context-providing reality beyond the bare recognition of the fact that we can't help acting as if it were real? First, then, we have to recognize that Kant's account of the argument from contingency is not quite what Aquinas or most modern interpreters of Aquinas would claim to be doing. Kant writes as though the point of the older argumentation were indeed to come to an indisputable first point in a series; and he seems to understand 'necessary' being as the kind of being that has to exist by definition – so that a claim about the existence of God as non-contingent becomes a claim to incontrovertible knowledge about what is beyond the realm of certainty.[22] As we have hinted, the point of the argument in its classical form is different – not that we are arguing from one kind of existent to another, let alone defining the kind of being that

20 *Critique of Practical Reason*, trans. Lewis White Beck (Indianapolis, IN: New York and Liberal Arts Press, 1958), pp. 128–36.

21 Ibid., p. 129.

22 See the whole of the chapter on 'The Ideal of Pure Reason' in the *First Critique* (Second Division, Book II, Chapter III), pp. 485–570, especially pp. 491–5.

can't help existing, but that we are faced with the question of whether we can manage to talk sensibly about a universe of contingent being without looking for some way of pointing to a ground or context in regard to which the language of contingency or dependence would not be intelligible. And, second, while Kant's positing of God as the unknowable point of coincidence between virtue and happiness does sound, on the face of it, at least congruent with Preller's formulation, quoted earlier, of the intellect being ordered to what it cannot know, the matter may turn out to be more complicated. Preller is interested in the paradox that it really is the *intellect* that we are talking about here: on his account, the human intellect is driven to a judgement that its resources are ultimately inadequate to what is before it; it acquires by grace a capacity to use the word 'God' in a sense that is not completely stupid, but that really is all.[23] But the point is that this is properly an *intellectual* judgement (which means that some of Preller's more mischievously agnostic formulations will not quite do); it is not, in Kant's sense, a judgement of 'practical reason' – not, that is, the positing of something we need in order to act but the acknowledgement of our inability to complete our judgements about what it is to *be*. And Preller, with other modern Thomists, would no doubt observe that Kant's schema requires God to be as God is in order to resolve an antinomy of our experience in or of the world; precisely why the Kantian God is to be regarded as the *source* of the world or the agency that sustains finite agency is not really elaborated in Kant's argument and this leaves his postulated divinity in an ontological no-man's land. Nothing can be said here about the character of finite being as such, and so nothing is said about the intellect and its proper use and object.

None the less, the chastened Thomism Preller argues would look different if Kant had never written. The two major points to make in this connection are, first, the substantive one that any claim to *know* God has to negotiate its way around a set of unprecedentedly sharp cautions about projecting beyond the material realm any of the mechanisms of physical relatedness, and, second, the methodological one of tracking where and

---

23 Apart from, obviously, what revelation may deliver to us: the important point for Preller is that natural theology provides no *positive* information about what God is like, but something like a system of warnings about the misuse of the language.

how language about God 'comes in' in relation to the undeniable and irresoluble inadequacies of description in terms of physical relatedness alone. And in a sense Kant's own method in the Second Critique has a certain similarity to what we have been considering as a way of shifting the agenda of natural theology away from the late scholastic assumptions that Kant rightly challenges in the First Critique. He is – to use the language used earlier – inviting us to develop the discourse of moral disinterestedness to the point where the mere appeal to the categorical authority of moral commands fails to carry what we need to say if we are to avoid a cosmology in which we are 'naturally' at odds with nature.

3

Perhaps the methodological issue might also be clarified if we draw on a very different reflective tradition. Buddhist meditational practice – specifically what is called 'insight' meditation, *vipassana* – requires the meditator to consider something that is claimed to belong to the nature of all phenomena: the truth that every apparent substance is the product of a hierarchy of synthesizing perceptions enacted by our minds. Everything has 'come to be'; it has no being in itself. The principle of 'dependent origination' is the axiom that 'all things exist dependent on determinants'[24]: the ensemble of all things constitutes a 'continuum or process' without a 'First Cause'[25] (i.e. a single *all*-determining agency). Insight is 'seeing what has come to be as having come to be'[26] It liberates because it allows us to recognize that the apparent world (including the apparent self) has no element of permanence or solidity: in the central paradox of Buddhist thought, the acknowledgement of universal determination opens the door to freedom. We understand how our minds put together perceptions, how perceptions arise from unacknowledged needs or longings, how needs and longings arise from a mythological picture of the self as some thing

24 Ajahn Passanno and Ajahn Amaro, *The Island: An Anthology of the Buddha's Teachings on Nibbana* (Redwood Valley, CA: Abhayagiri Monastic Foundation, 2009), p. 68 (a quotation from Bhikkhu Payutto).
25 Ibid.
26 Ibid., p. 105

that has to be satisfied, some thing that can claim a sort of ownership of what it knows. Thus, in the terms used by the Buddha in the Pali Canon, ignorance (of the self) leads to 'formation', the shaping of the world into discrete substances; formation leads to consciousness, consciousness leads to materiality (the impenetrable other that consciousness defines itself against), materiality to the six spheres of sense experience, the sense spheres to 'contact' (the sensing of these fantasized substances as solid objects for us), contact leads to feeling, feeling to craving, craving to clinging, clinging to becoming (the inexorable round of going on generating what we think is life), becoming to birth and birth to suffering.[27] *Vipassana* meditation exposes the imprisoning effect of taking the phenomenal world as a simple given, when in fact it is pure transaction, a pattern of universal dependence, including, crucially, dependence on our synthesizing habits of mind. What then remains if the world of our experience is seen in this way? The unconditioned or uncreated or unmoved; 'cessation', release, the stilling of the cycle: *nibbana*. The common translation of this as 'extinction' is deplored by most Buddhists as implying that something that used to exist stops existing. More accurately, it designates the state in which the self, by 'seeing through' itself and dismantling the burden of accumulated impression and longings, is freed from the agitation metaphorically represented by the burning of a flame, and is simply still. This stillness is not an individual state of mind, an experience among others that the mind 'has', but what a clumsy non-Buddhist vocabulary would probably try to characterize as a 'participation' in the stillness that is whatever the world of dependent origination is not; although, having said that, we have to unsay it, because it suggests either two realms side by side, or else a 'merging' of a finite substance with an infinite – neither of which models can be sustained in a Buddhist metaphysic.

For the Buddhist, the process of enlightenment begins when suffering is recognized as a problem, for oneself and for others. The world, in other words, does not provide its own justification; it does not answer the question of why suffering occurs. Or rather, it can give exhaustive accounts of why this or that situation occurs, why there are circumstances in which people suffer. But what it fails to do is explain why it is *suffering* we feel. So the

27 Ibid., pp. 59ff, 72–4.

proper response is to work through the causal chains of the world's actual being in order to bring to light the fact that we suffer because we conceive ourselves as solid subjects with clear requirements that dictate how we engage with our environment. If we are not subject to that dictatorship, we grasp that seeing the story of the world in terms of dependent origination allows us, unexpectedly, to be other than cogs in the machinery – not by giving us superhuman liberty but in allowing us to see that our complete and unequivocal immersion in the continuum of this world is our path into stillness. We do not look for somewhere else where we can be our 'real selves': here and now we see both the universality of causation and the sheer actuality of the moment, so that we enter the unconditioned state.

This is, in effect, another version of the invitation to develop a discourse to breaking point which we have referred to earlier. There is no attempt to arrest the process by identifying a single first moment or first principle within the system. There is no search for a gap into which a special supernatural agency can be fitted. There is only the exhaustive projection of causal explanation up to the point where you realize *both* that everything falls under the rubric of dependent origination *and* that this is not an ending, a closure on all possible strategies of conscious and free speaking or living. Something becomes possible that operates on another plane of awareness: not so much – perhaps not at all – anything like a further description, but a space to inhabit, a perspective, itself deeply resistant to description in the ordinary way. And the point for our purposes is that what has happened in this meditative process is not an argument but a *method*, a practice of thinking to the edge of what can be said. Think to the point where there seems nothing further to be said and see what happens. It is as far as could be from auto-suggestion, because there can be no prescription as to what does happen at such a point: enlightenment cannot be reduced to a technique. Part of the discipline is sitting for a long period with the insolubility of what is in front of you; and, in some forms of Buddhism, this is ritualized in the shape of the *koan*, a form of words that resists conceptual reduction and 'clarification' or rational restatement and so becomes a kind of condensation of what we confront at the edge of descriptive language.

The purpose of this brief excursion into Buddhist thought and practice is to prompt the question of whether it is more helpful to see not only Aquinas's Five Ways but the whole enterprise of a reconfigured natural theology as a *method*, perhaps even a skill. Natural theology is a practice – or at least outlines possible practices which bring us to the point at which we run out of things to say in the discourse we started with but recognize that this running-out is not simply an ending. What then supervenes is not, though, the 'vagueness' Leunig speaks of (and I don't actually think he means that religious speech is or should be vague as a matter of principle; he is observing the indeterminate way in which we are normally introduced to it). It is a different kind of accuracy or adequacy that is called for, something that is not descriptive in the usual sense yet is emphatically not arbitrary either. The challenge in speaking about God is the challenge of referring appropriately to what is not an object among others or a definable substance that can be 'isolated' and examined. Part of my argument in these chapters will be that the labour involved in scrutinizing and using language about God with integrity is bound up with the scrutiny of language itself, the recognition of the ways in which it puts questions to itself and destabilizes our expectations that we can settle or complete our thinking of the world we inhabit. Looking at the actual varieties of and stresses in our speech may give us some insight into how we honestly negotiate the territory beyond 'ordinary' description, the 'grammar' of the various sorts of incompleteness we have to confront.

4

To sum up so far: natural theology as an attempt to reach conclusions about the existence and character of God by arguing from features of the world was always an eccentric enterprise from the point of view of both philosophy and theology. But the challenge to start from somewhere other than claims to revelation is not necessarily nonsensical or impious. It obliges us to pay attention to the ways in which language about God actually finds its way into our speech, and so delivers us from discussing the language of belief in a vacuum. The classical so-called 'proofs' of God developed by Aquinas and others in fact sit very well with this: they are not arguing in the abstract towards an otherwise unheard-of conclusion, but charting some of the ways in which we comprehensively make sense of the workings of the world so as to suggest that, when we have done the most we can in this comprehensive mapping, we have not exhausted what we want to say or feel compelled to say. Thus, to draw up a 'map' illustrating the dependent or contingent character of all we experience leaves a question, not about how we provide an extra piece of causal explanation but about whether this style of description needs a context or frame that cannot be categorized within the limits of the discourse we have been using. This is not quite so vulnerable to Kant's criticisms of varieties of the cosmological argument, as it does not propose that we should be able to demonstrate a conclusion that cannot be otherwise, and does not seek to provide a final supplementary agency to complete a causal series. It has some points in common with Kant's own argument in the Second Critique, in so far as the latter represents a 'charting' of aspects of the intelligible environment in such a way as to leave a question about the framework within which this intelligible environment as a whole becomes intelligible at a different level; however, Kant's refusal to connect this with any sort of ontology remains a major divergence from the Thomist tradition. What is in view might, finally, be described as a recasting of natural theology as a *practice* not entirely unlike the insight meditation of Buddhist discipline, a structured thinking through of the universality of dependence so as to open the door to the possibility of a state of freedom from conditioning.

The reference to Buddhist practice in fact takes us back to the problem flagged at the start of this chapter, the problem of whether this evocation or gesturing to an unconditioned life or being leaves us with a God incapable of action and thus of revelation. If this is true, the entire project of recasting natural theology in the way suggested is a bit of a waste of time from the point of view of a theologian. I shall return to this question in later chapters, but for now simply observe that what we are talking about is a practice which chastens or relativizes any habits of speaking that aim at containing and 'fixing' what is being talked about; we might recall Cavell's language of 'yielding to what we know'. Such practice opens the speaker to what is not predicted or scripted: that which we now confront as the matter of our speech cannot be seen as simply passive to our commanding intellect. So, whatever exactly emerges from this, there is at least an opening to what can change the speaker, to what remains strange, resistant: is the rhetoric of 'yielding' just a turn of phrase? To translate terms like these into the language of divine action does take us to another level again; which is where the language of revelation comes in, as I hope we shall see in due course.

5

Meanwhile, we shall be looking at a succession of features of our human language in the light of the kind of suggestions Ernst and others have prompted, looking and listening for the elements in our ordinary practice – specifically our practice as speakers – that become extraordinary and strange the more we examine them. To begin with, there is a set of issues around language and *freedom*: what does it mean to see language as something other than a system of determined behaviour, something that is impossible to reduce to patterns of stimulus and response? There are a good many current philosophies which aim so to reduce it; are any of these sustainable in the face of what speech actually does? Next, we shall look at language as something located in *time*, something always temporally enacted, constantly accumulating through successive exchange, never finishing its account of its environment but always inviting fresh events of speaking and hearing. As such, it is of course also an *embodied* phenomenon, rooted in physical negotiations and transactions, both internal and external. How do embodied speakers, necessarily located here and not there, now and not then, create a linguistic environment where there is an assumption of convergent and continuous meanings and shared references? Then, fourth, there is the issue of the way language generates what I shall call '*excessive* speech', forms of utterance that go beyond what is functionally required and that, deliberately or not, put pressure on speakers to do or say more than is immediately comfortable or (apparently) reasonable, in order to enlarge the practices of communication. Excess in this sense covers both the uses of metaphor and the practical disciplines of poetry; and it also has some connections with the unavoidable strains of language in innovative science. In all these contexts, language is deployed to make us strangers to ourselves and then recognize our world afresh. Then, finally, we shall need to think about silence: about the particular ways in which speech is suspended in different contexts, not as a pure absence of utterance or an accidental gap, but as a strategy *in* the process of utterance; or perhaps rather as an unavoidable move 'outwards' in order to give what we say another kind of location, a particular sort of horizon or hinterland without which what we say would be vacuous.

All these questions carry a challenge to any idea that there is a 'primitive' literal level in our speech on whose foundation metaphor and symbol are built up. Without at this point going into the immense subject of the origin and acquisition of language,[28] we can at least say that it is associated with a particular moment in cultural evolution – made possible by a particular moment in the physical evolution of the cerebral cortex – at which *representation* became a shared human practice. But – and here is a crucial point – 'representation' does not mean some sort of reproduction of a particular set of data: to represent the environment by the means of sound is already a drastic step away from reproduction, creating what looks or sounds like the subject matter. And an environment that is capable of being represented in this sense is one in which the mind discerns a tension between the given shape of some aspect of its environment and a 'way of existing' that can be recaptured in another medium so that what represents it does not have to be in any simple way 'like' it. Using the terminology of the Jesuit philosopher Erich Przywara, itself clearly indebted to Heidegger,[29] we recognize a tension between the *Da* and the *So* of what confronts us, and thus recognize that our capacity to *think* what is there ('noetics') is neither separable from nor identical with the judgement that it is in fact there ('ontics'). There is some aspect of what is perceived that can be read into another moment in our seeing and speaking. The matter of our perceiving is not exactly 'raw' material; it is not a set of wholly discrete monads, nor a series of mutually oppositional moments, but a continuum of 'analogical' relations in which we can speak of one thing in terms of another, of participation existing between not only object and object in the world but between object and representing subject. To represent anything presupposes that some level or aspect of what is perceived can in fact 'come to be' in another medium. At the most abstract level, philosophers have spoken of the intelligible form of something; but that does not quite do justice to the perception that when an object is understood and spoken of – spoken

---

28 For a reliable and comprehensive overview, see Ray Jackendoff, *Foundations of Language: Brain, Meaning, Grammar, Evolution* (Oxford: Oxford University Press, 2002).

29 As found in Erich Przywara, *Analogia Entis. Metaphysics: Original Structure and Universal Rhythm*, trans. John R. Betz and David Bentley Hart (Grand Rapids, MI: Eerdmans, 2014) (the original German publication of the long core essay was in 1932; a new edition with some amendments appeared in 1962, accompanied by a number of Przywara's other pieces).

of either 'literally' or 'metaphorically' – there is a convergence or confluence of action between object and subject. What is understood and spoken of is present as modifying the subject's activity, both limiting its options in certain ways and expanding its capacity in others. But for agents to exercise agency (recognizable or intelligible as consistent with their agency on their 'home territory') in the agency of another we need a scheme that does not oblige us to think of monadic substances bumping into each other: we need the 'analogical' discourse that is able to identify continuity in material distinctness, continuity between discrete agents of a certain kind and between knower and known

So representation becomes a distinctly interesting matter. Not simply the copying, imitating or just registering of features, it presupposes, it seems, some notion of a characteristic *form of action* that can be activated in different media. And it is this notion that lies behind the persistent belief that names embody power, that words are not arbitrarily related to what they designate or evoke (in the sense that they at least crystallize the openness of the subject to being changed by the object). There are crude and magical versions of this, and it is a view that has at times acquired a deservedly bad name in theology, let alone philosophy,[30] but in all that follows it will be important to remember that this conviction about continuity or partici- pation between agents in relations of knowing is bound up in any properly nuanced account of representation. Literal and metaphorical speech are not related as more and less 'faithful' representations of an object: both seek to secure the intelligible presence of what is perceived. But it is arguable that the metaphorical, or at least the non-slavishly literal, has in some circum- stances a better chance of representing what is spoken of, in so far as it seeks to identify a form of action that is active within another phenomenal shape – so that the distinctive form appears (paradoxically) more plainly

---

30 For a very nuanced and creative discussion, see John Milbank, 'The Linguistic Turn as a Theological Turn', in *The Word Made Strange: Theology, Language, Culture* (Oxford: Blackwell, 1997), pp. 84–120, which traces the way in which early and mediaeval Christian theology attempted to walk a tightrope between mythological pictures of linguistic origins inherited from pre-Christian cosmology and purely functionalist and pragmatic accounts, with Aquinas representing something of a theological retrieval and revaluation of the non-arbitrary element in language (i.e. granting to the name a certain kind of participation in what it names).

when 'playing away from home', detached from its original specific embodiment and linked to another context; just as the distinctive feature of or
moment in the life of the 'host' subject becomes more itself when phrased
in a borrowed terminology. 'Weeping skies' cannot be a literal description,
but the association of a rainy day with grief points up something about
weeping by associating it with weather as well as pointing up something
about weather by recognizing its irresistible linkage with mood in our
habitual interpretation of it, our 'humanizing' of it as a phenomenon that
casts light on us as selves. Likewise (and this is pertinent to some of our
later themes), when we say 'money talks', we not only pose the – painfully
contemporary – question of how money establishes meanings of its own
and creates 'cultures', we also introduce into our understanding of language
a set of uncomfortable considerations about how far 'talking' is implicated
in power, in the control of human exchanges; about whether or not it has
a proper liberty from the function of negotiating relations of power and
advantage.

6

I am implying a working distinction between two ways of speaking about
what we encounter. There is a cluster of activities whose focus can be called
description, in the sense which I have generally been taking for granted so
far in these pages – a mapping exercise in which we assume that the task is
to produce a certain traceable structural parallel between what we say and
what we perceive. And then there is what I have so far called *representation*
– a way of speaking that may variously be said to seek to embody, translate,
make present or re-form what is perceived. The word has been used in a
wide and doubtfully compatible variety of ways by different philosophers
of language and aesthetics,[31] and it is a rather risky business proposing
a new usage which is not quite identical to any of these. I apologize for
the possible confusions, but the use I am here putting forward has the
advantage of being fairly simple in itself, and can claim some roots in
Max Black's discussion of 'the representational aspect of metaphor' as one

31 This is a dauntingly large subject, and I have offered a sketch of the territory in the
appendix to this book.

among several means of showing what there is in language that cannot be understood as 'substitutes for bundles of statements of fact' – ranging from photographs and realistic depiction (close to descriptive statements of fact) through to diagrams, charts and maps – and ultimately metaphors and other more challenging usages of speech.[32]

Reverting for a moment to Cornelius Ernst's arguments, what this kind of working distinction helps us to see is that truthful or truth-claiming speech is neither the pure reproduction of discrete elements nor a set of impressionistic 'tokenings', acts which arbitrarily label elements of the environment. The significantly generative moments in speech occur prior to any division between an atomistic account of facts described in what are supposed to be unadorned words used in their 'primary' meanings and the work that is done by words 'playing away from home', whether in straight-forward metaphor or in interconnected and schematic accounts. In the terms I am using, 'description' and 'representation' crystallize out of a very diverse and flexible set of responses. Neither is a degenerate or inadequate form of the other. To quote from a discussion by Michael Arbib and Mary Hesse in their Gifford Lectures of 1983, 'metaphorical shifts of meaning depending on similarities and differences between objects are pervasive in language, not deviant, and some of the mechanisms of metaphor are essential to the meaning of any descriptive language whatever'.[33] These authors use 'descriptive' more generously than I do here, but the point is clear enough. And Arbib and Hesse go on to spell out an account of understanding 'description' – and assessing its truth and adequacy – that requires a kind of speech which locates what's being referred to within a *schema* of understanding, a complex of use and association or resonance and recognition patterns or habits.[34] We do not seek to refer accurately just to an object in isolation; we need language that will carry reference to a schema. Such a schema may in the first place be a wider network of causal and 'process' description (moving towards what we properly call scientific

---

32 Max Black, 'More About Metaphor', in Andrew Ortony (ed.), *Metaphor and Thought* (Cambridge: Cambridge University Press, 1979), pp. 19–43 (quotation p. 41).
33 Michael Arbib and Mary Hesse, *The Construction of Reality* (Cambridge: Cambridge University Press, 1986), p. 152.
34 Ibid., pp. 58–61.

modelling) or, beyond that and more ambitiously, a symbolic pattern which does not seek to 'represent the state of the natural world for the purposes of prediction and control'.[35] Only if we hold that the primary and essential purpose of speech is 'prediction and control' will such symbolic schemata be seen as inferior or secondary. Representation, in the sense I have given the word, *may* be used in this way, but is not necessarily or even primarily directed thus. Representational speech will carry a good many features that are irrelevant to prediction and control, but answer to something more like a sheer desire to understand and to deploy verbal symbols in ways that enlarge the repertoire of communication that can be both purposive and more playful or (to use a loaded word) contemplative – attuned both to *scientia* and *sapientia* in the language St Augustine used to distinguish instrumental and reflective or contemplative knowing, knowing whose point is simply *knowing*, in the sense of intelligently enjoying the presence of the other.[36]

In the discussions that follow, I shall be assuming this characterization of representation as a wide-ranging strategy which touches on but is not confined by questions of how to manipulate the environment successfully, and is centred on language uses that are nearer metaphor than (what is imagined to be) literal description. As we shall be seeing again and again, questions about what spills over the frontier of 'description' are 'pervasive ... not deviant'. And the perceptive reader will have noticed that by this stage of the discussion a couple of strictly metaphysical principles have been eased into our thinking. These preliminary reflections on natural theology and human language have noted (i) the way we assume that dependence is an inalienable aspect of finite being; and they have further suggested – by way of thinking through the primitive presence of metaphor in our accounts of the world; (ii) a distinction between intelligible forms of action and the precise embodiments in which they are encountered. To speak at all about the life of the world around us, we presuppose both dependence and analogical fluidity as metaphysical basics. The latter, it is important to note, is not some sort of doctrine of separable forms, let alone a dualism of form and matter in the usual sense; it simply recognizes that even within a

---

35 Ibid., p. 161.
36 Augustine, *de trinitate* XII, especially xiv.22, on this distinction.

rigorously material account of the world, the communicative sense made by this or that object is not another feature of its material composition – as, to use the famous Wittgensteinian example, the expression (smile or frown) is not a material *feature* of the face, yet can only be intelligible *as* the shape of a material face (with due respect to Cheshire cats).

Going back to the earlier days of *homo sapiens*, we have ample evidence of a mindset for which representation, the life of one agent echoed or rekindled in the life of another, was a focal matter. The surviving art of the Ice Age (as witnessed in the remarkable British Museum exhibition of 2013) not only illustrates the prevalence of straightforward representation of animals and human subjects (notably fertile women) but also, tantalizingly, suggests the possibility of a sort of visual metaphorization in the statuettes of 'lion men', figures with lions' heads and human bodies – more precisely with lions' heads and human bodies partly shaped in leonine form.[37] The makers of such objects are engaged in a profoundly linguistic task: they are so depicting one thing that it 'speaks of' another, both blurring boundaries and sharpening definition; the sculptures are 'indicative of a mind capable of imagining new concepts rather than simply reproducing real [sic] forms'[38] and thus indicative of the presence of pre-frontal cortex activity in the brain. Whoever made the lion men must have been able to speak in a way not wholly dissimilar to ourselves. A characteristic intelligible form of life or action is identified and recognized at work in another living agent, and the representation creates a new hybrid material shape: this is a shape that describes nothing in the 'real' world in the ordinary sense of description, but is not simply a casual *jeu d'esprit* (not simply stitching a bit of one object on

---

37 Jill Cook, *Ice Age Art: Arrival of the Modern Mind* (London: British Museum Press, 2013), pp. 28–37 on this convention. The subtitle of the book is worth noting, suggesting, as it does, that certain modes of complex symbolization constitute 'modernity'. It might be more accurate to think of them as constituting human intellection as such, but that is a larger issue.

38 Ibid., pp. 28–30; c.f. p. 34: 'It is not necessary to have a brain with a complex pre-frontal cortex to form the mental image of a human or a lion. This development is necessary to conceive something like a lion man that does not exist, then externalize and communicate such a creature by reproducing that instinct, thought or dream in material form.' The image is thus a crystallization of relations between spheres of being, human, animal, divine, perhaps reflecting shamanistic practices (p. 35).

to another). The leonine style in which the figure's upper arms are portrayed subtly tells us that the artist is thinking through gradations of 'lion-likeness', thinking through how two significantly different shapes are to be shown as one. Human identity as a vehicle of leonine, leonine identity as a vehicle for human – there is no way of telling what exactly is at work here, but the point is clear enough as to the mental skills entailed. The skills involved are plainly in line with the Arbib-Hesse thesis about schematic knowledge: an Ice Age artist creating such an image is modelling more than what is 'directly' perceived, in that s/he is able to form an implicit heuristic account of what-it-is like-to-be-a-lion such that this what-it-is-like can be fused with what-it-is-like-to-be-a-man/woman. Leonine identity and human are to that extent grasped schematically, in relation to an unspecified range of environmental factors (lions are powerful, dangerous, dignified or whatever against their background).[39]

But this unspecified range is important in another way. Schematic perceiving is of its nature somewhat diverse: but the plurality of possible schemes within which a representation may work does not mean that there is no level at which exclusive truth claims may operate: certain representations fail to be credible, leave out central criteria for recognizability, override what is given and so on. We cannot in human discourse simply say what we please. Yet once we acknowledge that we are doing more than answering carefully prescribed questions about causal and operational issues – questions which admit a degree of finality in the answers – we face a possible variety of representative schemata not quickly exhausted. We cannot say in advance just how diverse may be the range of possible and recognizable schemata. We can only try it, and see where we fail to persuade some other speaker or perceiver of the recognizability of our version. An overwhelming number of cultures deliberately push this as a social and intellectual game: how obscure can you get before recognition disappears? Hence the riddles so popular in pre-modern cultures, in which elaborate metaphorical strategies are consciously developed to make recognition difficult, and so to extend still further the range of what can become part of a communicative exchange, as well as marking the boundaries of what counts as proficiency in a culture. Once again, we couldn't say in advance

39 Ibid., p 34.

how many possible riddling 'kennings' there might be for familiar objects. To anticipate some of what we shall be looking at in the next chapter, there is an indeterminate – or, perhaps better, underdetermined – element in representation so understood.

In the background of all this, as we have noted in passing here and there, is a set of issues in neuroscience. The familiar distinction between right-brain and left-brain activity has recently been explored and extended by Iain McGilchrist in a very remarkable book, *The Master and His Emissary*.[40] McGilchrist notes[41] that, although it is conventional wisdom to locate linguistic capacity in the parietal region of the brain's left hemisphere (the hemisphere more associated with collecting information, with handling 'description' in the terms I have been using), this can be a seriously misleading account of brain functioning: the right hemisphere is no less involved in language because it is involved in grasping the meaning of whole sentences and recognizing the tone or emotional register of an utterance – in activities that, in other words, relate to 'schematic' perception. Furthermore, 'lateralisation of brain function [i.e. specialization as between left and right hemispheres] and asymmetry of its structure, occurred without language or tool design';[42] that is to say, the particular physiological and neurological conditions that relate to language seem to predate the emergence of language and tool use. Linguistic development makes use of a pre-existing 'space' in the brain's capacity. There is a strong case, which McGilchrist sets out very lucidly,[43] for concluding that what initially makes that space is *music*, differentiated sound-production, adapting for an ever-growing range of expression and the building of relation, as a kind of 'social grooming'.[44] This is where we can identify the ultimate roots of speech. Even with the language of 'description', the primal origins of such

---

40 Iain McGilchrist, *The Master and His Emissary: The Divided Brain and the Making of the Western World* (New Haven, CT and London: Yale University Press, 2009). The 'master' of the title is the synoptic perspective of the right brain, which in a balanced cultural environment is served not dominated by the information-gathering and problem-solving left brain.

41 Ibid., pp. 99ff.

42 Ibid., p. 100.

43 Ibid., pp. 102–5.

44 Ibid., p. 106.

a function do not lie in a concern for simply communicating gobbets of *information* but as a means of laying out the contours of an environment so as to negotiate it more effectively,[45] utilizing the frontal-lobe capacity for producing 'virtual representation of reality',[46] disembodied versions of elements of the environment, which allow us to focus on how we most effectively model what is around us so as to use it, to find our way around it. This is, of course, a function with strong left-brain-type associations. But language itself as a whole system proceeds to 'compensate' for the losses in perception involved in this virtual depiction by reinstating something of the musical origin of speech through metaphor; that is, by speaking out of a more empathic and more consciously embodied attitude, drawing on right-brain capacity, on a more archaic repertoire. The origins of linguistic capacity lie in pitched and differentiated sound allied to gesture (including dance); the body enters into a process of seeking continuity with what is both sensed internally and perceived externally. This capacity is, on the one hand, refined into a mapping operation; but the recognition of sameness-in-otherness that we earlier noted as basic to metaphorical speech comes to pervade the left-brain (descriptive and analytical) operation that has developed, saving it from the total dysfunctionality that would occur if there were no synthesizing activity.[47] 'Language', writes McGilchrist, 'is a hybrid. It evolved from music and *in this part of its history* represented the urge to communicate; and to the extent that it retains right-hemisphere empathic elements, it still does. Its origins lie in the body and the world of experience. But referential language, with its huge vocabulary and sophis-ticated syntax, did not originate in a drive to communicate ... It has done everything it can to repudiate both its bodily origins and its dependency on experience – to become a world unto itself.'[48]

We shall be returning in a later chapter to the question of language's material base. But for the present, the point is to insist that what I have been calling representation, activity that assumes the possibility of one form of life existing in another, is a basic and distinctive human characteristic,

45 Ibid., pp. 113ff.
46 Ibid., p. 115.
47 Ibid., pp. 115–32, *passim*.
48 Ibid., p. 125

not reducible to the mapping exercise and functional goals of left-brain description. It is a commonplace among child psychologists that the representative urge surfaces very early indeed (and seems not to have any parallels in the activity of primates brought up in human care): 'the child does not mistake his or her creation for the real thing but is evolving a graphic logic that states that a simple unit, such as an oblong with facial features, can stand for another more complex unit, in this case a human or an animal'[49] – just as, we might add, the capacity to recognize an ensemble of actual physical features as a *face* is a skill surfacing at the origins of human consciousness.[50] What is most interesting is how the very idea of representation arises – the innate confidence that the hand is able to produce what is meant to be a version or a recognizable sign of what is seen. And, as noted earlier, the notion of representation by sound is even more surprising when we reflect on it. We can only say, it seems, that it is characteristic of human perceiving to associate perception itself with the need (not too strong a word) to express a continuity with what is known, to embody the perceived reality through one's own bodily activity. Such embodiment may or may not be in any sense an imitation; the child's 'graphic logic' reminds us that this is not simply about making something that looks like what is there. And to 'embody' in words what is perceived is something we ought to find odder than we often do. No account of language that neglects this dimension is going to be of any use, and, as McGilchrist observes, there is a definite limit to how far we can go with the doctrine of the arbitrary character of signifiers associated with Saussure.[51] The two features foregrounded by McGilchrist for understanding a linguistic practice that fully involves

49 Claire Golomb, *The Creation of Imaginary Worlds: The Role of Art, Magic and Dreams in Child Development* (London and Philadelphia, PA: Jessica Kingsley Publications, 2011), p. 20.

50 McGilchrist, op. cit., pp. 60 and 78.

51 Ibid., pp. 119–20; McGilchrist describes the doctrine of the arbitrary nature of the sign as 'fascinating and counterintuitive', and points to the well-known research which suggests that 'those with absolutely no knowledge of a language can nonetheless correctly guess which word – which of these supposedly arbitrary signs – goes with which object, in what has become known as the "kiki/bouba" effect ("kiki" suggesting a spiky-shaped object, where "bouba" suggests a softly rounded object' (119). These intuitions are evidently connected with bodily sensation and its evocation in sound.

both hemispheres were, we might recall, empathy and embodiment. The paradox – in some people's eyes – is that accounts of language, let alone knowledge, that focus on the reportage of 'material facts' are actually less embodied, in McGilchrist's sense. And the direction of this chapter's discussion is likewise to suggest that an account of our environment as a whole that reduces it to determined material transactions in fact loses touch with materiality, embodiment, including the embodiment of the knowing subject. More on this in Chapter 4.

7

We have travelled a fair distance from Aquinas and Kant. But I hope that some sense has been conveyed of why issues around both the practices of meditation and the models proposed by neuroscience are relevant to the reshaping of natural theology. We began by thinking provisionally of natural theology as a way of identifying where language about God 'came in' in the world of routine or everyday speech. Further exploration has complicated the idea of the everyday: there is not in fact a plain substrate of language that is without redundancies, symbolizations, appeals to schema or context. The everyday is odder than that. God is not the only thing that comes into discourse and unsettle its descriptive ambitions. But we need some crude rules of thumb here. First, we can grant that there *is* a register of speech that – quite simply – does not expect or routinely seem to require much in the way of schematic or representational treatment. For practical purposes we know pretty much what it means and how to deploy it; its metaphors are buried, no longer recognized as such. Granted that the literal-metaphorical duality is one that needs dismantling, we do, broadly, know when a metaphor has ceased to function in any very startling or disruptive ways. To speak of the hands of a clock causes no ripple on the surface of routine communication. So we can still distinguish between this register and the consciously 'excessive' or apparently eccentric voice that prompts unease with supposedly simple descriptive language and demands a better understanding of the representative task. Second, language about God is indeed not unique in having a disruptive effect, which is why it is in some measure illuminating to reflect about it in connection with the language of poetry or indeed certain kinds of science. But, as we shall see again in our discussions, it proposes the most serious disruption of all because it proposes certain understandings of the character of finite being itself – something, in other words, about all possible subjects of discourse. The implication of this is that it cannot be numbered among possible subjects of discourse in any obvious sense, so that what is said about it is going to be linguistically eccentric in a uniquely marked way, and the role of what we could call strategic silence becomes central (see Chapter 6).

To push the argument a little further, the model of representation sketched so far implies a relation between knower and object of knowledge in which the latter is active 'beyond' the grasp of the knower. Yet this is not to say that there is an unknowable interiority eternally defended from the knowing subject. As we move further into exploring what this activity beyond our grasp might be or how it might be talked of, that as yet unknown residue takes on, as we discover it, the contours of what can be thought, what can be understood. Hegel's much-misunderstood axiom that the real is the rational means that what is there for perception of any kind is there to be *thought*, to be rendered in concept and metaphor: it continues to offer a structured life in which the knower has a part, or which has a part in the knower.[52] Thus, wherever we find ourselves on the spectrum of knowing, we assume that what confronts us offers the possibility of some kind of ordered speech, some kind of representation. This, incidentally, is why the idea, fashionable in some philosophical and neurological circles,[53] that the world of our perception is, so to speak, a 'virtual' world, unrelated to 'what is actually there', manifestly incoherent. Apart from the difficulty of giving any content to the idea of a 'real world' without any formal connection to our acts of knowing (for this to make sense we'd have to have an heuristic discourse about 'reality' differentiated from the contents of our minds in ways we could not by definition adequately specify), we could give no very good account of why such a virtual world would repeatedly generate problems whose solutions formed a provisionally rational system, and at the

52 A first-class recent discussion in Nicholas Adams, *Eclipse of Grace: Divine and Human Action in Hegel* (Oxford: Wiley/Blackwell, 2013), especially chapter 2.
53 For a full critical treatment of these issues and a robust response to the lure of virtualism, see David Chalmers, *The Character of Consciousness* (Oxford: Oxford University Press, 2010), chapter 13.

same time repeatedly led to a reshaping of what counted as rationality. As we shall see shortly, the possibility of error in language is a metaphysically interesting question. Our minds are not instantly self-correcting mechanisms but take time to identify a difficulty and then to reorder concepts and protocols to deal with the difficulty.

But if there is such a dimension to knowing, the dimension of an indeterminate yet intelligible hinterland to every percept, we are led to another postulate of the highest generality: finite being is always dependent, so we have assumed; we now see grounds for the suspicion that it must also be always intelligible, representable in the widest sense. Whatever we encounter is something that triggers capacities for recognition and representation in our minds. And it is this insight, or something very like it, that has suggested to theologians the language of a finite reality that consistently 'gives' itself to be known. We advance in our engagement with our environment in the confidence that the activity we meet is congruent with our own to the degree that we can think it, and that it represents a feature of activity as such or being as such – a direction, if not towards us at least in tune with us, moving into our subjectivity as a presence that enlarges our capacity and serves our welfare. To go on in the 'quest for knowledge' under whatever form requires some version of this confidence. If our speech is consistently opening out on to the horizon of further questioning, we can begin to see how this trajectory, for practical purposes unlimited in prospect, may carry with it a shadow of the image of an infinite flow of activity characterized by what we can only think of as generosity. Or, in other words, the indeterminate diversity of representational possibility points us towards an abundance that is always bound up in understanding, always rooted in the intelligible, and also active in bestowing its activity on and in what it is not. The schema that is called up as these considerations are spelled out is, ultimately, that of an unlimited intelligence and love. If we characterize finite being as dependent, this model claims, what it depends on is what we can only speak of as an act of intelligent and beneficent 'bestowal'.

These points are made here in rather abbreviated form, but will recur as the discussion advances. What I hope to show is how the unfinished character of human language establishes us as speakers in a particular imaginative context, as subjects constantly seeking to respond to changing opportunities of participation in our environment and being variously enlarged by those responses. To speak of response is to gesture towards a prior reality of *address*, an address to which we are always 'subsequent', even a gift which we are always seeking to receive appropriately.[54] To speak of enlargement is to gesture towards an assumption that the relation between the knowing subject and its environment is fundamentally and irreducibly nourishing, making for growth – not exclusively (though importantly) growth in some controlling capacity but growth in an awareness of connection that allows not only a more successful negotiating of the environment but a *celebration* of its resource: language as a festive 'holding-up' of what is represented so that it can be see freshly, art and contemplation as well as *techne* and politics (which in turn has significant ethical consequences, although these will not be the main focus of discussion).

In the next chapter, we shall be looking specifically at various aspects of language as behaviour that is not simply determined. We begin with two points about language as we know it – that it is possible to say what is *not* the case, to create 'representations' that are at odds with what is there; and that language is always 'triangulated' between the sign, the signmaker and the signified. Much of the confusion that can attend our thinking about language, and indeed consciousness, arises from the attempt to reduce three terms to two. In trying to map more effectively the particular kind of freedom that belongs to human speech, we should find ourselves better able to understand how language advances through the processes of self-questioning. Preller, the reader may remember, spoke of the human intellect as ordered to what it could not know. In the light of what we are about to look at, we need to clarify this by saying that, as far as finite objects of knowing are concerned, our minds are 'ordered' to schemata that constantly reveal themselves to be problematic or at least tantalizingly capable of being 'read' in different ways when thoroughly explored – i.e. they reveal themselves as generating further questions, and so generating a recognition of what is not

---

54 The category of gift has become increasingly central for recent discussions of theologically framed ontology, thanks partly to Jean-Luc Marion (see, especially, *Being Given: Toward a Phenomenology of Givenness* (Redwood, CA: Stanford University Press, 2002) and John Milbank's seminal studies in *Being Reconciled: Ontology and Pardon* (London: Routledge, 2003).

known. And we could say further that, in regard to *infinite* being, we could only acknowledge our incapacity to form a concept – while at the same time enjoying a relation analogous to knowing in so far as we participate in an action directed towards us.[55] But in either case, the 'ordering to the unknown' clarifies what we might want to say about language's freedom: the relation between knower and known is not – whether in regard to a finite or an infinite context – a matter of a certain determinate set of facts or truths causing/triggering a certain determinate set of signs. On which, back to Michael Leunig for an almost-last word for now: 'The word "God" cannot be grasped scientifically, rationally or even theologically without it exploding. It can only be held lightly and poetically.'[56] Part of the point of what follows is to look at some of the phenomenology of explosions – the breakdown of speech when it turns to God and the breakdown of speech when it is unable to turn to God. Somewhere in between there is perhaps a way of 'holding'. Finding that is surely an aspect of what the renewed natural theology we are searching for might embody.

55 For some suggestive insights here, see Jean-Yves Lacoste, 'Perception, Transcendence and the Experience of God', in Peter M. Candler Jr and Conor Cunningham (eds), *Transcendence and Phenomenology* (London: SCM Press, 2007), pp. 1–20.
56 Leunig, op. cit., p. 237

2

CAN WE SAY WHAT WE LIKE? LANGUAGE, FREEDOM AND DETERMINISM

1

Speaking is a material phenomenon; it is a form of physical behaviour. And there have been those[1] who have not shrunk from the conclusion that it – like all other manifestations of a supposedly intentional consciousness – is therefore no less determined than any other form of physical behaviour. For such thinkers, in the last analysis, we have no choice about what we say. Our vocal cords obey the same inexorable physical laws as the rest of our organism. This does not, of course, mean that what we

---

1   For the most influential and sophisticated statement of the view that all representational states of consciousness (and thus all linguistic behaviour) are causally determined 'matter-of-factual relations', see the work of Wilfrid Sellars, especially *Science, Perception and Reality* (London: Routledge and Kegan Paul, 1963), and *Science and Metaphysics: Variations on Kantian Themes* (London: Routledge and Kegan Paul, 1968). On the whole set of issues around causal models of consciousness and the questions raised by different models of artificial intelligence, the texts and reading lists contained in Douglas R. Hofstadter and Daniel C. Dennett (eds), *The Mind's Eye: Fantasies and Reflections on Self and Soul* (Harmondsworth: Penguin Books, 1982) remain seminal, though the debate has gone on and the literature has expanded vastly. Chapter III of Chalmers. *The Character of Consciousness*, is helpful.

say necessarily *mirrors* or reproduces what the constraints that cause it to happen are actually *like*; why, after all, should the noises we make 'show' anything at all? The most we could say would be that a comprehensive study of causal factors and noises made would presumably display certain correlations: such and such a sequence of noises would coincide with such and such a set of stimuli. We should have no ground for supposing that the noises were anything but a rough guide for identifying the stimuli that were at work. There would be no particular reason for supposing that they informed us what the stimuli were like, or that there was some guaranteed continuity of shape or logical form, let alone any element of imitation in a more obvious sense (Wittgenstein and the Italian gesture again).

But there's the catch. A determinist theory of human utterance has to be expressed in words; and such a theory amounts to saying that one group of noises (this particular theory) is and one group of noises isn't reflective of what processes outside the self are 'like'. The noises by which we purport to construct a comprehensive picture of causal necessity are saved from the bonfire which consumes the claims of all other utterances to show a state of affairs truthfully – whereas, in strict consistency, these noises would be as susceptible as any others to an analysis that correlated them with causal factors beyond themselves. It is the central and vitiating Cretan paradox of determinism – that I should have to be *obliged* to say that everything is determined, while necessarily implying thereby that nothing I say can be relied on to reflect extra-mental truth. If it is true that all my utterances are determined in a way that denies any connection between what I say and what is the case, at least one must also be truthful – that all my utterances are determined. And any supportive arguments for the truth of that utterance must likewise be exempted from the overall discon- nection, if the claim is not to be wholly arbitrary. To give reasons for believing determinism is true is to undermine determinism. To articulate the evidence is to relativize it, because to assume that the noises I make in defending deter- minism have the property of causing you to believe it, or even disposing you to believe it, is manifestly unfounded, and dangerously near to being a flat contradiction of the warning *not* to assume that a state of belief can be caused by anything except a set of immediate physical causes.

All this is familiar enough as a riposte to determinism. But there is a further aspect to its internal problems. Grant for a moment that in principle (and everyone knows that this phrase is a bit of a get-out-of-jail card in this context) it may be possible to predict someone else's utterance at a specific point in time. Yet, as soon as this is said, the other person in question will be made aware of that action/utterance as a possible future course of action; and to be aware of a possible future course of action is also necessarily to entertain the possibility of other courses of action (because one of the logical properties of 'future courses of action' is that they are as yet undetermined). If I tell you that your next utterance will be 'Now I see that determinism is true', you are bound to be conscious of the possibility of *not* saying it; indeed, for a certain temperament, the inclination to say something different, whether or not you believe it, will be irresistible (they might even reply, if they have a taste for Moebius-strip type logical tangles, 'You only say that because you are wholly causally-conditioned to do so').[2] A person simply cannot entertain the prospect of a future action of his/ her own as if it were the prospect of the sun rising tomorrow, seeing it as an event with a high degree of certainty and one over which the person has no control whatsoever. Any future action, for a human agent, is a *possible* action, i.e. one proposed as something that I might or might not do: that is the grammar of speaking of the future action of a conscious agent. The prediction cannot therefore be articulated without its being rendered uncertain. And it does not greatly help that, of course, the act of predicting any particular outcome will itself be determined and cannot therefore be relied on as a truthful prediction.

In his brilliant and influential work, *Philosophy and the Mirror of Nature*,[3] Richard Rorty argued a strong case for distinguishing between the (as he saw it, unavoidably) determinist account we have to give of physical causality and the radically undetermined possibilities of meaning, so that a determinist picture of the actual history of linguistic activity would not be helpful or relevant to the history of meaning. 'Even if we could predict the sounds made by the community of scientific inquirers of the year 4000, we should not yet be in a position to join in their conversation.'[4] It is not,

2   C.f. R. S. Thomas, 'Biography', in *Experimenting With An Amen* (London: Macmillan, 1986), p. 17: 'turning left when you should have gone right / to prove determinism to be in error'.

3   *Philosophy and the Mirror of Nature* (Princeton, NJ: Princeton University Press, 1980).

4   Ibid., p. 355.

he insists, that there is actually something about human beings that allows them the internal liberty of deciding what they mean or what they are going to say: the ontology he assumes means that '[s]ome atoms-and-the-void account of micro-processes within individual human beings will permit the prediction of every sound and inscription which will ever be uttered'.[5] It is simply that we shall go on using the language of 'deciding' or 'inventing', knowing what we mean by that. The point is 'the difference between a language suitable for coping with neurones and one suitable for coping with people', not any kind of ontological divide.[6] But this does not really spring us from the trap. To say that I have the sense of deciding when in fact I do not is something different from saying that I decide: I know the difference in normal speech between these two things, and I can say in retrospect (perhaps in therapy?) that, while I thought I was deciding, it is now clear to me that I wasn't, that I was acting under compulsions I didn't understand. If Rorty is correct, I should have to be perpetually in a state in which this kind of discrimination would not be open to me.

Perhaps more seriously, I should have solid grounds for being suspicious of anyone else's claim to be 'deciding' about their speech or actions; the respect I should be bound to give to someone else's account of their reasons for doing something or their needs and priorities would have to be a wholly arbitrary choice, perhaps a self-interested one (if I want my account of such things to be taken seriously, I should probably at least pretend to take someone else's claims seriously). But if I am not in a position where I need that kind of reciprocal recognition, if I am in a position where, for example, I have some clearly defined power over another individual or group, what ground is there for according any respect to someone else's self-description, someone else's version of their needs or interests? How can the liberal polity and culture Rorty commends be rationally derived from his basic position? This morally unsettling implication of Rorty's scheme has not had as much discussion as it needs, although it is touched on in the

5   Ibid., p. 387.
6   Ibid., p. 355 and chapter II, *passim* (e.g. p. 125, 'These so-called ontological categories [the free and the determined, the mental and the physical] are simply the ways of packaging rather heterogeneous notions ... which were convenient for Descartes' own purposes' – the assumption being, apparently, that a Cartesian dualism of parallel kinds of substance is the only *ontological* alternative to physicalism; c.f note 68 below).

critique offered by Roy Bhaskar, about which we shall hear more shortly. It is not quite enough to say that we would somehow instinctively know where the boundaries lay between the languages suitable for two contexts, neurone-language and people-language, if one of those languages is making exhaustive claims that are wholly incompatible with the intelligent and self-aware practice of the other. If reference to what is 'suitable for coping with people' is without any ontological content – if, that is, what is said about people is a 'surface' discourse, a sort of optional extra to the real analysis, which is always to do with neurones – it is always going to be up for negotiation; it has no controls other than what happens to make sense to a speaker at any particular moment, or, worse, what happens to suit the interest of a particular speaker at a particular moment. In such a situation, the superficial register of language that purports to refer to that particular organization of neurones we call a person adds nothing but a kind of sentimental colouring to the basic account. And, because this is not simply about how I perceive my own actions but about how I read and respond to the actions of others – not simply about inhabiting my own determined identity with the playful irony that Rorty so eloquently commends but a potential ground for refusing any other person's account of their own agency – it is a position with such morally worrying implications that we might well be driven back to probing with extra care the cogency of the underlying philosophical case.

Such energetic probing has been undertaken by Roy Bhaskar in his *Philosophy and the Idea of Freedom*,[7] where he picks up the question of whether the neurophysiology of an individual is the sort of closed system for which comprehensive prediction is possible. If, for example, the newsagent hands me a copy of the newspaper I have asked for, would his actions have been the same had I not asked for it? And, if not, can we say that my asking causes him to hand it to me? Neither is satisfactory: the former is manifestly nonsense, the latter either claims that words spoken act as determining causal agencies or allow a culturally mediated element to enter in: the newsagent hands me the paper because he recognizes a request and is willing and able to respond. In the latter case, we have an action not determined by simple physical processes, unless we want to

---

7   *Philosophy and the Idea of Freedom* (Oxford: Blackwell, 1991), see especially p. 48ff.

adopt the comprehensive determinism that assumes every conceivable action in the universe is foreordained, and 'each person's microstructure is so synchronized with every other's that it appears *just as if* they were talking and dancing, batting and bowling, laughing and crying.'[8] So a closed-system determinism is impossible to sustain; we cannot avoid assuming that we are responsible for at least some of our physical actions, and our linguistic behaviour is one of the prime candidates for such responsible behaviour. If it is true that we should not be able to understand what people are saying in 4000 even if we knew what it would sound like, this is indeed no more than the consequence of our lack of cultural familiarity with that specific setting.

Rorty's fundamental problem, Bhaskar argues, is that he seeks to hold together a completely exhaustive and exact realism at one level (all physical processes are determined and predictable) with a radical 'existentialist' voluntarism on the other, in which we create the meanings and definitions we choose. Freedom is the ability we sense in ourselves to redescribe anything and everything, and this is the only form of power over 'the world' that we can have.[9] What Rorty's scheme does not help us with is how we make a difference to the material circumstances we find ourselves in – our purposive interaction with the environment, our restless adjustments of social relationship and power. In a way that is – as Bhaskar points out[10] – quite at odds with his ambitious celebration of the human capacity constantly to reinvent what can be said and imagined, Rorty seems to be assuming that we live within a set of determined constraints that cannot be *materially* affected by our liberty to say what we choose. Our speaking will not relate to anything 'out there'; 'Poetry makes nothing happen'[11] becomes a general principle about all utterance. And we might press a little further, noting a point Bhaskar does not actually take up: if we do live in a world of physically determined events, then the neural activity underlying not only our speech but the representation to ourselves of what we say, our imagining and planning, our redescriptions of the environment, must also

8   Ibid., p. 49.
9   Ibid., chapter 5, *passim*.
10   E.g. ibid., chapter 8.
11   The phrase is from W. H. Auden, 'In Memory of W. B. Yeats', *Collected Poems* (London: Faber and Faber, 1976), p. 197.

be determinate – otherwise we have simply introduced into the material system a set of uncaused phenomena, the neural firings that give us the illusion of meaning something by what we say. In short, a thorough-going determinist ontology will finally demand more than Rorty is prepared to concede; and if a liberty of imagining is granted, it must in the last analysis be as illusory as any other liberty. Rorty has been seduced by the strong inherited mythology of the divide between material fact and mental interpretation, 'hard' and 'soft' kinds of speaking about phenomena.[12] But physicalist determinism is undoubtedly more of a universal acid than this allows: all 'soft', humanistic or imaginative varieties of speech are going to be consumed, sooner or later.

We shall be revisiting other aspects of Bhaskar's argument later on. For now, we should simply conclude that whatever we want to say about language as underdetermined must avoid the confusion and the possible self-contradiction inherent in Rortian dualism. The idea that we are free to give what account of 'reality' we choose, that there is no difference between 'telling a story' and 'reflecting the world',[13] fails to deal with the actual constraints that speech works with. In plain terms, it gives no account of *difficulty*, of the element of struggle involved in working on language so that it is purged of idleness, self-indulgence and self-referentiality, superstition (however defined) and so on, and becomes an increasingly sustainable tool for common reflection and common labour. The fact that we work on our words in such a way that we come to trust one another, to be confident that what we are talking about is what another speaker is talking about, so that we can negotiate shared activities – this tells very seriously against the idea that 'describing things as we please' could be a constitutive strategy of our language. We shall always have *learned* how to identify and describe; if we then go on to revise the descriptions we have learned, it is because the world of common action (including shared speech about the object) reveals over time various lacunae or tangles of sense that need labour. The Hegelian

---

12 Bhaskar, op. cit., chapter 3 and c.f. p. 135. On Rorty's formulation of 'hard' scientific knowledge, see also p. 20: 'Rorty operates a characteristic dilemmatic disjunction here: *either* science is algorithmic [reducible to strict and repeatable formulaic analysis] *or* it is unmethodical. We are offered a choice between a rigid fundamentalist demand and a soft deflationary option.'

13 Ibid., p. 111.

pattern of positing, critiquing and re-founding what we say about anything at all is a far more fruitful and faithful version of how we speak than any mythology of a single 'creative' speaker reinventing his or her world. We continue to learn, and part of fully setting out the meaning of a description may in many cases be a matter of setting out how we have learned to use the language we now use. After all, scientific *narrative* is a central feature of scientific justification. And the fascination of examining a poet's or novelist's notebooks is the opportunity to see how a writer learns something, moves away from initial statements in response to a usually invisible and imagined partner in speech, or at least to a kind of pressure that is not simply generated by the speaker's conscious agenda. There is always a struggle to make what we say both recognizable and defensible: speech that aims at truthfulness is speech that invites responsive testing, to establish if it is really recognizable.

2

Yet – and here is the salience of Rorty's picture – we know that what we say is not actually *dictated* by what is simply there. We know that what I have been calling description is constantly edging towards more ambitious varieties of utterance, towards representation, the rebirth of what is 'given' in another context of meaning or another medium of showing. A representation that contradicts or wholly ignores the history of how the relevant description has been learned is obviously problematic; we could do worse in our attempts to capture what is claimed for relations of truth or reference than appeal to this as a touchstone: does what is said make it impossible to go on telling this particular story of how, experimentally, we came to say this rather than that about an object?[14] Yet there is another history of learning, one in which we are repeatedly challenged to configure more comprehensively and connectedly the specific impressions that have been identified as elements of description (remember the 'schemata' of Arbib and Hesse discussed in Chapter 1). And this of course introduces into our speech a new dimension: what we say is no longer an attempt (if it ever was)

---

14 C.f. Chapter 6 below for the significance of the history lying behind any particular utterance – or non-utterance.

at reproducing a catalogue of juxtaposed elements, but involves ascribing to what we are talking about a coherent 'life' with some continuity over time and some interweaving with other 'lives' (the scare quotes simply mean that this applies to what we should call inanimate as well as animate objects). Our speech declares its distance from simple reproductive listing: what we can say is more than what we might be obliged to say in creating a formal picture of a set of elements. As I have indicated, we are pointed back to Wittgenstein's breakthrough from his early 'picture theory' (utterances as logical maps of the elements of what is the case). The gesture that made Wittgenstein think again is, of course, still further down the road away from plain description; but as soon as we move away from identifying 'elements of description', we are well on this road. I should make it clear that what I am talking about is not some kind of narrative of consciousness that begins with bare sense impressions or whatever and moves to abstraction and talk about essences; as our discussion in Chapter 1 shows, the origins of language seem to lie in a more dialectical to and fro between right- and left-brain functionality. It might be better to say, not 'as soon as we start to speak of "reproductive" discourse', but 'as soon as we are reflectively aware of the diversity between the two already operating kinds of function and register'. The important point is that to notice what we are doing when we speak is to notice the interplay between registers. I do not find it helpful to characterize this as Rorty does in terms of 'normal' and 'abnormal' speech;[15] this is a question-begging locution if ever there was one. But he is right in highlighting the fundamental fact that we habitually use language in a way that is not demonstrably tied to what is in front of us; and that using language this way complicates what we have to say about truth in certain important respects.

What we say is – to state the obvious – an action that we perform. Cataloguing elements of perception, describing, is a particular mode of responsive action. Imagining the schemata in which that description fits is another, more complex, mode which comes into focus if we are concerned not only to *register* what is perceived but to *engage* with it, to find our way around it, so to speak, and even to discern the patterns of its own activity in such a way

15 Rorty, op. cit., pp. 322ff. and 386–9. The terminology derives from Thomas Kuhn, but is given a distinctive twist by Rorty.

as to cooperate with, modify or divert those patterns. We need linguistic and conceptual tools that allow us to see a continuing identity over time in what confronts us, and a 'schematic' consistency in clusters of phenomena. Refining these tools is a matter of learning, trying out schemata, exposing them to be tested; and that testing is not only in terms of practical success but also and inseparably in terms of recognizability in the exchange of speech with other speakers – what we colloquially and significantly call 'making sense' to others. And this is an area of uncertainty or risk: we are not in a position simply to point to an agreed set of atomized phenomena. Cultures or 'natural languages' divide up the perceived world rather differently: it is notoriously difficult to establish exact translations for certain colour words, and some cultures have immensely sophisticated classification schemes for, say, diversities of weather or terrain and extremely limited taxonomies for animals.[16] The sheer fact of the diversity of natural languages already alerts us to the underdetermined character of the relation of observed phenomena to representation. It seems that, to understand how language works, we have to understand its riskiness, its unstable connection with what it engages with. Notice that I am not talking about the relation of 'language' with 'the world': once again, this begs a question, assuming that there is somewhere a straightforward catalogue of neutral phenomena to be isolated as what is basically *there*, and that anything else is what we choose to say, or at best what we vaguely and intuitively decide to add to the iron rations of description. As we have already seen in this chapter, such a distinction is unworkable; and the instability or uncertain 'fit' of what we say to the environment we inhabit and with which we negotiate is not a mark of its arbitrariness. We test our schemata, we criticize and enlarge and rework our representational structures, transforming both our relationships with each other and our capacity to negotiate with the environment. We claim to move from less to more adequate representation, not only – as Rorty and others suggest – from one imaginative experiment to another.

Yet once this instability has been named, we have to think through the implications. What we say is capable of being not only a representation

<hr/>

16 The second and third chapters of George Steiner, *After Babel: Aspects of Language and Translation* (Oxford: Oxford University Press, 1975), still offer a rich background for considering these questions, despite a drip-feed of criticism from more risk-averse analysts.

but a misrepresentation; the elements of description may be assembled in ways that bear no relation to what has been encountered or engaged. We noted in the first chapter that the Ice Age image of a 'lion man' displays not only a capacity to render an accurate reproduction of the features of a lion and a human being but also the ability to disaggregate those features and recombine some of them so as to suggest a fusion of the overall quality or essence of both of the kinds of life involved. It is possible to create a representation that corresponds to nothing that is actually *there* as a single object in the environment, yet which – we have to presume, given that the type is repeated in different places – 'made sense' to those who saw and handled such images. We can, in word or artefact, reorder what is given. Speech can, to put it in the most dramatic way, rebel against any attempt to install a tyranny of description. As George Steiner put it many years ago in a classic discussion of problems around reference, truth and translation, most modern accounts of truth do not provide any very helpful insights on the question of *falsity*, saying what is not so. Steiner, very boldly, claims that this question is actually fundamental for an adequate theory of what makes human language what it is: 'I believe', he writes, 'that the question of the nature and history of falsity is of crucial importance to an understanding of language and of culture. Falsity is not, except in the most formal or internally systematic sense, a mere miscorrespondence with a fact. It is itself an active, creative agent. The human capacity to utter falsehood, to lie, to negate what is the case, stands at the heart of speech and of the reciprocities between words and world ... We are a mammal who can bear false witness.'[17]

3

Steiner goes on to note the importance in philosophy of propositions that cannot be simply verified by appeal to what can be 'descriptively' established. Counterfactuals and subjunctive conditionals ('If x had done y, he would have ...'), statements containing 'if' and 'can', are all essential tools in what Steiner illuminatingly calls the 'protean stability'[18] of our speech, its capacity to extend the possibilities of action by extending what we can

17 Steiner, op. cit., p. 214.
18 Ibid., p. 215.

narrate as thinkable courses of actions for ourselves and other agents and to refuse simply to accept what happens to be so as the endpoint of what we can say, to stay on 'the treadmill of the present', in another of Steiner's memorable phrases.[19] The truth is (an ironic idiom in this context) that relatively little of what we say is strictly descriptive. And an over-neat moral dualism between speaking truly and speaking 'falsely' does not greatly help us in calibrating which of the countless utterances that go beyond the flatly descriptive are genuinely morally problematic. As Steiner says, there are differences of emphasis here between classical and early Christian authors, even between Christian authors themselves. And, to take up a point I have touched on in another context,[20] we need a nuanced approach to the role of controlled or securely bounded fantasy in the psychological development of children; we should not assume that there is a simple moral superiority in the kind of speaking or writing that reflects only what a child may be familiar with.

Steiner is, of course, provocatively blurring some comfortable boundaries between two rather different things – asserting what is not the case *as if it were*, and asserting propositions corresponding to no actual state of affairs but not designed to mislead. But he is surely right to provoke: the boundaries are not instantly self-evident, and appeals to whether or not there is an intention to deceive will not settle the issues immediately. And he is right to note a diversity of philosophical and theological judgement on this. Paul Griffiths, in a recent and wonderfully lucid discussion of Augustine's view of lying,[21] maps the diverse approaches within the spectrum of patristic and mediaeval theology, concluding that Augustine alone takes the issue of lying with full theological seriousness in his absolute prohibition of any untrue utterance, even if it is made with the intention of protecting the innocent or avoiding catastrophe: 'Augustine takes it to be clear ... that no temporal good, not even the saving of life or protection from rape, can warrant the lie.' [22] This is because he begins from a conviction about speech

---

19 Ibid., p. 218.
20 Rowan Williams, *Lost Icons: Reflections on Cultural Bereavement* (Edinburgh: T. and T. Clark, 2000), pp. 12–22.
21 *Lying: An Augustinian Theology of Duplicity* (Grand Rapids, MI: Brazos Press, 2004).
22 Ibid., p. 96.

itself: truthful speech is a participation in the life of God the Holy Trinity. Just as the eternal Word of God is generated instantly, timelessly, from the Father, so our thought is generated out of the depths of our *memoria*, the inner 'deposit' of all we have received, as an image of that *memoria*; and the rendering of thought into speech echoes the incarnation of the Word in flesh. It is the clothing of thought in external form, accessible to other material and historical subjects; and so its content is properly no more than and no different from the content of what is thought. 'Any change in this relation is therefore a rupture of the divine image in us.'[23] Griffiths contrasts this with the teaching of nearly every other patristic writer, as well as with Aquinas, Kant and Newman. but he stresses that Augustine is not recommending a rigorist moral approach to truthfulness so much as inviting us to imagine what speech would be like without evasion or self-serving – what speech would be like if it were nothing but 'confession and adoration', a realm of words entirely transparent to the eternal reality which language-using creatures are created to manifest.[24] The avoidance of the lie can only be realized when we are overwhelmed by the gift of God's grace, because we have to recognize that we are habitually liars and can only cease to be so when we let go of the 'ownership' of our speech and surrender to the language of confession, testimony to the beauty of God.[25]

Even granted that Augustine does not completely rule out the creative use of speech, in poetry or epic,[26] this is a singularly austere position. We may agree with Augustine and Griffiths that the utterly habitual untruthfulness of human intercourse, the party chatter, the gossip and self-excusing and self-promoting we are accustomed to (and accustomed to not thinking about in moral terms) is an abuse of language and a tacit but serious betrayal of the image of God in us. We may agree that lying under pressure to save ourselves from unpleasant consequences is, however common, not an acceptable strategy for anyone who believes what Augustine believes about the nature of language,[27] and probably not for anyone who thinks of the use

23 Ibid., p. 84.
24 Ibid., pp. 85–92, 225.
25 Ibid., chapter 5, *passim*.
26 Ibid., chapter 6, *passim*.
27 Ibid., pp. 98–9.

of language as a moral question at all. And Griffiths's powerful conclusion that speech is most truthfully itself when it – so to speak – resigns its powers and ambitions is indeed a resonant characterization of what most Christian writers, including poets, dramatists and novelists, have hoped and prayed they were doing. Yet the great counterintuitive claim that any kind of conscious deception is unmitigated sin, even if performed in order to save the innocent, needs a little more probing. The classic case of the person interrogated by the Gestapo as to the whereabouts of a Jewish family concealed in his house continues to nag at the imagination. Augustine discusses[28] such a case and recommends refusing to answer – or saying, 'I know where they are but I'm not telling you' – and inviting the persecutors to do their worst: silence, for Augustine, is always a moral option, indeed *the* moral option in such a case. And Griffiths rightly follows Augustine in warning[29] against using this sort of instance to suggest that there are times when only a sin on your part will prevent a sin on someone else's. However, there are a few considerations that might make us pause. First, it is not insignificant that the case under review is one in which I am not distorting truth primarily for my own safety or profit; and to read the moral coordinates of the situation as essentially and centrally about whether I as an individual am adequately witnessing to the divine image risks obscuring that image just as damagingly as any conscious falsehood. It is not easily glossed as a straightforward case of whether or not I am dispossessing myself of sinful power. Even silence is not so straightforward: what will a persecutor deduce from my silence? Am I sure that I can resist pressure to break that silence, threats against my own family, perhaps, or torture? Would such a certainty itself be a case of trying to 'possess' a future that is intrinsically uncertain? Most important of all, is the theologically motivated impulse to manifest my thought as faithfully as possible the only consideration in an ethic of speaking? If our speech is given us as a means of challenging what is the case in the name of an imagined world of greater justice or mercy or joy, if what it is to manifest is not only a static mental content but a divine purpose or desire, can we say that a saving fiction is invariably impermissible? To manifest an Augustinian mental content ('The family is in the basement')

28 Augustine, *de mendacio* xiii, PL 40, 504–5.
29 Op. cit., pp. 95–6.

unquestionably provides the occasion for a dreadful and unjust act to occur; it cannot be without guilt, as I know with a high degree of moral certainty what awaits the family if discovered. I have a choice and must act; that act has clear consequences. One does not have to be a simple consequentialist to conclude that there is no unambiguously right option available and that the prudential calculating of near-certain harm has to enter in. Augustine may have said that temporal harms – to others as well as myself – are less grave than the spiritual betrayal involved in lying; but surely he under-rates the spiritual betrayal involved in so relativizing the avoidable hurt of another, obliging others to pay with their lives for my own truthfulness, colluding with a powerful and pervasive injustice. Is this really a dispossession of speech? Griffiths eloquently asserts[30] that such cases show how the gift of God's grace is a 'violent' disruption of our secure consciences; yet how can we be sure that adhesion to Augustinian truthfulness will not be, in the hands of anyone less passionate about the priority of grace, simply a way of identifying an unambiguously right course of action that will soothe our consciences rather than disturb them? Plainly, how do we know that this hideously costly truthfulness will not be the occasion of smugness rather than anguish?

Once we allow that the relation of mental content to words is not the simple mirroring that Augustine seems to assume in this context (not in all, it might be said), the theological point becomes more nuanced. What speech is equipped (or even 'called'?) to represent here is not just a state of affairs, but a possible, an imaginable state of affairs: fidelity to what is perceived, fidelity, in Augustine's terms, to the God-givenness of truth, requires not just a faithful reproduction of data but a faithful alignment with whatever can be discerned or received of a merciful purpose, of the eternal generosity of the threefold divine life; and that may leave us a little more open to taking the risk of fiction when confronted with the hard cases Augustine wrestles with, well aware that this is a moment of apparent transgression that leaves a marked streak of grey in the moral map. Melodramatic speculations of a Graham Greeneish variety about unavoidable sins or sins committed out of charity are not the point here: the question is rather whether the 'saving fiction' is sinful in precisely the sense that a deliberate

30 Op. cit., p. 230.

refusal of God's loving purpose for myself or another is sinful. Augustine, and perhaps Griffiths, would clearly want to say that it is. But the counter-case is not just about sentimental relativism or the comforting acceptance of what a spiritually unformed conscience delivers. What if the truth I am struggling to manifest is that the Jewish family in the basement is, precisely, the object of the unconditional love that generates the eternal Word (and all our own words in and with it)? And what if the only way of changing a profoundly and systematically untruthful linguistic environment is to refuse its demands for the 'manifestation' of facts, even to the point of producing fiction?

This last question may help to explain why I have taken time with a prolonged discussion of Griffiths's book and Augustine's argument. If all we have to discuss in the construction of a theology or moral philosophy of language is the function of manifesting what is the case, we miss a range of difficult but essential themes, pertinent to the overall argument of these lectures. For example, it is a more complicated question than it seems to ask what it is that creates and maintains *trust* in the exchange of language: the obvious answer (telling the truth) is not quite enough. Someone who was known to tell the truth unfailingly in situations like the Jewish family in the basement case would not necessarily invite trust (except among members of the Gestapo or their equivalent). One would be hesitant about entrusting information to them; so that, paradoxically, a rigid adherence to manifesting the facts would encourage less rather than more truthful sharing of infor-mation. We could say that what fostered trust was something more like an adherence to the truth about human beings before God and a systematic resistance to the prevailing outrages against that truth in current political practice. Or, to take a slightly different instance, think of the scenario portrayed in Ibsen's play, *The Wild Duck*: an idealistic and morally absolute character judges it his duty to expose skeletons in the family cupboard, with devastatingly destructive results. Is Ibsen's Gregers Werle a person whose speech commands *trust*? Surely not. His truthfulness is pursued without attention to the actual feelings and needs of those around, and so can hardly be seen in Griffiths's terms as a disowned or dispossessed language. This is not to echo the sentimental claptrap that would prefer 'a lie that brings a smile' to 'a truth that brings a tear' (hands up all who have dabbed at their eyes while watching *Miracle on 34th Street*). The problem with Ibsen's

Gregers is that he has a frighteningly simplistic idea of the automatically liberating effect of truthfulness wholly uninformed by any sense of what can be heard by others and how it is heard. And once we have granted that there is an ethical question about 'what can be heard' – as an aspect of the imperative to self-forgetting attentiveness – we have introduced into our moral reflection the recognition of language as more than a making visible/audible of a single mental content.

This does not tell us that lying is all right, or that truthfulness is too complicated to attain; but it poses the question of what enters in to an 'adequate' representing of the reality we encounter, and takes us back to George Steiner's provoking notion that what is most distinctive about human speech is its capacity to 'bear false witness'. Speech *can* betray (it is significant that Steiner chooses such a resonant biblical phrase); what did it mean for the earliest language users to discover that the sounds they made could conceal as well as manifest, that they could recombine the elements they named? How would we explain to someone from a radically different culture or to the proverbial Martian that this was among the uses of speech? There are certainly cultures for which the conscious elaboration of fiction – culminating in the novel or the drama – is almost unimaginable.[31] But it seems we must say that language is from the beginning *capable* of such use, for the simple reason that it presents us with choices about how we make representations – even how we 'describe', in fact. And once we are conscious of choices, we are conscious of what is not to be said, and so of the space in which alternative discourses could be generated, whether in the relatively unproblematic shape of a metaphorical rendering, or in sheer counterfactual assertion. And as to the latter, counterfactual assertion may be intended to deceive, but may equally be meant simply to provoke new possibilities into life. On any account, it is a move away from anything like a dependable and stable relation between what is 'given' and what is said as the fundamental nature of speech.

31 Steiner, op. cit., p. 218, refers to Jonathan Swift's Gulliver attempting to explain to the Houyhnhnms why humans ever speak anything but the truth. C.f. A. N. Wilson's novel, *The Potter's Hand* (London: Atlantic Books, 2012), pp. 78–81, for a similar attempt by an eighteenth-century Englishman to explain to a Native American what satire and theatre are; an attempt met with Augustinian incomprehension and disapproval.

4

Speech is not – to borrow the vocabulary developed by Walker Percy, the American novelist, in his essays on language and reference – one pole of a 'dyadic' relationship, a simple cause and effect doublet. Percy, in several of these essays,[32] builds on the way in which C. S. Peirce, one of the major figures of American pragmatic philosophy, elaborates the distinction between 'dyadic' and 'triadic' relations. Dyadic relations are those between forces or agencies, interactions between different elements in an environment. As Percy says,[33] this can be rendered in more contemporary terms as 'energy exchanges ... subatomic particles colliding, chemical reactions, actions of force-fields on bodies, physical and chemical transactions across biological membranes, neuron discharges, etc.' In this world, certain phenomena may be 'indices' of other phenomena: if this phenomenon is perceived, we conclude to that; if smoke, then fire. So, in human behaviour, some of the sounds we make are indices: a person has toothache and groans. But another person says 'Ouch!' and another says 'My tooth hurts'. 'It may be unexceptionable', says Percy,[34] 'to say that all ... emitted responses, the first a wired-in response, the second and third learned responses.' But what it is that distinguishes the learned responses from the 'wired-in' variety needs something more than an energy exchange model to account for it; to treat language as susceptible to 'dyadic' analysis only is not to have a science of language at all.

What is at issue is the difference between the index and the *symbol*. Symbolizing is a triadic relation, between language user, object and symbol, with the symbol as an element that is not naturally 'like' what it refers to. 'A symbol must be unlike what it symbolizes in order that it may be trans-formed and "become" what it symbolizes.'[35] Thus a word takes on the 'feel', the associations of what it points to, even though it is not a thing lying to hand that we use to symbolize another thing because it intrinsically reminds us of that other thing. An utterance in a natural language establishes a *world*,

32 Walker Percy, *The Message in the Bottle: How Queer Man Is, How Queer Language Is, and What One Has to Do with the Other* (New York: Farrar, Straus and Giroux, 1975).
33 Ibid., p. 162.
34 Ibid., pp. 164–5.
35 Ibid., p. 169.

which is importantly different, Percy argues, from an 'environment';[36] a world is a scheme of sentences proposing a coherent set of relations, which may be actual or fictive, present, past or future (it should be clear, of course, that the sense of 'world' here is different from the one that seeks to characterize the environment as opposed to the speaker, the sense I challenged a little while back). Which of these it is will be settled by a complex process taking place in a community of speakers. What we can be sure of, though, is that it cannot be settled by an account of linguistic behaviour that treats it as a series of responses to stimuli. We noted earlier in this chapter that the *form* of an utterance cannot in itself tell us what is the case; the relation between the noises we make and any states of affairs in our environment is anything but straightforward, and the very idea of a representation, or even a description, of states of affairs by way of noises highlights the point about fundamental unlikenesses between what is represented and the symbolic medium of representation. Thus we can describe an environment as a system of energy exchanges; but a 'world' requires something more. In a dyadic system of energy exchange, the same stimulus will produce the same response, but this will not work for language – either in terms of the relation between object and utterance or in terms of the relation between utterance and hearer. As Percy observes,[37] the sentence 'I need you' can provoke a very wide range of responses depending on the 'world' in which it occurs. And, as he goes on to argue, there are 'normative' dimensions to sentences which go well beyond a simple true-or-false polarity: the same words may be spoken as literal, as metaphor, as trite metaphor or fresh metaphor, as significant or banal, appropriate or inappropriate. As we noted in regard to Griffiths's version of Augustine, the plain binary scheme of truth or falsehood may reflect very little of what is involved in speaking truthfully or adequately. And if we think further about some of the varieties of speech failing to represent truthfully, we need also to reflect on the diverse ways in which we can claim to identify *mistakes*. Once we start asking what is meant by a mistake, we realize that we are again well beyond any stimulus–response pattern: Percy neatly describes the Freudian slip as 'a dyadic irruption of unconscious forces into triadic behaviour' and so not a *mistake* in any

36 Ibid., p. 173.
37 Ibid., p. 176.

interesting sense.[38] A mistake may be any one of a broad spectrum of missed connections, faulty readings of what was imagined to be a shared world but turns out not to be, clashes of register or tone and so on.

In fact, as Percy observes in another essay,[39] the idea of a mistake is in one sense fundamental to understanding language. The very act of symbolization – relating ourselves to a given phenomenon by proposing a potentially complex utterance that represents it, over and above any strict account of its identifiably distinct elements – is a basic 'error' according to some accounts of language, in that it turns away from the simplicity of the dyadic or the mere indexical reflection so as to hold what has been perceived/encountered in the medium of something else. The temptation is to seek to reverse this turning away as if it were the original sin of language, and to try to restore an unmediated reflection of what is there, a sort of unfallen descriptive clarity; and this must be resisted.[40] The more we think about metaphor itself, the more we grasp that it is a symptom – an index? – of that restlessness with which we as speakers approach our environment. A boy in the country apprehends the unique movement of a bird's flight, perceives clearly and comprehensively what is going on, but then 'having perfectly perceived the flight of the hawk, now suffers a sort of disability, a tension, even a sense of imminence.'[41] Something 'needs' to be said or done. But what more does naming the bird add? Is the release of tension that comes with finding a name, and, further down the line, finding a way of representing the bird, just another instance of practical needs being satisfied or energy imbalances adjusted? By pairing the apprehended thing with another thing, a cluster of sounds that may have other pairings and resonances, I shift the bird, in Percy's terms, from environment to world. To *know* the bird is to set it in the context of the echoes and resonances that come with utterance.

Percy takes this further by giving us an extreme case of representational oddity from the American South, a case of 'accidental' metaphor, the sometimes bizarre mishearing of words that create chance associations – in

38   Ibid., p. 178; c.f. pp. 181–8 for a fuller exposition of this.
39   Ibid., p. 81.
40   Ibid., p. 82.
41   Ibid., p. 67.

this instance, the mishearing of the hawk's original designation ('blue darter hawk') as what seems to be a startlingly compressed and bizarre image ('blue-dollar hawk'), which takes over as the normal dialect form. It is this latter, dialect, name that gives the more intense sense of what the hawk is, says Percy, because it is not just describing the bird's behaviour. It presents the hawk as dense with significance, as puzzling and inviting, and so as independently real in an intensified way. We might take Percy's argument a stage further and say that when the hawk – or whatever else – is presented to me as a puzzle, as something designated by an impenetrable name which does not simply reflect what I think I see, it acquires a status as 'over against' my act of perceiving which establishes that my speaking is exploratory and incomplete in respect of what I am encountering. The error of mishearing points to the deeper 'error' of moving out of description and reflection towards this exploratory enterprise, the constant searching for connections in the company of other speakers. [42]

Walker Percy's treatment of these issues is often painfully compressed and rather tangled, and it is clear that it reflects just the process he is trying to set out – the repeated struggle to chart the territory of what is perceived from one angle after another, with no final statement possible. It has also attracted its share of criticism from professional philosophers.[43] Yet it remains one of the most suggestive – and deplorably neglected – meditations on language in the last half-century or so. I shall return to some of his arguments in the next chapter when we shall examine more closely the material character of language. But what he contributes to the specific point of this chapter is the insistence that what we earlier called the instability of the relation between linguistic behaviour and the described environment is at the centre of how

---

42 Ibid., pp. 64, 69–72, 81–2: the 'accidental blundering into authentic poetic experience both in folk mistakes and mistaken readings of poetry are explored for what light they may shed on the function of metaphor in man's fundamental symbolic orientation in the world. The "wrongness" of metaphor is seen to be not a vagary of poets but a special case of that mysterious "error" which is the very condition of knowing anything at all' (p. 81).

43 Thomas Nagel reviewed *The Message in the Bottle* very sharply in the *New York Review of Books*, 18 September 1975, pp. 54–6; for a summary of this, see Jay Tolson, *Pilgrim in the Ruins: A Life of Walker Percy* (Chapel Hill, NC and London: University of North Carolina Press, 1992), pp. 400–1.

we think about linguistic behaviour itself. Conventional semiotics alone
– i.e. the analysis of signs as if they were indices of invariable connections
in the causal nexus – will not give us a proper theory of language. And,
Percy claims,[44] this conventional semiotics is blinkered by its nervousness
of metaphysics: look at how symbolization actually works, and you are up
against two difficult, unavoidable questions – how can one thing 'be' in
another? and what is the role of the community of speakers in establishing
meanings? Participation and intersubjectivity are substantive metaphysical
issues; it may feel a lot easier not to have to deal with them. But not to deal
with them is to abandon all hope of an adequate account of what we do
when we speak. Percy enumerates a variety of theories that seek to avoid this
dimension, including those that see identification between word and thing
as 'wrong' – that is, as a mistake[45]: the irony is that the very idea of a mistake
presupposes just that intentional character in language, the proposing of an
assertion for scrutiny and agreement or disagreement, that such a theory
denies. And to approach this as though 'real' relations were always between
non-intentional agents or agencies, and as though semantic relations were
somehow illusory in which meanings were probed and negotiated between
conscious speakers, is to refuse to attend to the facts of linguistic behaviour.
And, as we have already seen, if a linguistic exchange is simply a phenomenon,
a happening in an environment, what is the scientific observer of language
to say about that particular happening which is her own investigation?
'What does the scientist think of science as a phenomenon, not, what does
he do as a scientist as he practices his science, assembles his data, sets up a
controlled experiment, makes pointer readings, puzzles over discrepancies,
gets a hunch, tries a new hypothesis, etc. – but what does he think of science
as a happening in the world which takes its place among other happenings?'[46]
This is, in Percy's words, an 'antinomy' in the scientific study of language:
on a stimulus-and-response view of speech, the assumptions that have to be
made by a practising scientist in order to practise intelligently conflict with
the framework in which explanation is permitted.

And Percy's catalogue of the typical practices of science reminds us of a

44 Op. cit., p. 246.
45 Ibid., p. 226.
46 Ibid., p. 231

point touched on earlier. 'Puzzling over discrepancies' means that the investigator confronts difficulty. The scientist moves forward by identifying what is difficult, what does not fit in an existing framework, but what account of such difficulty can be given in a purely dyadic, causal picture of language? We do not have to go to the laboratory to find instances of this. Any serious interpersonal exchange involves moments when we struggle for words; when emotion of one kind or another leaves us baffled and inarticulate; when we cannot without a sense of dishonesty reproduce what we have said or heard in other circumstances apparently similar. Cordelia's embarrassment at her father's demand for protestations of love at the beginning of *King Lear* is painfully recognizable. And – to anticipate issues discussed in Chapter 5 – the deliberately invited difficulty of poetry, the conscious complicating of what has to be said by imposing the requirements of metre or rhyme or metaphorical patterning, is no more and no less than the extrapolation of this hesitation, this reluctance to tie up a situation in words too quickly or glibly. It is this hesitation, this embarrassment, that in some circumstances is the only thing that can reveal or at least suggest truth. Stanley Cavell's justly celebrated essay on *King Lear*[47] notes that Cordelia's response to her father exposes Lear's 'terror of being loved, of needing love'; and his discussion of this leads him to that central insight of his philosophical reading of Shakespeare which we have already mentioned, the insight that these (and other) dramas put 'the question how acknowledgment is to be expressed, that is, how we are to put ourselves in another's presence.'[48] The fact that we experience such anguish at times in being thus visible to each other should make us deeply wary of any theory of language or meaning that sees the central or normative practice as a simple articulation of what is 'in our minds.' And Cavell argues that drama – both comedy and tragedy, in wholly diverse ways – makes us present to the other's absolute difference for the simple but radical reason that I cannot *intervene* in the events that are presented to me on the stage. And so I am brought face to face with what I do not want to grasp or apprehend – my own limits as they border on the limits of agents who are absolutely and inaccessibly other. Paradoxically

47 Stanley Cavell, 'The Avoidance of Love: A Reading of *King Lear*', in *Disowning Knowledge* (Cambridge University Press, 2003), pp. 39–123; quotation from p. 62.
48 Ibid., p. 104.

and crucially, I discover solidarity in encountering this difference. What brings me closest to my fellow-humans is the fact that we are all incapable of making ourselves transparent, all faced with the limits of bodiliness and mortality and the diversity of our histories and everything else. Faced with the drama that shows me the most extreme case of my incapacity to invade another's life and sort it out, I am brought back to the need to listen and indeed to puzzle over my neighbour's address to me and my relation to him or her. More or less remotely, we are put back in touch with 'nature' or even 'With Being, I would say, if I knew how'.[49]

Difficulty thus works at several levels: Cordelia's inarticulacy reveals what Lear does not want revealed; what is the case is shown not by description but by the most paradoxical kind of representation, the spectacle of someone stammering and at a loss. But that difficulty enacted on the stage becomes another kind of difficulty: I as a spectator can say nothing; I must look at the other on stage as the extreme instance of human otherness, someone who speaks but not to me and to whom I cannot speak. And so I too have revealed to me what I might prefer to be hidden. 'Puzzling over discrepancies': it is not just a matter of recognizing that a problem is more intractable than I first thought and that the 'answer' is further away. It is confronting some kinds of intractable difficulties about what can be said and acknowledging that this confrontation may uncover things we did not know or did not choose to know. And – to return for a moment to poetry and drama – what the poet seeks to do is something quite close to provoking a 'crisis' in the language she is using or the linguistic situation she is setting out, so that a new perception is pushed into being. By stepping up the pressure on what can be said, by deliberately generating puzzlement, the poet aims to generate some kind of discovery – a discovery of 'nature' or 'Being', as Cavell cannot quite bring himself to say. We are taken back here to the point touched on in the first chapter about the uses of paradox and verbal tension in traditions of meditation, especially in Buddhism.

A theory of language that declines to make room for these sorts of difficulty will remain unhelpfully static; whether we are talking about the practices of experimental science or the practices of managing and understanding the setback of verbal performance in the ways discussed,

49 Ibid., p. 110.

what seems to come through is a picture of truth-telling that is a great deal broader than the manifestation of what is the case by sets of adequately descriptive words (Max Black's 'bundles of statements of fact') – and which assumes that speech 'moves into' its subject matter over time and through a variety of invited and uninvited pressures. We are looking at practices of handling frustration and bafflement. And yet to speak in these terms about speech is also to affirm the freedom of our speaking in a way that is both metaphysically and morally significant. The instability of the word–fact relation – to use an unhelpfully crude terminology – allows us to think in terms of a speaking agent who is for certain purposes able to move out from the nexus of stimulus and response and to create afresh in an alien medium the life of what is perceived. And because that capacity to create a representation by bringing a new difference into being is only intelligible as an act that I own and plan, even if I don't wholly control it, there is an ethical 'default setting' in our exchange of words which prompts me to regard the other's speaking as something I must treat *as* other, as making certain demands and having a certain hinterland (we shall be returning to this theme). The person I speak with must be assumed to own their words as I do mine; even a theoretical assumption that I can 'own' my analytic take on the speech of another in a way they do not own their words, that I can understand them as they do not understand themselves, is an irony too far for moral comfort.

5

To say that language is characterized by 'freedom' is thus quite a complex matter. It is not a licence to say whatever we choose; as we shall see in later chapters, the sheer inescapability of making interpersonal sense makes this impossible from the start. But it is also important to recognize the ways in which difficulty works – the uncovering of truth by acknowledging what it means to struggle for words in various contexts. And, perhaps paradoxically, it is the sense of difficulty that most clearly underlines what language's freedom means. To struggle, to test and reject and revise, is to experience language as a project requiring intelligent discernment, choice and action: language cannot be left to the realm of fixed and predictable responses to the environment. It creates a world, and so entails a constant losing and rediscovering of what is encountered. The connectedness of language to what is not language is a shifting pattern of correlation, not an index-like relation of cause and effect. We cannot easily imagine human speaking without the risk of metaphor, without the possibility of error and misprision, without the possibility of fiction, whether simple lying or cooperative fantasy. In other words, the human speaker takes the world as itself a 'project': the environment is there not as a fixed object for describing and managing but as a tantalizing set of invitations, material offered for reworking and enlarging. The intelligibility of the environment is not simply in the fact that it can be reduced to this or that pattern of causal sequence but in its capacity to generate fresh schemata and fresh ways of expressing one identity through another. And, accordingly, our own intelligence manifests not only as the capacity to chart or map but as the ability to absorb the life of what is encountered at a level that makes it possible both to recognize and to represent that life in another form. As speakers, we *make things other than themselves*: so far from constructing a definitively demarcated territory, a sort of Versailles Treaty version of the matter of our discourse, we constantly re-draw boundaries – or rather, perhaps, introduce migrants into different territories and make them speak new dialects and wear new clothes. The unceasing effort to re-work perceptions as our means of exploring what it is for something to be 'there' for us is both free, in the sense that it is never accounted for by an energy-exchange model, and deeply constrained, in the sense that we are always trying to allow what is there to show itself – an ethical and not only an epistemological point, as it requires a systematic questioning of our own starting point, our own interest.

Mistakes, the capacity to recognize and build on mistakes, fictions and projections, all these tell us more about language than any dyadic interpretation. Our sense of what is distinctively human is, it seems, bound up with our ability to be *wrong* or even untruthful in our representing of the environment. This should not be overstated: an animal may experience faulty recognition of some phenomenon (the fish 'thinking' the angler's bait is a minnow), and may act so as to mislead another animal (the mother bird dragging her wing as if injured to draw a predator away from her nest). But animals do not make representations of their environment that may be more or less adequate. The misrecognition of some feature of the environment is, in Percy's terms, a dyadic affair. It is a case of two or more similar causal prompts producing confusion, and potentially leading to an inappropriate response; inducing such confusion or misreading by feigning a state of affairs (the bird pretending that it is wounded) is tantalizingly close to what we might call a linguistic fiction, but doesn't seem obviously to involve *symbolization*, only a manipulating of 'indices'. We appear to be distinct from other animals not so much in the sheer development of our communication skills but in the fact that these skills include the ability to miscommunicate, to cut links with the environment (deliberately or otherwise), and also to scrutinize the nature of those links and repeatedly reimagine them – though even if it turned out that we could ascribe genuine symbolization (and thus deliberate fiction) to non-human animals, this would simply intensify the problem over the roots of language and make this sign of human distinctiveness more clearly a matter of degree than of kind .

Human evolution has thus produced what is often called (usually in a rather minimizing spirit) a 'feedback' capacity, a reflexive dimension; which means that it has developed a capacity to stand apart from the material causal nexus to the extent that it can represent itself – including its location in the material causal nexus. As Walker Percy repeatedly insists, a theory of language that does not reckon with the phenomenon of our awareness of this standing apart is not a theory of language at all. Even if we say that the sense of being aware is 'illusory', we are using language drawn from the realm of language and consciousness (the realm in which we know how to distinguish truth from illusion) to deny language and consciousness. There is no escape from this constraint any more than there is from the self-contradictions of strict determinism. But if we do indeed have to come to terms with the awareness of our location, we also have to reckon with the fact that the way we learn, and represent what we have learned, is by working with various schemata which do not map neatly on to each other, and by projecting structures of representation which allow diverse aspects of what is encountered to emerge into view. We learn and represent our learning, in other words, in a mode that (i) assumes we have no single final perspective on what is encountered (there is always more to say) and (ii) assumes that what we say itself alters what we can say *next*, so that the deposit of one essay in representation affects and (hopefully) enlarges what we go on to say. At one end of the learning–knowing relation stands an object which is constantly being uncovered at different levels or in different perspectives, as if there is in principle no end to the ways in which it can be understood and represented; at the other is a subject which is constantly involved in drawing out the life of what is represented by more and more initiatives in 'reading' the object through one medium after another. In short, at both ends we have an indeterminate horizon: the object is not to be exhausted by the multiple representations that keep being generated; the subject is not to be constrained by the limits of description or reflection. We could say that the object is consistently 'proposing' more than any one account of itself will capture – metaphorically, that it continues to 'give itself' for new kinds of knowing. It is there as an irreducible other, never to be finally absorbed into the knower's version of things. Likewise the subject is continuously capable of responding to this otherness by connecting diverse parts of the field of environmental stimulus in new schemata. This *analogical* process or nexus which subject and object inhabit is one in which the world is known in ways that are both fluid (because there is no final vantage point, no final representation) and accountable to what is given (because – simply – the working through of analogical speech is *difficult*).

In the context of the overall argument of this book, what is important is that the 'freedom' of language requires an anthropology, a picture of what is distinctively human in terms of receptiveness to a set of signals from the environment that do not allow of a final and ideally complete reading. To go back one more time to Walker Percy, the problem with both physical and cultural anthropology is that they have 'everything except an anthropology';[50] they offer an account of culture without raising the question of what it is in the human constitution that makes culture possible, that gives us some purchase on 'assertory behaviour',[51] the human habit of claiming to remake the environment by naming and representing. If we hold on to the two poles of indeterminacy I have mentioned, we imply that what is 'given' to us to understand in our environment is not simply a set of intelligible formulae which provide a grid for explanation: it is a complex of actual and

50 Op. cit., p. 239.
51 Ibid., p. 240: a properly 'scientific' account of language 'cannot disqualify as a datum the very phenomenon of which it is itself a mode'.

potential life, of structures breeding not only complexity but different levels of unity. The formulae claimed as basic, the essential numbers or ratios in the universe about which so much has been so well written in recent years,[52] inexorably produce clusters of data not reducible in their joint properties to the properties of their constituents. And when we as speakers get hold of them, we reorganize them in patterns and schemes that allow them to 'live' in other media, including the unlikely medium of noises made by human mouths and larynxes. What we call understanding moves 'down' to the level of basic ratios, the level of mathematics; but it equally moves 'up' to the various analogical representations that are sparked into life, made possible by the phenomena before us. The challenge for a reductive doctrine of humanity and its knowing, for the idea that there must be only one significant level at which we account for and interpret our environment, is in this potential for mathematical relations to generate not merely the complexity of living organisms, not merely the bewildering feedback capacity of the brain, but also the power of speech to cut loose from what is given and to recombine the data in ever more resourceful and surprising patterns. If I am right in arguing that what I have defined as 'representation' – the practice of transporting kinds of perceived life across the territorial boundaries of initial strict description – is the crucial distinctive ability of the linguistic animal, the final ontological question is how we do justice to the 'being' that produces such ability. We shall be coming back to the whole issue of what it means to think in terms of a world in which we cannot – apparently – talk about the relations of fundamental causal agencies in our biology without shamelessly borrowing linguistic terminology: information, coding and so on. It is obvious, for example, that to identify something as a coded message implies that there is a receptor able to decipher it: the unity of a particular string of DNA as a 'code' depends on what is there to recognize it; it does not have an independent identity as a unit apart from this.[53] But if we apply the same principle to whatever it is in the life of the objects of

52 See, for example, Martin Rees, *Just Six Numbers: The Deep Forces That Shape the Universe* (New York: Basic Books, 1999).
53 Once again, there are insightful observations in Steiner, op. cit., pp. 126–7; see also Conor Cunningham, *Darwin's Pious Idea: Why the Ultra-Darwinists and Creationists Both Get It Wrong* (Grand Rapids, MI: Eerdmans, 2010), pp. 71–4, and chapter 6, *passim*.

our speech that enables the upward spiral of partnership with our language to produce new representation – apparently without any final state of 'adequacy' – something of the same point emerges. There are dimensions in what we encounter that require recognition in the imaginative world of our speaking, over and above whatever initial register we have found useful or 'natural'. The life of what we encounter is a many layered complex of invitations to that imagination.

Strict argument will not take us much further: but this is one of those points where the questions generated by our linguistic life reach out in the direction of certain themes in theology. The environment we inhabit is, on the basis of what we have just been considering, irreducibly charged with intelligibility: the relations that make up this environment are conceived as the mutual adjustment and readjustment of meaningful communications and intelligent receptors. We are oriented to picking up and decoding intelligible messages. And, in religious discourses, the notion of an unbounded creative intelligence has regularly been associated with the idea that the elements of the universe we know are crystallizations of the unbounded intelligence perceiving the innumerable ways in which its own life may be reflected in bounded form. 'God's knowledge is the cause of things', in a familiar Thomist phrase[54] (we shall be coming back to this in the fourth chapter): that the unbounded intelligence is able to condense aspects of its own unified life into an abundance of specific forms, specific limited structures, is the rationale of there being anything at all in this metaphysical framework. If we are oriented to perceiving intelligibility, theology proposes further that we are oriented to an ultimate intelligible energy shaping the intelligible particulars in the universe. And since each limited structure is inseparable from the limitless life that brings it into being, that structure, though finite, is always going to resist final capture in terms of some basic and exclusive explanation: there will always be more to be said about it, and there will always be relations between it and other presences in the finite

---

54 See the *Summa Theologiae* I.xiv.8 for a discussion: God's knowledge is the cause of created things in a sense parallel to that in which the craftsman's knowledge is the cause of what he makes, as the principle by which his intelligence works. Furthermore, God's knowledge is inseparable from his essence and so from his will and love: what he knows is what he brings to be through his creative love, so that we can call his knowledge a 'knowledge of approbation' (*scientia approbationis*).

universe that need to be uncovered and represented. To make sense of the idea of a life that unceasingly generates more and more levels of 'represent-ability', more and more to be imagined and spoken, needs some opening out on to the horizon of what we could call intelligible abundance, an inexhaustible life which is itself unboundedly open to diversity of representation and at the same time supremely resistant to representation. Eckhart wrote of God as *omninominabile* and *innominabile*, the terminus of all acts of naming but also that which is incapable of being named. Taking seriously the freedom of language, its escape from the categories of stimulus and response, or even those of descriptive accuracy and inaccuracy, begins to point us to that paradoxical Eckhartian characterizing of actuality itself.

In our next chapter, we shall be looking a little further at the implications of language as something that never arrives at finality. Essentially a time-related thing, speech also refuses to work with deadlines for final representation. And in examining the issues that arise in this connection, we shall be introduced to the consequent questions about language as a physical affair which will, I hope, bring us back to some of the matters already touched on in relation to the 'excesses' of speech – and so, finally, to the question of where silence belongs in all this.

3

SPEECH AND TIME: THE UNFINISHABLE BUSINESS OF LANGUAGE

1

Towards the end of David Lodge's satirical novel, *Small World*,[1] the main characters are assembled in New York for a conference on literary theory. Everyone knows that their performance at this conference will determine whether or not they are plausible candidates for the coveted UNESCO Chair of Literary Criticism. When each has given his or her presentation, questions are invited; and the engagingly naïf young Irish scholar, Persse McGarrigle, asks, 'What follows if everyone agrees with you?' All are silenced except for the aged Arthur Kingfisher, who has been devoid of any critical ideas for many years. 'You imply', he replies, 'that what matters in the field of critical practice is not truth but difference. If everybody were convinced by your arguments, they would have to do the same as you and then there would be no satisfaction in doing it. To win is to lose the game.'

It's a neat academic joke – the Holy Grail of academic life, represented by the UNESCO Chair, the impotent Fisher-King of Arthurian legend, the innocent young Sir Percival who is charged with asking the question about the meaning of the sacred objects

1 *Small World: An Academic Romance* (London: Secker and Warburg, 1984), pp. 318–19.

displayed in the Grail Castle, the healing of the King and his land that follows when the question is asked, all allied with Lodge's quizzical but penetrating evocation of the complex byways of literary theory in the 1980s. Kingfisher's response is cast in highly problematic terms (and Persse is not at all sure that the answer is persuasive, only that the question is important): it presupposes only the context of an academic discipline, a 'game' that may be won or lost, and it takes truth and difference as mutually incompatible goals in this game. But the question could be addressed on a much broader canvas. What follows if everyone agrees is the cessation of the labour and difficulty of representing. The next generation of humans perceiving and interacting with their environment will be under no compulsion to *add* anything to what has been said. All perspectives have, as it were, merged for practical purposes. We do not, in any particular future generation, need the unfamiliar voice or standpoint to enhance what we perceive. While we are used to arriving at a necessary degree of convergence in what is said, so that we have ways of (mostly informally) determining whether we mean the same, 'meaning the same' is always a phrase that carries the shadow of actual articulated difference. Convergence is not guaranteed, never complete and always suggesting new possibilities of *divergence*. It is not (*pace* Arthur Kingfisher) that winning is losing the game; more that whatever 'victories' of convergence may emerge, they do not simply end the game you happen to be playing, they establish the possibility of new and different 'games' or, better, practices of shared speech. Even if we claim to be repeating some form of words that has been settled on as expressing perfect convergence, we have to deal with the problem that we cannot ever simply say the same words twice with absolutely precisely the same meaning.

The problem is familiar to philosophers: I say, 'There is a mouse in the kitchen'; you then also say, 'There is a mouse in the kitchen.' Do we mean the same thing? You can't be doing exactly what I'm doing, simply sharing information about what we might expect to see in the kitchen. You may be checking that you've heard correctly, probably with a small upward inflection at the end of the sentence ('There's a mouse in the kitchen?'). You may be expressing shock at the news: 'There's a *mouse* in the kitchen?' (I'm terrified of mice / what does the cat think we pay her for?) or 'There's a mouse in the *kitchen*?' (I've just left a plate of toast on the table / I thought we'd got rid of the mice indoors and they were only in the garage / the environmental health people are due in the hotel this morning). Notoriously, if someone else repeats what I have just said, that does not normally work as a guarantee that they have understood my utterance; quite often it may mean the exact opposite ('What do you mean by telling me this? What conclusions am I supposed to draw?'). If – to echo the phraseology of the last chapter – the relation between words and what we encounter or have to deal with were a 'stable' one, to repeat the same words would be to say the same thing; the fact that repetition does not guarantee understanding reinforces the point that there is a fluidity in the relation, and that the passage of *time* makes a difference. Saturday's performance of the school play is not the same as Friday's: the same words are said in the same order (with luck, if everyone has learned their lines), but there will be differences bound up with the fact that 24 hours have elapsed. When Tanya speaks her lines in Act 2, she is at some level aware of where she got a laugh last night, of the fact that her grandmother is in the audience tonight and will be shocked when she has to swear on stage, that she grasped for the first time last night why the other character on stage at this point reacts as he does so that she will tonight be expecting his reaction in a slightly different way. At a much more professional level, the conductor preparing to take the Academy of St Martin in the Fields through a Mozart piano concerto will have digested a substantial discography as well as all the performances he or she has heard, and knows perfectly well that 'playing the same notes as last time' is no kind of account of what will be going on. What is said, performed, enacted becomes 'material' to the next utterance or performance, so that this latter cannot be in any very interesting sense the same.

Now: put these observations together with the argument that 'understanding' an utterance or performance may be best understood as a matter of *knowing what to do or say next*. Rather than being a matter of gaining insight into a timeless mental content 'behind' or 'within' what is said, it is being able to exhibit the next step in a continuing pattern. Wittgenstein, in a well-known passage in the *Philosophical Investigations*,[2] describes what happens when someone, watching another person writing down a sequence of numbers, suddenly grasps how the series is developing: 'Now I can go on!' The principle of the series will be expressible in a formula; yet it is

2   *Philosophical Investigations. The German Text with a Revised English Translation*, trans. G. E. M. Anscombe, 3rd edn (Oxford: Blackwell, 2001), pp. 151ff.

not, says Wittgenstein, that 'a formula occurs to [the observer]' when the observer successfully continues the series. Understanding is not in that sense a 'mental process', the summoning up of a key principle by conscious thought, it is the skill or confidence to go on, to follow the series through; a skill in the exercise of a habit, if you like. It is, as Wittgenstein goes on to argue,[3] like the experience of reading. We don't apply a procedure in our minds, a series of operations that allows us to move from seeing a sign to making a noise or at least imagining making a noise; we simply exercise a skill, closer to knowing how to ride a bicycle than performing a calculation.

So, if understanding is knowing how to 'go on', how to follow what has been said or done with an intelligible next move, linguistic activity is always going to be something that moves in time. There is an irreversible trajectory in language: what has been said cannot be unsaid, and what is now to be said has to reckon not only with the environment as such but with the speech of others which makes the environment we encounter always already *represented*. The world we inhabit is already a symbolized world, a world that has been and is being taken up into a process of speaking and making sense together; and what we say cannot be understood except as an event that requires further speaking, 'following'. What I articulate in this moment is a perception and perspective that confesses its own unfinished character by the sheer fact of being *spoken*, in words that belong to an ongoing flow of linguistic activity; by being there, they can be echoed, agreed with (although never, as we have seen, simply or neutrally repeated), challenged, contradicted. They do not stand still as fixed tokens of the distinct objects they refer to. The challenge we have already discussed, to move from description to representation, is implied in the decision to 'stake' a position, to venture a perception in language, knowing that what you say will not and cannot be the last word.

'Staking' a position is an idea explored particularly by the British Hegelian philosopher, Gillian Rose, in several works of the 1980s and 1990s.[4]

---

3   Ibid., pp. 156ff.
4   See especially *The Broken Middle: Out of Our Ancient Society* (Oxford: Blackwell, 1992), pp. 147–52, and chapter 6 *passim* on the imperative of refusing a mythology that allows me to represent myself as absolved from moral risk in the name of some clear and unambiguous fusion of politics and ethics. For a full and eloquent discussion of this theme, see Andrew Shanks, *Against Innocence: Gillian Rose's Reception and Gift of Faith* (London: SCM Press, 2008).

Her distinctive reading of Hegel presented the dialectical philosophy as an unending sequence of ventures, in which we begin with the 'natural' errors of pre-speculative recognition and move into the business of renegotiating what we say that we see in the tensions and contradictions of shared speech: 'entertain the particular in its strangeness, and out of that will, properly, come the speculative recognition of the unsustainable character of the "natural"'.[5] To stake a position, to articulate a perception, is to acknowledge that my judgement of my perception is not self-contained and self-justifying; it is to be exposed to contradiction, to the verbal challenge and probing of partners in the language world, and thus to the 'speculative' development that returns us finally to where we started but with a completely different kind of awareness. Our perceiving has been sown to be historical and metaphysical: we see how the passage of time has enabled us to see differently, and what we see is a reality that is inextricably bound up with our linguistic response and our linguistic partners. To pick up a point touched on earlier, the Hegelian principle that 'the real is the rational' is easily misunderstood.[6] It does not claim that what happens to be the case is 'rationally' determined (and thus beyond challenge). It does mean that what we talk about is always a reality that is talked about – that has been, is being and will be talked about, that requires to be talked about and cannot be talked about without talking of the talking, thinking of the thinking, that engages with it, and that therefore also entails thinking the social relations in which talking occurs.[7] What is real is what is available for speech – not in the sense that we should be able to find adequate verbal tokens or logical pictures for all that is there in the world, but (almost the contrary) that the encountered environment is 'real' for us as and only as it insists on establishing itself in our language and stirring that language to constant readjustment and new kinds of representation. And this, as I have suggested in earlier discussions of Rose,[8] is at the heart of how history and metaphysics coincide in a clarified and reworked Hegelian

5   Rowan Williams, 'Between Politics and Metaphysics: Reflections in the Wake of Gillian Rose, *Wrestling With Angels: Conversations in Modern Theology*, ed. Mike Higton (London: SCM Press, 2007), pp. 53–76 (quotation p. 61).

6   Above, Chapter 1, note 52.

7   See Gillian Rose, *Hegel Contra Sociology* (London: Athlone Press, 1981), and 2nd edn (London: Verso, 2009), especially pp. 84–97.

8   Particularly the essay quoted in above note 5.

context. To understand is to be able to survey and inhabit a narrative of *learning* and thus also to see the immediate task of understanding as a matter of knowing how to follow, to go on. 'What follows if everyone agrees with you?' The answer has to be literally 'nothing': the very idea of 'following' means that what has just been said is not final and that there is no agreement about how we speak of whatever is before us. Which is not – we'd better be clear – to say that our linguistic practice is constantly characterized by open conflict and mutually exclusive utterances (a Hegelianism which read Hegel as insisting on *opposition* as the grammar of speculative advance would be a serious misunderstanding of his logic[9]). A lack of agreement may be sharply conflictual. It may also be a less dramatic set of discomforts with available perspectives and representations. Not all difference is simply opposition in the sense of mutual exclusivity or excluded middles.

Many years ago, I heard a distinguished sculptor saying that he had discovered his vocation when visiting a gallery in his teens. 'I knew', he said, 'that there was something missing from that gallery, and it was *my work*.' The gallery had been showing a set of exhibition pieces designed to lead up to the work of Rodin; the teenage visitor had sensed that he knew *how to go on* from Rodin, so that his work would be the obvious next step in a story. You could say that he did not 'agree' that Rodin should be where the story ended; but that does not add up to a rejection of Rodin, and that indeed was as far as possible from the younger man's intention. In his own terms, he had understood Rodin better than anyone who simply looked at Rodin as a phenomenon without any conviction that this was a story in which s/he belonged; sensing a pressure to respond and continue is the mark of understanding what is perceived in this context, not least because sensing such a pressure implies apprehending what is before you as in some sense an address and invitation. And while this sort of idiom makes reasonably obvious sense when we are talking about the intentional work of another human agent, we can recognize that there are analogies in the way we react to the environment overall. The innovative scientist is impelled to ask the hitherto unasked question and propose the new explanatory structure and/or interpretative schema: it is not fanciful to speak here of a sense of 'pressure to continue'. The simplest strategic

9   See again Nicholas Adams, *Eclipse of Grace* (Chapter 1, above, note 52).

development that allows us to solve a problem that might otherwise be lived with – a problem that does not absolutely have to be solved for our survival – reflects something of the same response. A technical advance allows new tools to be developed which allow and stimulate fresh questions to be asked. In our scientific and technical lives, we behave as if this were an environment in which we were constantly encouraged to 'go on', to follow what has been said and done with new utterances. And all this is inseparable from the recognition that we cannot speak about our *selves* without narrative, without the hinterland of allusion to the time it takes to shape or establish what we can call a self by new utterance, new determinations of who is speaking.

2

Richard Sennett, in his excellent and innovative book, *The Craftsman*,[10] discusses at some length what he calls 'Material Consciousness', the entire complex process of transformation that unfolds in a tradition of making, a tradition of reshaping an environment. He identifies three elements to this transformative pattern: 'the internal evolution of a type-form', that is, a generic structure for what is produced that is repeatedly altering in response to failure; the process of 'judgment about mixture and synthesis', that is, decisions as to whether blending different materials or binding them together works better in a particular context; and 'domain shift', the recognition of 'how a tool initially used for one purpose can be applied to another task, or how the principle guiding one practice can be applied to quite another activity'.[11] Material consciousness is that kind of human awareness which moves steadily through engagement with time and matter, accumulating experience, acknowledging connection,[12] involved in 'a continual

---

10 *The Craftsman* (New Haven, CT and London: Yale University Press, 2008).
11 Ibid., p. 127.
12 See also Sennett's *The Culture of the New Capitalism* (New Haven, CT and London: Yale University Press, 2006), on the pressures towards radical disconnection with other agents in contemporary social and economic practice. His most recent book, *Together: The Rituals, Pleasures and Politics of Co-operation* (London: Allen Lane, 2012), explores this further.

dialogue with materials':[13] there is no sharp disjunction between seeing and doing; once again, to understand is to be in a position to act, to follow. Philosophy, says Sennett, is readily persuaded that the observer's interpretative skill is somehow more important than that of the worker in materials, because we are always in search of what is not vulnerable to the change and decay of the material world; yet the craftsman exercising the sort of material consciousness Sennett sketches is in fact answering the question about permanence and impermanence in his or her own way. The three elements of material consciousness display what continuity in and through material difference might mean in practice; this, we could say, is analogy in action, and our active inhabiting of the material environment as human agents is fundamentally characterized by this analogical skill-set.

We shall return to the question of the material context of intelligence in the next chapter; the point of referring at this stage to Sennett's discussion is to underline the irreducibly time-bound nature of the human sense of self. We have of course become used to uncertainties being expressed about the notion of a 'continuous' self; but these uncertainties reflect a culture seriously out of touch with the kind of consciousness Sennett is exploring, a culture marked by compulsive withdrawal into a world of symbols that can be endlessly exchanged and manipulated, symbols that have lost their anchorage in a genuinely representation-oriented (and therefore critical and exploratory) engagement with the environment. Not to labour the point, this is manifestly part of the toxic fascination of those games with virtual wealth that have threatened the economic viability of whole nations in recent years. To be aware of oneself *as* a self is to think of a continuing 'conversation' with material data in the course of which (to return to Cornelius Ernst's formulation, quoted in the first chapter) the world to which we belong becomes the world that belongs to us. Our practices 'furnish' an environment whose shape both moulds our activity and is moulded by it. And the consistency of those practices is a central aspect of being able to see and speak of ourselves as subjects whose present capacity is made what it is by the accumulation of learning, of practices tested and altered, challenged and improved and constantly extending in

13 Sennett, *The Craftsman*, p. 125.

scope and 'domain-shifting' flexibility. And, as Sennett hints, it is against this background that we need to think about thinking and about speaking.

Speech, as already noted more than once, is itself a material activity; and it is, crucially, a practice which can be seen in terms of the material consciousness described by Sennett. It evolves type-forms, structures of representation that are reworked in the extended process of engagement with the environment and are subject to correction and/or enlargement; it operates a process analogous to the discernment around mixture and synthesis which characterizes material consciousness – that is, it recognizes some words and phrases as capable of more or less indiscriminate interchangeability and others as significantly and irreducibly diverse in meaning; it displays capacities for domain-shifting, importing images and categories from one area into another, using metaphor at level after level of reference and representation. Linguistic intelligence embodies that cumulative sense of self which emerges in the process of learning what viable interactions with an environment look like. And just as we can say that a particular product of material craft is admirable of its kind, even 'finished' in its way, yet never the last possible thing that can be done in that mode, so with language we can say that such and such a formulation, whether scientific or poetic, is 'finished', 'beautiful', 'well-formed', we acknowledge that it is not and can't be the last word that will be said. In the case of a material work, the object made becomes a datum for the community of craftsmen and women; it suggests new possibilities. So too in language, what is said becomes a datum, allows something different to be said. And in the awareness of all this, what we call the awareness of self is born. We recognize that we have learned strategies for negotiating our environment, that we have encoded those strategies in the sounds we make and record, that such strategies are constantly being tested and are open to varying degrees of revision. What's more, such openness to revision is not just a matter of solving unexpected operational difficulties that arise, though that is undoubtedly part of the impulse. 'Simple imitation', writes Sennett,[14] 'is not a sustaining satisfaction; the skill has to evolve. The slowness of craft time serves as a source of satisfaction; practice beds in, making the skill one's own. Slow craft time also enables the work of reflection and imagination.' The familiar theme recurs:

14 Ibid., p. 295.

the typical product of reflective apprehension of an act/utterance is not plain repetition; such repetition is not yet (in the vocabulary we have been using) representation. Saying what has just been said, doing what has just been done, is not a good index of understanding. A craftsman who does nothing but imitate step by step what has been done will not yet necessarily have grasped the logic of the process, which emerges only when the principles of the process are deployed to produce something different, even if only slightly. The parallel with what has been extensively discussed in relation to language acquisition is clear.[15]

Performance generates new possibilities of performance (and, as we shall see later in Chapter 5, commonly does so by deliberately intensifying stresses in what has already been said or done, actually creating new problems or challenges); and if the 'sense of self' arises out of the awareness of a cumulative process of developing strategies, verbal and tactile, then the consciousness of being a self *now* is the consciousness of being able to 'perform' in certain ways, to add to the cumulative sum of enacted strategies. Being self-aware is being aware of one's ability to complicate the world further. It is also important, though, to note, with a further glance at the Buddhist tradition, that the disciplines of self-forgetfulness in meditation or contemplation are about recognizing and bracketing in certain circumstances this capacity to complicate the world, to generate fresh data – so that we do not get so compulsively enchanted by the creative capacity of mind that we in fact come to be in thrall to its own inventive interactions with the environment.[16] We shall look at some further implications of this in Chapter 6. 'Consciousness as an experiencing self is the evanescent moving point between memory and anticipation', as William

---

15 Language acquisition, as analysed by modern theorists such as Chomsky, is the process of becoming able to form intelligible sentences *that you have not heard before* – but also to become able to distinguish context, aspect, tone and so forth, so as to recognize when apparent verbal identity conceals irony or challenge. For a lively discussion of what Chomsky's – and some other contemporary – theories of language acquisition do and do not illuminate in this connection, see Ian Robinson, *The New Grammarians' Funeral: A Critique of Noam Chomsky's Linguistics* (Cambridge: Cambridge University Press, 1975).

16 Passanno and Amaro, *The Island* (see Chapter 1, note 24), chapters 4 and 5.

Downes puts it in a very helpful and wide-ranging recent book[17]: but the context of this 'moving point' is an environment sufficiently stable to allow a sense of duration to inform the sense of the transition point between what has been and what might be. That is, to put this in terms close to those I have been using here, I am able in the present moment to form the idea of acting in the future according to a strategy because I am able to trace a cumulative pattern in what I remember – this action was informed by that, this decision was shaped by those words or actions. 'The self explains itself and gives reasons for what it does ... The conscious self is the first person of stories about the past pivoting around the evanescent transition and projected into the future.'[18] What Downes calls the 'meta-representation' of the self is the attempt to hold together all the various tokens of 'myself' which figure in the narratives I remember, to see them as 'a lineage, a family of representations'.[19] This meta-represented self is, in Downes's terms, an 'aesthetic' concept, an ideal limit; no space–time reality could contain the infinite plurality of possibility and the manifold inconsistencies bound up in the representation, but we cannot function without some concept that halts an infinite 'regression of representing selves' in relation to both present and past – here am I looking at myself (as I am) looking at myself (as I was) looking at myself.[20] We speak as if there were a 'terminus' of experiences that remained constant over time, and we cannot help speaking so.

This leaves us with a considerable mental challenge. To say that we cannot avoid speaking about the self – the bearer of a continuous narrative – is not to say that we must identify the self as some sort of object; and, on the other hand, to say that the self is not an object in space–time is not to say that it is a fiction. It may be more helpful, suggests Downes, to say that what we mean by (mind-independent) reality is itself indeterminate: 'The species-mind seems compelled to some variety of realism, although it doesn't agree what is ultimately real.'[21] Speaking of a continuous self lands us in the realm of irreducible mystery: we cannot dispense with the question

17 William Downes, *Language and Religion: A Journey into the Human Mind* (Cambridge: Cambridge University Press, 2011), p. 191.
18 Ibid., p. 192.
19 Ibid.
20 Ibid., p. 193.
21 Ibid., p. 259.

of what warrants what we say, but equally cannot pin it down as an element or set of elements in the space–time world. We must therefore be content with a 'philosophy of uncertainty',[22] allowing that there may be facts that warrant what we say but that they may be radically inaccessible to us. 'With respect to mysteries, we don't *know* which can be naturalized, ultimately become tractable problems, and which will forever remain mysteries and are therefore in the permanent domain of philosophy, religion and art'.[23] But I wonder whether Downes's complex and finely articulated argument does entire justice to the point that he himself grants so readily – the essentially temporal character of self-awareness and the consequently cumulative character of what we call knowing. The difficulty is this. If our habitual self-awareness is as it has been discussed here, a matter of familiarity with an existing range of verbal and other strategies evolved for negotiating a path through the material environment; and if understanding is tied up with the sense of how to go on, to follow – then we may need to probe a little just what the level of 'uncertainty' involved here amounts to. Or, in plainer words, what more can we do/we look for? Does it in fact make sense to talk about 'agreeing on what is ultimately real'? If we are looking for a way of identifying the 'real' in a way that is somehow detached from the continuing processes of representation, we shall be looking for a chimera: it is simply that *this* is how we display 'realism', by 'following' what has been said and done in ways that are open to continuing scrutiny and revision. We show that we are serious about the extra-mental by certain features of our linguistic behaviour – by the exposure of our representations to response and correction or expansion, by behaving as though they were accountable to something more than their own inner logic or the convenience of the speaker.

Thus I suspect we ought to be a bit more cautious about the distinction between what is capable of being 'naturalized' and what remains mysterious. As we have seen, what can be naturalized, in the sense of being rendered as a set of soluble problems, does not lend itself to final or definitive representation any more than anything else: when the explanatory/descriptive work has been done and credible and sustainable explanatory structures

22 Ibid., p. 261.
23 Ibid., p. 262.

have been elaborated (what we could call 'first-level schemata' to borrow the language of Arbib and Hesse), that does not mean that there is no more to say, that those structures offer an exhaustive account of what is there in the phenomena under discussion. And this is not to postulate a mysterious underlay in things to which mind or language never attain; it is only to say that there will always be another possible representation, another possible way of locating the phenomena. What is there is always capable of entering into new relations with what is around, including new relations of representation; indeed, Downes notes as much at one point in his work.[24] So the question, 'Are there realities incapable of being represented?'[25] is a more complex one than we might suppose (granted that his use of 'representation' is slightly different from my own). One advantage of the somewhat extended sense I have given to the word 'representation' in these pages is that it allows us to use the term for whatever in our linguistic and symbolic world registers some kind of active presence and transmits something of its effect. On the basis of this usage, we do not need to invoke a non-representable level of reality – a strictly non-*speakable* level of agency. It is more a matter of recognition that the process by which we establish that we are 'accountable' to more than the contents of our heads may be more or less protracted, more or less capable of being pinned down to easily measurable criteria, so that 'satisfactory' representation will be constantly deferred. The boundary between 'tractable problems' and the province of philosophy, religion and art is less secure than at first it may seem. But Downes's discussion invaluably highlights the dangers of speaking as though 'naturalized' description were not merely the gold standard but the only genuine currency for claims to reliable knowledge of the environment. The book contains much useful treatment of what it is for a proposition or what he calls a semi-proposition (a form of words that clearly intends to refer but does not contain enough determination of its terms to be evaluated properly) to be 'relevant' (best able to improve our representational repertoire) in the process of pursuing an enquiry, settling a dispute and so on.[26] And the account of what is involved in believing 'semi-understood' propositions – propositions that

24 Ibid., p. 135.
25 Ibid., pp. 183–8.
26 Ibid., pp. 133ff.

are held to be true on the authority of their source even when we do not fully grasp the meaning of the words used[27] – is illuminating. But I remain unsure about the clear demarcation between realities that do and realities that don't lend themselves to definitive explanation: it is possible to take Downes's points and still to argue that this disjunction breaks down when pressed too hard, and that the idea of the non-representable leaves a fair number of conceptual loose ends.

Understanding, so we have been arguing, involves seeing that there is now something further to be said/done; that there is a future for *this* particular line of engagement. It is very different from a definitive act of penetration into the inner workings of an object so as to lay bare its 'essential' mechanism. When once we have articulated a response of any intelligent kind, we have both recognized something that we are 'accountable to' in the world (we have denied ourselves the liberty to say what we please) and staked a position, a perspective that we now expose to challenge and possible revision (we have denied ourselves the security of claiming that there is no more to be said). *What we do not know* is not so much an elusive interiority as the range of possible relations in which the object stands or may stand. And this means that the only way of augmenting or refining our knowledge is to 'go on', to continue the process of inviting further speaking. It is in this connection that we imagine the self as a necessarily time-related reality – while at the same time recognizing that it cannot be rendered as one object among others in the time–space continuum, as Downes affirms. To know myself or understand myself is to be involved in a narrative exercise: I do not look for a timeless true self at the heart of all I do or say, but I do look for a sequence of encounters I can narrate in which specific ways of seeing my history became available for me (and, presumably, specific versions of that history *ceased* to be available, versions that I must now characterize as fantasy). I cannot sit down and decide I will embark on a search for my real self by thinking hard about what is essential to my mental life; I can only approach whatever the term 'real self' designates by sifting through remembered narratives in which I identify my problems or failures as arising from self-deception or self-protection, from some sort of flight from the real.

And to do this is normally something I undertake when I am concerned that I may be falling back into self-deceiving or self-protecting habits; I am

27   Ibid., pp. 146–7.

not looking for an object I have misplaced or overlooked or suspect may be around somewhere (except in a strongly metaphorical sense: 'where have I left my conscience?'). Nor can I speak of self-awareness in the simple temporal way I speak of other actions. 'I was sitting in the kitchen at the time' is a different kind of statement from 'I was understanding myself at the time'. This latter phrase might look tempting because of its apparent analogy with 'I was looking out of the window at the time'; but the analogy will not work. I do not have a 'self' upon which I can fix my attention as on a window, any more than I have a self to which I can relate as to a chair to sit on. If I say, as I sometimes do, '*then* I understood ...', or even, '*then* I knew ...', I am claiming that there was a moment when my awareness of my possibilities altered substantially and I was able to think of a distinctive future. I am setting out a narrative of a certain kind, not suggesting that self-knowledge is a 'conscious mental going-on' extended over a particular period. And my puzzlement over how I can know that my knowledge is not illusory is, as Stanley Cavell eloquently explains,[28] a (doomed) attempt to establish a connection between what I say and what is there when in fact I have deprived myself of all the routine means of making such a connection. 'The reason we cannot say what the thing is in itself is not that there is something we do not in fact know, but that we have deprived ourselves of the conditions for saying anything in particular.'[29] In other words, we cannot talk about what something is like when we're not talking about it; we cannot talk about an object in a way that avoids the staking of a position and the opening of an intelligible future of debate and exchange.

It is not – to labour the point again – that there are unrepresentable realities that would ground what we say if only we could get at them; it is that the way we know and understand is by representing, and then risking the form of our representation in shared discourse as time unfolds. The self I may claim to know is always the active first person of a narrative; and the first person notoriously has as little of a clear location as the eye does in the field of vision. It is not an object for inspection; but then neither is it to be characterized simply as a reality we cannot represent, a reality that, if we only knew how to speak of it, we could after all locate in such a

28 Cavell, *The Claim of Reason*, p. 238.
29 Ibid., p. 239.

way as to justify truth claims about it. The truth is that we do in some sort 'represent' the first person in the bare fact of continuing to put it at the centre of narratives. What is the 'real' self? The only defensible answer in this context, it seems, is to say that it is the action that here and now gathers events narrated from the past and possible courses of action in the future into one story that is unceasingly being revised from one utterance to the next. It is an instance where the difference between description and representation (in the senses in which they are used here) is exceptionally clear. And I suspect that Downes's interest in the non-representable conflates the perfectly correct point that there are realities we speak of that cannot be treated as if they were items in a list of what is contained in the space–time continuum with the more contentious and, I think, less defensible claim that there are states of affairs which would warrant certain true statements but about which we could say nothing. Recognizing some of the difficulties, Downes intriguingly scouts the possibility that 'Un-representable realities might be so un-representable that they may not even be in the form of "states of affairs",'[30] but I have no real idea what this might add up to (and, as he disarmingly admits, neither has he). I fully grant that some of the problems arise from how we are to define representation itself, a question he addresses carefully in terms of different levels of explicit logical and propositional form.[31] And my reservations about this are to do with how we deal with the range of symbolic vehicles that may count as representations of one kind or another – issues already touched on and to which we shall come back in Chapter 5. As we shall shortly see, I believe there is in fact a need to examine the grammar of the unrepresentable, if not quite in the sense that Downes has in mind.

3

The implication of locating the self firmly in this temporal context is of course to locate it also in the processes of linguistic *exchange* that are initiated by a venture of understanding. To be a time-conditioned self is also to be a *social* self, a self formed in interaction. Who I believe myself to be is

30 Downes, op. cit., p. 186.
31 Ibid., p. 130.

inseparable from what I have heard, the possibilities offered me in relation and conversation – consciously remembered or not; I may well insist with some vehemence that I am *not* simply the sum total of other people's perceptions or projections, but merely to say this is to enter the world of exchange, converse, challenge and so on. I want to assert my independence in words that will be recognizable to others. As Stanley Cavell argues in the monumental essay 'Between Acknowledgment and Avoidance', which makes up the final section of *The Claim of Reason*,[32] the apparently abstract discussions of scepticism and certainty in the philosophical literature of early modernity can be read as so many ways of handling the far from abstract question of what it is for me to see and to be seen, to know and to be known, in the risky territory of personal communication. How do you 'let yourself matter' to another human subject? 'To let yourself matter is to acknowledge not merely how it is with you, and hence to acknowledge that you want the other to care, at least to care to know. It is equally to acknowledge that your expressions in fact express you, that they are yours, that you are in them. This means allowing yourself to be comprehended, something you can always deny. Not to deny it is, I would like to say, to acknowledge your body, and the body of your expressions, to be yours, you on earth, all there will ever *be* of you.'[33] The overcoming of scepticism is not a matter of some clinching argument to establish a state of affairs capable of grounding a rational belief in the reality of other minds or an external world; it is something more like a discipline of speech and sensibility that persistently identifies and challenges our various strategies of retreat from being present in our words, from the risks of being recognized. To relate this more closely to the discussion of the present chapter, it is to acknowledge that the self now speaking is a 'project': I set out in my words and acts an identity formed out of my history of interaction with other speakers and implicitly ask if I am intelligible, recognizable. Is there a future for whatever it is that speaks from this position? Is what I am saying the kind of discourse that can be replied to?

To think of personal identity in terms of gathering and presenting what I hope may be worth recognizing and answering carries with it some

---

32 Pp. 329–495 (incorporating – pp. 481ff. – the essay on *Othello* also published in *Disowning Knowledge*, pp. 125–42).

33 Ibid., p. 383.

cautions about other versions of identity that lead to serious conceptual and imaginative difficulties. If my selfhood is fixed at the point of utterance, that utterance is in no sense a request for acknowledgment; if my selfhood is determined from outside, if (to think back to some of the arguments in the preceding chapter) it simply plays out a determined script, I am not in fact 'uttering' at all: I am performing an operation whose outcomes are in principle predictable. Either of these perspectives would be an avoidance of risk, of the moment of self-abandoning uncertainty involved in actually saying who I am – allowing myself to be comprehended, in Cavell's phrase, and owning my expression as mine. And, in the light of this, we can perhaps see how the unitary self both is and is not 'something' in the space–time world. In one sense it is certainly true to say that the imagined self, the stable terminus of all actual and possible experience for me, is not an inhabitant of the world and not open to the sort of scrutiny I give to objects ('I' is not the name of a *thing*). But, at the same time, we can say that it is very specifically a *speaking body* here and now, the focal point of a situation, an agent involved in symbol-making activity. By virtue of working with the symbolic accumulation of the past, with what has been understood (and thus followed out, in the sense outlined earlier), and by making appeal to the symbol-recognizing capacity of other language users in the immediate vicinity (and ultimately further afield), I declare that there is a self *here*, my body or rather – Cavell again – 'the body of my expressions'. And I commit myself, by speaking and inviting a response, to a continuing temporal development of the body of my expressions, the repertoire with which I seek to make myself present to others. The next chapter will discuss this in more detail.

Our fascination with both narrative and ritual – including the rituals of drama and storytelling – reflects our desire to develop that 'repertoire' not only in the habitual exchanges of conversation but in intensified forms. A narrative, perhaps especially a dramatic one, displays the way in which persons move and grow, acquire fresh dimensions to their self-presentations. But in contrast to our own narrative about ourselves, it will – if it is a good narrative – be charged with significance moment by moment (whereas our self-narration will have to select from a background of not obviously significant material). Drama shows us what is going on in our own self-construction without our knowing it by making us follow a narrative in which every moment is manifestly part of the construction of a sustained and developing meaning. Cavell, writing about drama,[34] compares it to the 'directed motion' of a musical composition: we don't know why it begins where it does or how it is going to end, we are presented with a situation demanding our closest attention because the directedness of the motion means that every moment will in some way contribute to an outcome. 'The perception or attitude demanded in following this drama is one which demands a continuous attention to what is happening at each here and now, as if everything of significance is happening at this moment, while each thing that happens turns a leaf of time.'[35] Drama highlights what we recognize to be true of our existence as human agents in general, the fact that our self-awareness is always of a moment of transition, as things move into an irrecoverable past and shape an unseen future. And, while we may watch a drama whose plot we know perfectly well, so that the outcome is not in doubt, we shall still be attending with the same intensity to see better how *this* moment opens and closes possibilities for the next (and beyond), hoping as we attend to see something of how it is that people 'go on', follow what is said and done. We are hoping to understand human agency and interaction, hoping to see more clearly how and why this leads to that and so to become aware of larger possibilities for our own 'going on' in understanding. The dramatist or novelist proposes a pattern of temporal movement and transformation which I can recognize as (in principle) like what I am aware of living in. In attending to this unfolding pattern, I am assisted to attend to my own narrative – perhaps to recover aspects of that story which I have ignored or buried, perhaps to 'read' my actions or those of others with new questions, new suspicions, so that my decisions and in particular my own utterances are formed by larger and more various factors than hitherto.

Ritual includes elements of drama, but is not identical with it. Building on definitions offered by Richard Sennett, we could say that ritual is repetitive, transformative and publicly theatrical. It traces the same pattern of performance in different enactments over time; it makes ordinary physical stuff (including words and gestures) carry meanings that are not intrinsic

34 *Disowning Knowledge*, pp. 92–3.
35 Ibid., p. 93.

to themselves; it involves us in performance that is about more than what happens to be in our individual minds. It has a nuanced relationship to the passage of time: rituals are conserved over time, so that it appears that we are doing the same thing at different moments in time, and the time of the ritual itself provides a narrative sequence that does not vary; yet the reason they *are* conserved is that they are believed to be pertinent to a constantly changing context of human action and utterance. To return again to a ritual form is to bring together my/our current situation, choices made or to be made, so as to allow them to be informed by patterns of intelligible act and speech which are not directly conditioned by that present situation. In other words, the story of my/our current doings is located against the backdrop of another and supposedly broader narrative canvas. When we join in a celebration of Remembrance Day in the UK, we juxtapose our current lives with the record and collective memory of major international conflicts, so that issues around our corporate identity, vision and wellbeing are configured differently. When Christians join in a celebration of the Eucharist, they allow themselves to be interrogated by the story of Christ's self-sacrifice, to be questioned as to whether their present lives are recognizably linked with Christ's and to be reconnected with the story of Christ's death and resurrection by the renewing gift of the Holy Spirit. So the awareness here and now of how my life is unfolding, and my reflection on what I am going to put 'out there' in linguistic exchange to be recognized and responded to is confronted and enhanced by a story whose form is already fixed: a story which *has* happened, in such a way that my present options are extended or altered. Effective ritual is a matter of holding myself to account, not of retreating to a comforting alternative time-track in which everything is resolved.

Part of seeing the speaking self as time-bound is thus also seeing the self as capable of being 'brought to account' in ways like these. The self's development normally moves in dialogue with 'normative' discourses,[36] internalizing the values ascribed to this or that action or style of living; but these normative points of reference are themselves regularly embodied in narrative, drama, ritual. To grow as a reflective speaker and agent is to learn how to engage with these; to become 'conversant' with the worlds

36 Downes, op. cit., pp. 28–30, 82, 235–8.

of imagination they present in order to continue to be able to *imagine oneself* – to go on projecting possible futures of acting and speaking. To let yourself be questioned is, as we have seen, integral to the whole business of intelligent speech; and this is all the more significant when we are thinking of the fundamental questions of what we value or how honest we are that arise when we seriously try to 'let ourselves matter' to others. The varieties of ritual imagination exist to enable and equip that questioning. It's an instance of that deliberate complicating or 'stressing' of discourse which we practise in order to extend our imaginative and moral reach (as we shall see in more detail in Chapter 5). And when we think about the processes by which we educate our feelings and reactions, our sensibilities, we commonly think in terms of exposure to an increasingly resourceful set of narratives, dramas and rituals. We might, in the context of British culture, reflect about what was the best time to introduce a child or young adult to his or her first 'proper' theatre outing, to a Dickens novel, a funeral, a football match, a rock concert or even a visit to family abroad, perhaps living in a more formal and traditional setting (there are several British cultures, after all). And we think about such things in order to assist a younger generation in understanding how to 'go on' in various contexts by showing them what an intelligible flow of action looks like in these highly formalized environments. We say, in effect, 'This is – in intensified form – what it is to grow up as a human agent/speaker: to become increasingly aware of ways in which we can continue an exchange, a discourse we are sharing.' And it is in this connection that we may start thinking about what the inescapably temporal character of our speaking has to do with language about God or the sacred.

4

Our speaking is always time-related; it is always incomplete, and in search of the perspective of another; it is characteristically engaged not only with other speakers in the same direct environment but with the more radical sorts of otherness represented by ritual and fictional narrative or drama; it is in search of tools for the critique and enrichment of its 'repertoire' – and quite often in full flight from such resources when they threaten to become excessively critical and unsettling. Speaking in a way that is conscious of the time-related nature of language requires a measure of humility and of courage, a mixture of reticence and bold affirmation (the staking of a position). In what ways does all this bear upon the affirmations of religious faith? It might be thought that faith has an investment in 'finished' stories and the avoidance of the kind of risk we have been thinking about; and there are undoubtedly varieties of religiousness that work in just such a way. However, this is a monumental misreading of the issue. What we have been exploring in this chapter are the implications of knowing that I am finite – that my thoughts and words are learned over time, that my utterances are open to the – perhaps abrasive – responses of others, that I do not have the resources as an individual to sustain meaning or honesty in my own practice. Choosing finitude, says Cavell,[37] is 'the choice of community, of autonomous moral existence'; that is, to be an autonomous moral agent is, counterintuitively, to be an agent aware of choices that are real because they are limited, limited by the sheer thereness of others and by the factors that have as a matter of fact made me the agent I am. Adult autonomy – contrary to what is lazily assumed by much of our culture – is never the liberty to decide in abstraction from what others are, what others say. It is not, after all, the exclusive opposite of dependence. It is the 'staking' of ourselves precisely in recognition of the non-transparent thereness of others, committed to the risky business of being there with or for them in their radical difference.

But this means that if we are to speak honestly about ourselves, we are committed to a more and more far-reaching investigation of dependence. We are, as speakers, in search of the most *dependable* and comprehensive resource for our truthfulness and clarity; we are moving in the direction of something to which we can be unequivocally present, by which we can 'allow ourselves to be comprehended' in the most extensive sense imaginable. This is not something we can depict: to depict it would be to reduce it to the scale of what our minds can construct. And even to 'represent' it, in the specialized sense I have given to that word, is a complex and risky enterprise. We can say that it is the invisible end of a trajectory whose beginnings we can trace, the trajectory of exposure to an other whose presence both assures and challenges. And for such an other to be a presence that is not merely the presence of another *interest*, a point of view that itself

37 *The Claim of Reason*, p. 464.

needs assurance and challenge, it cannot be reduced to being represented as a further item in the list of things that there are. It cannot have interests that are in competition with the things that there are in the universe. To hark back for a moment to Downes's argument, whatever it is that would make this aspect of our linguistic practice fully intelligible and adequately grounded would have to be 'unrepresentable', in an even stronger sense than the unitary self.[38] Simone Weil famously said[39] that she was 'absolutely certain that there is a God, in the sense that I am absolutely certain that my love is not illusory' and equally 'absolutely certain that there is not a God in the sense that there is nothing real which bears a resemblance to what I am able to conceive when I pronounce that name'. The implication is that to speak of a 'divine' other is in an important sense more even than projecting an infinite line out of the trajectory we now discern, but at least we have a basis for some sort of linguistic representation in so far as we *can* talk about the imagined effect of an other to whom we were unconditionally present, in terms of an unconditional permission to question and reimagine the self without any anxiety that the project would ultimately run out or terminally fail or undermine itself. To live and speak from such a place of non-anxiety is one plausible account of 'faith'; and it is the point of connection between the process of repeatedly 'staking' oneself in the incompleteness of language and the stability of faith.

Whether we conclude with Downes that this simply leaves us with a 'philosophy of uncertainty' and no hint one way or the other as to whether what we are here talking about has a life independent of our talking is a complex issue. In one sense he is clearly right: that there is an identifiable trajectory does not tell us that its direction is towards what is mind-independently the case. And it is clear from religious as well as agnostic reflection that to take seriously the notion of a trajectory 'giving on to' the unconditional perspective imagined is necessarily to agree that the otherness involved is not the otherness of another item in the universe. Downes further notes in passing, responding to 'non-realist' accounts of

---

38 See above, notes 25, 27 and 30; also op. cit., pp. 188–97.

39 *The Notebooks of Simone Weil* (London: Routledge and Kegan Paul, 1956), p. 127; for a fuller reflection on this and similar statements of hers, see Rowan Williams, 'Simone Weil and the Necessary Non-existence of God', *Wrestling With Angels*, pp. 203–27.

Christian faith such as Don Cupitt's, that there is a significant difference between treating God as a 'useful fiction' and responding to an invitation to act 'as if', cultivating the attitudes that would generate in us the particular strengths, virtues and habits that would be appropriate responses to a really existent God: 'a commitment to a concept one claims is fictional isn't exactly the same thing as either a regulative idea or a pragmatic warrant'.[40] Yet this is where we may reasonably return to points touched on earlier. What is it that is *displayed* in the actual phenomena of religious language? If it shows signs of working with difficulty, of having criteria for self-scrutiny and self-correction, it is certainly operating 'as if' it were dealing with something mind-independent. And, by the same token, if the search for what I called the most dependable and comprehensive resource in our own self-positing and self-questioning shows the marks of dealing with difficulty and reinventing itself in response to difficulty, we have to face the possibility that we cannot fully make sense of the temporal, unfinished, cooperative character of our speech without raising the ontological question – in effect, the question of whether we can in any way speak of what is not dependent, not originated, not an item among others in the universe; the question of 'Being', if you will, as something other than the sum total or supreme exemplification of the existence we habitually talk about. And one thing that certain kinds of religious language do is to suggest that, paradoxical as it may sound, the best way of representing the unrepresentable presence of 'Being', the unconditional witness to which/whom I seek to be open, is not by any concept – though we may chart some of the territory by tactically *negating* certain key concepts – but by a return to narrative. Thus (to look forward to a theme we shall be revisiting in Chapter 5) we could see the parables of Jesus as 'representations' of the unconditional presence in that they display situations in which the choices made turn out to be choices as to whether or not to continue being open to the grace of the unspoken and unsystematized. And we could see the 'parable' of Jesus' own life and death as precisely the narrative that Jesus' own stories lead up to, the displaying of the consequences of having the unconditional spoken and enacted in a human life. And the normative narrative of Christian discipleship is one of growing in the recognition that in our relation with the narrated figure of

40 Downes, op. cit., p. 108.

Jesus we are growing in our exposure to the 'infinite resource' of God, the reality or presence that has no interest to pursue and no selfhood to defend.

That's as may be; the philosophical argument alone will not take us to quite that point. But I have been trying to suggest that it can show where the language of grace or absolution or transfiguration may appear as an intelligible way of 'going on', once you have accepted the finite position of a speaker whose work as speaker is always incomplete, always inviting something else. And it is important also to note what the problems may be if the religious register is forgotten. Cavell has an interesting passage towards the end of *The Claim of Reason*[41] where he looks at the long-term effect of ceasing to think about a creator of the universe. We are still 'stuck with the idea of the human being as a *creature*, meaning a living thing, something procreated; but meaning equally something created'. And so we either abandon the resonances of the word 'created', thus 'naturalizing' human identity as part of an indifferent order, or else we install ourselves as self-creators in God's place. Yet however hard we try to locate ourselves solely in a natural order, we cannot help rediscovering ourselves over against nature ('whether for Descartes's reasons or for Rousseau's or for Kant's or for Blake's or for Wordsworth's or for Marx's or for Thoreau's'); and however hard we try to see ourselves as authors of ourselves, we cannot accept that our present state is what we have desired: 'We are apt to turn upon our creation in anger, as, according to us – and who knows this better? – the Creator did.'[42] Connecting this specifically to what we are arguing about language, we could say that it is the lived complexity of our position as language users that pulls us away from a 'naturalizing' strategy (as we saw in the preceding chapter) and also warns us against the myths of self-creation. And if it is indeed our language use that steers us away from the pathologies Cavell diagnoses, there seems to be some connection between language and the acknowledgement of a creator; as if the sense of finitude and dependence combined with the sense of not being a deter-mined vehicle of natural processes were inextricably involved in using words in the way we do. To labour the point again, this is not an open-and-shut argument for an extra-mental non-finite reality, but it is a way of

41 Pp. 465–6.
42 Ibid., p. 466.

identifying where the concepts and images of theology and religious belief touch the basic questions about how we make sense of what we as humans characteristically do.

We speak because we are in search of recognition; we want to be heard and understood. And, on the basis of what we have said so far about understanding itself, this must mean that we want to have opened for us the possibility of new kinds of shared action, ways of 'going on' in the company of others. In seeking to be heard and changed by whatever presence it is that does not compete or exclude (i.e. does not behave as if it were another agent or subject like myself), I am also seeking to open myself to a kind of agency that is active beyond the plain realm of specific causal processes. We represent this only with the greatest risk and difficulty and habitually trivialize it by trying to display it as another and more effective causal factor in the world, a power that can override any other power. What we *want* to say is something more like a claim that there will be, for any imaginable future we could have, a context of 'grace', of absolution and renewal for our failures and of growing alignment with such an agency so that we become channels of its absolving and renewing operations. As we shall see in Chapter 5, there are aspects of language that will press us to think harder about matters like grace, mercy and trust. And the way in which a theological account of language warns us off the toxic territories of both self-creation and reductionism opens up the vital issue of how a robust and coherent understanding of language is freighted with significant moral and political insight.

We began this chapter with a reference to the idea that critical engagement with the meanings of texts seeks 'not truth but difference'; if everyone agrees with you, there is nothing more to do or say. But in thinking through what is involved in a hermeneutic practice that never comes to a final conclusion, we have been taken to a rather different place. The search for meaning – that is, the search to understand what is said, written, depicted, the search to 'make sense' of it as something to which I can respond, the search to grasp it as part of a practice in which I can find my own human place – is always a search for the next thing to say. But that 'next thing' cannot be just anything. We can, of course, make what noises or gestures we please when we encounter a noise or gesture that seems to make some claim on our attention; but to make what we know to be a simply arbitrary noise/gesture is to foreclose any further response except just another arbitrary utterance. Normally, we are trying to make the noise or gesture that will prompt sufficient and appropriate acknowledgement on the part of another – an acknowledgment from an earlier noise-maker that we have heard correctly or an acknowledgment on the part of another noise-maker that *I* have been correctly heard. To be in search of 'meaning' is to be in search of this sort of recognition. Mere difference (dissimilar noises) is not enough; to use the slightly trivializing language of Lodge's professor, there is not even a game if all that is involved is difference. And once we have moved beyond the idea that difference is all that matters, the question of truth comes back – and we are once again confronted with the seminal question of what makes speaking *difficult*. If it is difficult to know how to make the sort of noise/gesture that will secure recognition and continuation of the practice, we are recognizing that our speech is 'engaged', that it is not without relation to what is given. The givenness is initially a matter of what is already spoken by another; but the search for under-standing and recognition equally presupposes that what is already spoken is itself open to question and to challenge in the context of a world that is more than a series of arbitrarily juxtaposed noises. I recognize what is said and I look for recognition of what I say; and that recognition assumes – as Walker Percy's speculations on this subject suggest – a point between or beyond speakers, a point to which both are gesturing.

I am once again – rather obviously – trying to avoid speaking of a 'world' beyond language, if only to avoid a not very helpful word/world dualism which encourages us to think of language as the labelling of a passive environment. My argument so far should show why I am unhappy with this, and the next chapter will spell this out further. But the unfin-ishedness of language, the fact of never having said a last word and of seeking to continue a practice, will not allow us easily to settle down with an account of language that treats it as a purely self-generated thing: its difficulties are bound up with the fact that one aspect of what we recognize in each other as speakers is a shared agenda of wrestling with what belongs to neither of us. And, as we shall see more fully later on, this, when explored further, gives us some purchase on what we might mean by the 'sacred'. It is as if – and this is awkwardly vague – all our speaking is done in the wake of a given quality in what we encounter, as if we were always catching up with a reality never seen as standing still enough to be absorbed or fully embraced or mastered. I referred earlier[43] to Cavell's faintly embarrassed comment on what is happening in tragic drama and the knowledge it brings: 'It is by responding to this knowledge that the community keeps itself in touch with nature. (With Being, I would say, if I knew how.)' What he is pointing to is something like this: as spectators of drama, we suspend our capacity to act, to join in a practice, to 'go on', as we watch; we give over this time to a recognition of the inaccessible otherness of what is done on stage. And it is this that keeps the community attentive to what it is itself, what it is that gives it its identity as a community. Paradoxically, a community of speakers recognizes itself as a community when it finds the kind of ritual form that enacts its character as a coming-together, a unity, of separate speakers, separate 'centres of situations', who will never be able simply to stand in each other's place. The ritual of suspending action and response declares that we must regularly and consciously acknowledge together that we live by incompleteness of understanding, that we are not transparent to each other; and that this, so far from being a handicap, is how we begin to get some grasp of the meanings of love, or attention or respect – or whatever we want to say about that *hesitation* before each other which stops us eating one another up, in one mode of fantasy or another.[44] We are put in touch with 'Being' in the sense that we see ourselves as limited, as opaque to each other, as always summoned to the search for the shared practice that is entailed in understanding – and so as located in a context we cannot master and must approach with receptive care. That we do not 'know how' to name Being is an inevitable corollary of how we speak: 'Being' is both the condition of where and how we are and that which never comes into view as an object for the perceiving mind. If, 'between or beyond' speakers, there appears a datum to which both are in some sense accountable, to which both seek to do justice, that appearing opens out ultimately on to the horizon of an agency that has no reaction, no conditioning, and is

---

43 Chapter 2, note 48.
44 'Hesitation' is another borrowing from Simone Weil; see her essay on 'The Iliad or the Poem of Force', trans. Mary McCarthy, reprinted in *The Chicago Review*, 18:2 (1965), pp. 5–30. The theme is very helpfully clarified in Peter Winch, *Simone Weil: The Just Balance* (Cambridge: Cambridge University Press, 1989), pp. 105–8, 164–5.

therefore, as we noted earlier, beyond any notion of rivalry. And once we have found, not a descriptive account of 'Being', but a means of mapping where questions about it enter our discourse, we have a new level of access to self-questioning, to the tools that bring us back to realism and humility about who and how we are. It is this gesturing towards what appears beyond and between speakers engaged in the unceasing exchanges of language that grounds our knowledge of ourselves as distinctively human, both radically limited and radically innovative.

And to speak of limitedness draws us back to consideration of what it is for us to speak as *bodily* agents or subjects. In the next chapter, we shall be examining how our location as bodies fills out the themes sketched in the argument so far, reinforcing the recognition that our speech is necessarily both collaborative and incomplete; and, in the light of this, we shall look briefly at some of those near-metaphysical or para-metaphysical proposals that have come from certain areas in the philosophy of science, and that yet again bring us up against the question of what it is that cannot be described yet invites representation of the kind we have been thinking about.

4

INTELLIGENT BODIES: LANGUAGE AS MATERIAL PRACTICE

'Suppose that I have ASD [Autistic Spectrum Disorder] and severe learning disabilities. I cannot make sense of the kaleidoscopic world I live in. My environment swirls round me and noises boom in my ears ... Sometimes I am swept by painful surges from my own nervous system. When these are more than I can bear I try banging my head or lashing out at the people/things that overload my senses, to stop the over-stimulation. I retreat to my own world and focus on a particular sensory stimulation.'[1] Phoebe Caldwell, one of the most creative interpreters of ASD in recent years, has explored in depth the roots of autistic behaviour in the crisis of sensory overload, and has underlined the crucial importance, in working with people who live with such conditions, of establishing what feels like a controllable level of feedback – mostly by a closely focused attention to the particular coping strategies developed by people with ASD, so that the supporter or therapist can echo and extend those patterns of behaviour and create a

1   Phoebe Caldwell, *Finding You Finding Me: Using Intensive Interaction to Get in Touch with People Whose Severe Learning Disabilities are Combined with Autistic Spectrum Disorder* (London: Jessica Kingsley, 2006), p. 117.

situation where communication is possible. Caldwell movingly describes how this works in a number of specific cases: a person expresses their distress by banging the helper's arm, and she in response bangs the arm of her chair. This is a way of recognizing that what is going on is the attempt to contain distress by finding a physical focus – as we may cling on to something unconsciously in moments of acute anxiety,[2] but it also opens a way out of the distressed person's world by mirroring the action, saying, in effect, 'what you are doing is not just yours; it is heard and can be followed. His brain is put in the position of saying, "Hey, that's my sound (or rhythm) but I did not make it". I want him to look outside himself for the source of "his" utterances.'[3]

What we are seeing in the interactions described by Phoebe Caldwell is the formation of a language: what is uttered is received and followed; after a certain point of mutual acknowledgement is reached, rhythms can be subtly altered and extended. What is fed back is not chaotic and threatening but recognizable. And, as Caldwell insists, to learn how to respond to a person with an acute ASD condition requires a high degree of 'dispossession' in the helper, who has to learn another language and will do so only if they are ready for some very disorienting and vulnerable patches. Our 'normal' ability to see that our patterns of activity (including noise-making) are reflected elsewhere in the sensory world keeps most of us away from a realm of anxiously monitored self-stimulation; and the identification of 'mirror neurones' in the brain[4] shows the physiological basis for this. The same set of neural connections happens both when I do something and when I perceive it done outside myself. Even more strikingly, this pattern of connection can be reproduced when the same rhythm or sequence is enacted in a different mode or medium. For most of us, this is a routine aspect of our learning and communicating; for the person with ASD, there is an apparent absence of this process of neural connection. They will recognize and respond to imitations of *their own* behaviour; so that, for example, when a person with ASD engages in repetitive or 'stereotyped' behaviour, he or she is likely to

2   Phoebe Caldwell, *Delicious Conversations: Reflections on Autism, Intimacy and Communication* (Brighton: Pavilion Publishing, 2012), pp. 28ff.
3   *Finding You Finding Me,* p. 115.
4   See McGilchrist, *The Master and His Emissary*, pp. 58, 111–12, for a summary, with references to the scientific literature.

be attempting a highly controlled form of communication to which the only acceptable response is some sort of mirroring on the part of the other person involved. The person with ASD will not imitate another person in performing an unfamiliar action, 'because it is outside the well-worn path of his repertoire'.[5] It is only when the person with ASD 'recognizes what it is that he uses to talk to himself' that he is able to interact;[6] so anyone seeking an interaction has to decode what such a person thinks of as 'talking to himself' in the patterns of repetitive speech or gesture. 'I answer by imitation, confirming that I have not only received and taken on board her gesture, but, perhaps more importantly, that it means something to me.'[7]

The point of this excursion into the intriguing and rapidly developing field of the study of autistic conditions is to underline the fact that our conversational practice rests on a closely woven scheme of physical interaction – the elusive process whereby the firing of our neurons reflects the neuronal activity of another, confirming that what we perceive is recognizable as the same sort of thing as what we do, the ways in which we can reinforce or indeed frustrate recognition in the degree to which we understand what another is 'saying' to herself and shape our physical behaviour accordingly, the methods we evolve of containing or controlling potentially menacing situations by physical, gestural strategies of which we are not fully conscious. Just as in neuroscience generally, so here: we learn certain fundamental insights about awareness and communication by attending closely to what happens when the system is functioning eccentrically. Understanding autism is a powerfully useful key to understanding certain things about language itself and about ourselves as language users. One of these things is that – once again, contrary to any simple stimulus-and-response model of how language works – our communicative activity normally selects and organizes stimuli and, when overloaded, narrows and focuses that activity in self-defensive ways; and, further, this communicative activity also normally functions by a process of reinforcing ('checking' is not quite the right word) its own workings in relation to the reflections it perceives in others. A potentially overwhelming environment is made

5   Caldwell, *Finding you Finding Me*, p. 121.
6   Ibid.; c.f. Caldwell, *Delicious Conversations*, pp. 68–9.
7   *Delicious Conversations*, p. 65.

manageable through these two strategies. We select what to attend to and we are encouraged to depend on the viability of our selection by seeing it in some measure reflected in the agency of others. When the selection capacity is for any reason adversely affected, we no longer know what to look for in the activity of others; and it is only the patient work described by Caldwell – the labour of working out what are the rhythms devised in order to protect the raw and overstimulated brain – that can begin to restore some level of expected communication skills.

This implies that the process in which we shape a coherent model of the physical world is a variously layered matter. We select, we check, we coordinate with other perceivers; we are involved in interweaving various material operations in brain and physiology and various relational strategies so as to identify objects that are perceived in common. As I develop physically, I develop a set of strategies for finding my way around what confronts me. I learn how not to bump into things, and thus create an internalized map and set of rules encoding my environment, increasingly sophisticated and differentiated: this bit of the territory presents *this* kind of obstacle, this bit presents *that* kind. The bare fact of binocular vision already presents me with a plurality of possible perspectives; and working through what this entails alerts me from the start to *depth* as a feature of my perceptual field. In tandem with this, I am being provided with confirmatory or non-confirmatory material from other agents whose visible strategies for managing the environment resemble mine (this is where the role of mirror neurons comes in). I discover not only the points at which the physical environment resists my motion, but – by following the comparable reactions of others – where this environment resists other agents as well. The primitive concept of a physical object is very far from being the straightforward presentation of a set of material stimuli to an individual brain. It is the product of a more involved response in which diverse patterns of identifying 'resistance' in the environment are held together. The very notion of a three-dimensional object assumes such a convergence of different possible points of view and points where resistance is met. And as perception becomes more conscious, such different possible points of view come to include the idea of continuity over time as well as the unity of different points in space. I shall have acquired a map of my environment in which I can locate myself in relation to other physical presences, I shall have recognized something of the paradoxical character of my own physical presence, which I perceive in a unique way. In the language of the most painstaking twentieth-century exponent of this approach to understanding perception, Maurice Merleau-Ponty, I shall have recognized my 'bodily intentionality', my presence in the world as an 'intelligent orientation'.[8] And, against such a background, language has to be understood as something more and other than a tool for getting information from one container to another. In Merleau-Ponty's words,[9] it manifests a link between human agents and between agents and the world. As we noted when discussing Iain McGilchrist's analysis of the origins of speech,[10] it is a mistake to think of speech originating in the (practical) need to communicate information: it has roots in simply articulating and testing mutual recognition, inviting response of an ever more differentiated kind. Which is why Phoebe Caldwell's ventures in establishing communication with people living with autistic conditions tell us so much about language itself. Communication is not, in this context, passing on information but establishing a world in common, where someone who is radically unsure as to whether their own response to the environment is recognizable and viable can find assurance that they are not isolated. The vicious circle of anxiety and inward-turning strategies can be broken.

'Language takes on meaning for a child when it *establishes a situation*', says Merleau-Ponty[11] in a phrase we have already been using. Hence, he argues, words are fundamentally not objects designed somehow to depict other objects, but practices – 'a certain use made of my phonatory equipment, a certain modulation of my body as a being in the world'.[12] It is a specific modification of the ensemble of physical variables, constituting the continuance of an object's life in the world in another medium: 'it is ... the aspect

8   Taylor Carman, 'Sensation, Judgement, and the Phenomenal Field', in Taylor Carman and Mark B. M. Hansen (eds), *The Cambridge Companion to Merleau-Ponty* (Cambridge: Cambridge University Press, 2005), pp. 50–73 (quotation from p. 71); c.f. Maurice Merleau-Ponty, *Phenomenology of Perception*, trans. Colin Smith (London: Routledge and Kegan Paul, 1962), p. 196, Part One, sections 3 and 4 and Part Two, section 2.

9   *Phenomenology of Perception*, p. 196.

10 Above, pp. 27–9.

11 *Phenomenology of Perception*, p. 401.

12 Ibid., p. 403.

take on by the object in human experience.'[13] But, as the argument goes on to make plain, this in turn means that I apprehend an object precisely as something shared: there is no point at which I have to make some conscious or half-conscious move outside a private frame of reference to a shared one.[14] My awareness of and my speech in respect of an object in my environment are not the product of some fusion between an internal sense of what I am experiencing and a process of inspired guesswork about 'the contents of another mind'. Seeing something and speaking about something are practices in which I take a particular place in a flow of activity that embraces myself and my neighbour. To refer back again to McGilchrist's characterization of the origins and nature of language, the body seeks a mode of action that moves with the perceived movement of the environment, seeks to continue the 'style' of action or energy it reflects or represents, through gesture as well as sound. Although the example has worn almost to a cliché, Bruce Chatwin's account of Australian aborigines 'singing up' the landscape comes to mind[15]: the landscape of a particular route through almost trackless wilderness is encoded as the length of time it takes to sing a specific sequence of sound. The sounds *are* the mode in which the landscape is effectively present in the subject. And so the representation of the landscape is inseparably bound up with a time-taking physical action worked out in response to a range of environmental triggers and clues. It would be odd to call it a description of the landscape, yet it is undoubtedly 'accountable' to a series of material stimuli from outside the brain and provides reliable knowledge of how to (in this case literally) 'go on'. And it is also the deposit of collaborative activity, an inherited practice tested in shared activity. It carries information, but cannot be reduced to a set of 'facts' separable from the complex material enactment of walking and singing. The practice might well be described in Merleau-Ponty's phrase as the form that the object (the landscape) takes in human experience, the object's life in another medium – or, to salvage an older metaphysical vocabulary, the life of intelligible form within a particular human intelligence.

The implication of what McGilchrist, Merleau-Ponty and Phoebe Caldwell, along with a fair number of others, have to say about the body and

13 Ibid.
14 Ibid., p. 405.
15 Bruce Chatwin, *The Songlines*, new edn (London: Vintage Classics, 1998).

language is that one of the philosophical myths we need to be most wary of is the habit of opposing purely active subject to passive object, of referring to an active mind's perception of mindless and passive process as the basic paradigm of knowledge. A coherent material object is, we have seen, a concept emerging from a fairly intricate interplay of processes, bringing in the physiological fact of binocular vision, the mutually confirmatory strategies registered in the activity of mirror neurons and articulated as speech is mastered, and the awareness both of time passing and of the availability of past impression and interactions in speech and other memory-related operations. Material objects and the material world as such are always already 'saturated' with the workings of mind; we cannot abstract the object we examine from the means we are using to examine it (this may be another commonplace, but if so it seems that it has not yet been fully absorbed by many who write popularizing texts on scientific method). When the evolutionary biologist Pier Luigi Luisi asserts that 'It is human consciousness that makes possible the emergence of objects of the outside world',[16] he is reinforcing Merleau-Ponty's analysis of the process of intelligent selection by which the brain decodes multiple stimuli into consistent structuring patterns, and warning against the idea that the only basic and dependable form of knowledge is the accurate registering of the simplest available level of material causal interaction. That 'simplest available level' is as much the product of complex mental operation as the most elaborate metaphysical version; what is more, such simple levels of interaction already presuppose a material order in which there are agencies that we can only describe metaphorically as 'seeking solutions' and producing innovative structures as paths to future goals, agencies moving towards new and optimally intelligible convergence. These are agencies making themselves 'understood' in more and more complete and effective ways. As Conor Cunningham notes in his admirable essay on the theological implications of Darwin's scheme,[17] 'something analogous to intelligence' has to be assumed in the way even plant life adapts to its environment: the entire system 'learns' and

16 *The Emergence of Life: From Chemical Origins to Synthetic Biology* (Cambridge: Cambridge University Press, 2006), p. 173; quoted by Conor Cunningham, *Darwin's Pious Idea,* p. 158.

17 Cunningham, op. cit., pp. 163ff.

'plans'. So far from consciousness or human intelligence being a somewhat embarrassing excrescence on the surface of rational material processes, it would be better to say that intelligence is literally the only phenomenon in the universe that makes sense of the overall direction of material existence towards coherent, sustainable, innovative, adaptable forms. If, to pick up a word I have used occasionally in earlier discussion, the story of the material world is one of 'negotiation', systems finding their way in interacting with one another and constantly refining and elaborating this rather than settling in an eternal equilibrium, conscious life, the knowing subject, is a development entirely consistent with this story. Indeed, we could not conceive of the story without the model provided by consciousness itself, the *awareness* of negotiation.

And one implication is that *language* must similarly be seen as the natural integrating factor in the evolving material universe. Rather than looking to material processes, understood in a mechanical fashion, as the key to understanding what language is, it would be nearer the truth to say that we look to language to show us what matter is. That is, language exhibits a pattern of cooperative agency in which the structure of life or action in one medium is rendered afresh (translated) in another. The material universe appears as an essentially *symbolic* complex. It is an exchange of 'messages', a universe of coherent process and temporal stability, of form and motion, an *intelligible* universe, because the unfolding story of material evolution leads to speech, to the expression and sharing of intelligible structure, both a communicating of information and a reinforcing of mutual human cohesion which allows more and more creative 'negotiating' with other parts of the environment. It is not an accident that the vocabulary of the natural sciences, not least biology, is littered with linguistic metaphors, as we have noted in passing. To take just one area: the notion of a genetic code and the immensely sophisticated concept of the genome take it for granted that there are in our genetic material regularities that can be identified as significant by other material receptors. A gene is not a small item, not even in the rather refined sense in which we could still just say this of an atom, but a shorthand symbol for a pattern of recurring elements within the ensemble of genetic material activating cell tissues; but it *becomes* a pattern only when there is a receiving and decoding 'partner'. The immense tracts of genetic material identified in the Human Genome Project whose significance is as yet wholly unknown simply remind us that to identify a significant pattern confidently we need to see how this or that particular cluster of elements is 'recognized' and acted on.[18] As all cryptographers know, a coded message may contain a number of apparent regularities that are red herrings in the definitive process of decoding. When we begin to see something of where a message is headed, we can begin to weed out significant from insignificant clusters. What has been unkindly called 'genetic astrology', the belief that it is possible to identify isolated genes which determine the behaviour of complex organisms,[19] relied on the completely mythological notion that a gene was a kind of agent, separated from other pseudo-agents within the ensemble of genetic material; whereas to think of a gene as a particular sequence of elements which, when recognized, combines in a particular way with other sequences or clusters in a way which is notably fruitful in understanding developmental processes in the genealogy of organisms – this keeps our minds on the fact that it is cooperation and 'recognition' (receiving information *as* information) that are the effective motors of the evolutionary story. Only the fact of language provides the models we need to grasp these processes in the non-human world. So far from matter being by definition mindless, it seems we have no choice but to talk about it as a linguistic or symbolic reality, whose processes we can only understand by analogy with our own conscious systems of recognition and collaboration.

2

We are so accustomed to using the rhetoric of 'dead' or 'mindless' matter that the idea of matter itself as inherently symbolic – in the sense that it is structured as a complex of patterns inviting recognition and constantly generating new combinations of intelligible structures – is likely to seem odd or fanciful. Yet this is the clear implication of the most advanced researches currently conducted on the material world, such as the Human

18 The point was made by – once again – Steiner in *After Babel*, p. 127: 'In both the genetic and the linguistic scheme an appropriate receptor or auditor is needed to complete the message. Without the concordat interface or surrounding field structure, the gene-sequence cannot "communicate".'

19 Ibid., pp. 50ff.

Genome Project. The idea of a fundamental, irreducible description of the 'real' stuff of the world, the interaction of basic particles, now seems painfully crude. Several decades ago, David Bohm's *Wholeness and the Implicate Order*[20] outlined a picture of the 'material' world in terms of what he called 'holomovement', a connected system in which every local sub-totality of agencies carried the informational content of the whole: we could properly isolate this or that field of agency for analysis when we had identified adequately stable 'patterns of order and measure' in a particular locality, but should not forget that this kind of consideration in terms of separable entities is 'approximate' and in a sense provisional, given that an adequate mapping of the processes of the universe would need to be one that laid out the way in which the entire cosmic order came to coalesce in this particular way at this particular point – a goal 'probably unknowable'.[21] To speak of an 'implicate' order for the universe is to recognize that the whole pattern is folded in to every part: we make distinctions between ensembles of elements as a way of identifying certain *situations* in which the holomovement crystallizes in such and such a way for a period. The tempting error is to suppose that we have identified enduring and solid building blocks in this making of distinctions.[22] It is more helpful, Bohm suggests, to think of the analogy, say, of two photographic images of a fish tank taken from different angles: we see distinct images, with some obvious correlation between them, but we should only understand what was actually being shown when we imagined the three-dimensional medium in which the process was one and undivided. So when we observe correlated behaviour in two atoms at a distance, with no apparent causal connection as we normally understand the term, it is most helpful to think of a further dimensionality in which the observed behaviour was one event.[23]

Bohm has already, earlier in his book,[24] noted that we can be imprisoned by the conventional structures of most of our languages, with their 'subject–verb–object' patterns implying that there are fixed

20 *Wholeness and the Implicate Order* (2nd edn, corrected) (London: Routledge and Kegan Paul, 1981).
21 Ibid., pp. 178, 179.
22 Ibid., e.g. pp. 183–4.
23 Ibid., pp. 186–9.
24 Ibid., pp. 28ff.

substances exerting their agency upon other fixed substances, but the saving eccentricity of language is that it is itself constantly subversive of this pattern. We use language in ways that unsettle the simple notion of basic solid elements, notably by metaphor and other supposedly non-standard forms of utterance. Perhaps, Bohm proposes, we need a quite different mode of speech, or at least of logical representation, which leaves us less enslaved to the primitive and unsustainable metaphysic of things doing things to other things; and he christens this the 'rheomode' (from the Greek word for 'flow'), a style of discourse that refuses to absolutize the isolated substantial agent. Something similar is advanced in a celebrated but prohibitively difficult paper by Margaret Masterman on 'Metaphysical and Ideographic Language',[25] in which a technique shaped by the use of Chinese ideographs is used to model how we might construct logical representations of states of affairs that will avoid the errors to which Bohm draws attention. Thus[26] we are shown how a statement can be rendered in terms of identifying a situation qualified by certain contextual factors, qualified in turn by other and wider factors. Masterman gives as an example the way in which you would build up a complex identifying clause meant to refer to 'The playing of the impromptu cadenza of the last movement of the first performance of so-and-so's Horn Concerto at the 1955 Edinburgh Festival'; in the 'ideographic' logical structure proposed, this becomes '1955-Edinburgh-Music-Festival-So-and-So-Horn-Concerto-First-Performance-Last-Movement-Impromptu-Cadenza-Play'. 'Play' (the act of performing music on a specific occasion) has been qualified by a string of definitions so that 'an originally verb-like concept, "Play" ... has become a final positional verbal noun, "Playing"; then ... an indexical symbol'.[27] The reader familiar with German will recognize a partly comparable pattern of building up a complex definition by the successive qualifying of an act or phenomenon.[28] What emerges from this discussion is that

25 In C. A. Mace, ed. *British Philosophy in the Mid-Century* (London: Allen and Unwin, 1957), pp. 283–357.
26 Op. cit., p. 332.
27 Ibid., p. 335.
28 Some readers may recall the apocryphal German newspaper headline referring to a bottle of ink being thrown at the female relative of a visiting African head of state: *Hottentotenpotentatentantentintenattentat ...*

metaphysical discourse is focused on what Masterman calls 'clusters' rather than statements[29] – that is, it works by displaying states-of-affairs in their most comprehensively imagined contexts rather than simply describing the condition of a primitive solid unit here and now. In Bohmian terms, it is about finding a symbolic form that expresses the sense of a situation in which the universal order is in-folded in *this* unique way.

And however much our 'normal' language unavoidably works with nouns and verbs, subjects and objects, it repeatedly pushes us back towards this apprehension of a universal fluidity 'caught' in specific clusters of significance, whose component elements ceaselessly recombine to generate new moments of clustering. Our next chapter will explore further some of the ways in which this habitually happens. But in regard to the theme of the present chapter, the salient point is that the more our speech attends to and understands its continuities with the material environment, the clearer it becomes (i) that it is not a system for depicting isolated subjects acting on each other in a void (this is where the causal determinism so casually signalled by Rorty and so fervently pressed by more recent secular apologists appears so profoundly at odds with what we know of material existence itself) and (ii) that the position of the embodied speaker is not that of a detached recorder of such mechanical interactions. The act of speaking and making sense in speaking is itself one of those clusters of 'significant crystallization' in the flux of the implicate order. Or, to put it another way, the act of speaking/making sense is inseparably part of the order of things; it is, as we have insisted earlier, not an alien importation into a mechanical universe, an epiphenomenon that causes minor embarrassment to right-minded materialists. Conor Cunningham sums up a long series of quotations from various physicists and cognitive theorists in the words: 'In the beginning there were only probabilities or potentialities, and they were only actualized when a mind observed them'[30]: the 'capture' of the world in language, in the articulation of regularity and connection and the capacity to generate new connectivities and structures, is continuous with, inseparable from, the way in which the 'holomovement' of the universe gathers itself into significant clusters, that is, clusters recognizable by minds as

29 Masterman, op. cit., p. 342.
30 Cunningham, *Darwin's Pious Idea*, p. 374.

being intelligibly structured. To repeat the point: we cannot think or speak intelligently about the 'material' world without speaking/thinking about ourselves as speakers; we cannot talk about 'matter' without presupposing 'mind' – granting that the two nouns don't help us much in holding on to a defensible account of our reality; and we badly need to free ourselves from the decadent Cartesianism of supposing the universe to be divided between impenetrably solid stuff and the immaterial content, whatever its value or truth may be, of the noises we make.

Two words of caution may be in order here, though. The first is to say that Bohm's 'implication' needs to be distinguished from that form of rather degenerate idealism, attacked by G. E. Moore and others,[31] which maintains that every true proposition must *logically* entail and be entailed by every other true proposition and that therefore every relational property of a subject is an essential part of the definition of that subject. We can know that Paris is the capital of France without having to know that water is composed of hydrogen and oxygen. We can know that this is Socrates without having to know that he is the husband of Xanthippe. To claim that every state of affairs is ultimately related to every other state of affairs in such a way that no 'complete' account of situation x could be offered without an account of situation y is to claim – almost trivially – that we can never isolate one strand of causal explication as wholly self-standing. It is not to say that we are unable to identify x and the propositions that happen to be true of it without strictly implying all that is true of y. Nor is it to claim that, if we had all the relevant information about y, we could deduce x as a necessary logical consequence. If the fundamental 'energies' of the universe are gathered into this 'knot' here and that 'knot' there, we operate a variety of simple rules to distinguish between the two knots and to trace what connects them. But we do not and cannot say that by naming and spelling out identity conditions for one of the knots we automatically define the other. To go back to Masterman's example, we may well acknowledge that a full specification of this particular act of performing so-and-so's Horn Concerto would expand to an impossible scale of framing or qualifying

---

31 See Moore's famous paper on 'External and Internal Relations' in his *Philosophical Studies* (London: Routledge and Kegan Paul, 1922), pp. 276–309.

definitions,[32] but that cannot mean that this full specification would by implication tell us about someone else's performance on another occasion of the same concerto or a different concerto or a piece of jazz improvisation.

The second caution is that it is fatally easy to misunderstand all this as a licence for imprecision, for loose claims that definition and limit are unimportant or unreal because the 'real' essence of all things is ('just') some sort of indivisible life-force. But the truth is that the account just offered – with the detailed outworkings by Bohm or Masterman – insists upon a more rather than less exact attention to the limited specificity of situations. Each intelligible cluster poses a set of demanding questions about its relationships with others in the same stream; each – as the crystallizing of a universal flow of activity – is going to open out on to such a wide assortment of connections that its representation is never finalized. Relating this to earlier discussions, we can say that the work of finding more and more comprehensive or sustainable representative forms is formidable and unfinishable. And this means that our representative forms will be constantly in search of new levels of adequacy or exactitude; to recognize their imperfect and challengeable character does not mean settling for vagueness but the very opposite. What is more, the attention demanded of me as speaker is intense. If I acknowledge the inexhaustibility of what is before me, it is not that I am imagining a mystical hinterland within a fixed object, but that I recognize the impossibility of mapping all the relations in which this situation stands in respect of others. I am inescapably involved in a temporal continuum shared with the object, never frozen. And to assume a continuity of agency or energy in which all share – all objects alike, 'object' and 'subject' alike – is not to deny the radical and disturbing otherness of what I confront in any specific moment. As knower and speaker, I must come to terms with finitude, with limit: I shall not master this object given for my apprehension because it is a specific in-folding of an unlimited flow of action. Both myself as knower/speaker and the object

---

32 Masterman, op. cit., pp. 335–6: 'within the universe of discourse of ideographic language, ... the trouble is not to make the flow of speech go on, but to get it, logically speaking, ever to cease'. In seeking to refer truthfully, we are always 'cut off short' and require 'cluster-forming' conventions to make our language manageable.

are 'journeying through time', in Merleau-Ponty's phrase.[33] I work to characterize and transmit the specificity of what is there through the medium of
my speech; I accept that this is always a provisional task in the sense that
there will always be other angles from which to look, and that my own
attempt at characterizing will therefore always be in need of other perspectives, other connections that can intelligibly be made. I speak from and only
from the limited specificity – the 'clustering' – that is this intelligent body,
in this moment, with this history.

This is importantly different from the notion that speaking as such
itself embodies a necessarily inadequate relation with what is there, a kind
of failure. If we say, as we must, that language is constantly 'transcending'
its current limitations, it is crucial to stress that this is nothing to do with
some goal of transcending limit itself; and this is essential in seeing off the
confused but pervasive idea that language itself is somehow an obstacle to
proper and full truthfulness.[34] The problem is not that words stand between
us and reality; it is that (as the last chapter noted) our speech can never
close itself off from further response and so any form of words will be open
to development; what I now say is not the last word. And the conclusion
should not be that language is an imperfect tool – as if there could be a
better or more transparent way of apprehending and representing what we
are engaging with; simply that there is no such thing as a fixed relationship
between two different things called language and fact. The reality we
inhabit is impinging upon us in constantly new ways, requiring more
from us as speakers; what we say is the unceasing process of shaping the
distinctive material event that is speech to the material events that prompt
but do not determine it, as a way of prolonging or extending in another
mode the life of the environment we inhabit.

This is in one sense to agree with the old doctrine that words carry
the life of what they relate to or represent. But it is not to imply a 'magical'
relation between word and world such that to know a name is to know and

---

33 *Phenomenology of Perception*, p. 407.
34 See, for example, D. Z. Phillips, *Death and Immortality* (London: Macmillan, 1970),
    p. 14 for a brief but perceptive critique of this view; also his essay 'Epistemological
    Mysteries', in *Faith After Foundationalism: Critiques and Alternatives* (London:
    Routledge, 1988), pp. 255–72.

possess an 'essence', to have something at one's disposal. It would be more true to say that what is being spoken of has the speaker at its disposal, at least to the extent that the speaker's stance in the world is for the moment of speaking defined by the presence of what is spoken of – a roundabout way of paraphrasing the Aristotelian and Thomist model of the action of an object's 'form' on the knowing subject. However exactly we put it, the point is that we need to set aside two profoundly unhelpful and misleading models of how speech and thought relate to their environment. One is that we are the recipients of individualized sets of material stimuli which we then translate into expression or communication, offering them somewhat tentatively to other speakers, never sure that their individual set of stimuli corresponds to ours. The other is that we are given access to the hidden interior essences of what we encounter by some mystically complete and effective image or sound. Both models share some of the same basic misconceptions: they assume a certain kind of gap between mind and object, let alone between one mind and another, and so assume that there is a distance to be crossed between mind and world. Magical thinking affirms that this can be crossed by the transfer of an essential content from one place to another, giving the subject unlimited access to the object; more conventional modern epistemologies envisage a processing and synthesizing of intrinsically neutral or meaningless material data – with the pervasive background anxiety that what is 'really' there eludes us and that we can have no certainty that our perceptions are shared. In contrast, the approach advocated here acknowledges that, if there is no primitive set of atomistic data to be labelled or catalogued, speech is always looking for means of representing an event and in some measure therefore prolonging or re-enacting an event (because adequate representation cannot be restricted to a simple reflection of the moment of appearing; an event is non-negotiably part of a continuum, and its prior conditions and after-life are bound to enter into representation). What we say is moulded according to how an event goes; it shows the impact of an event, at a number of very different levels, from the apparently straightforward record of sensory impressions through to various kinds of significance for a human cultural context. That speech in this sense extends the form of activity at work in an event is far from saying that it is a magical 'capturing of essences'; but it has some resonance at least with the linguistic speculations of some of the Russian religious philosophers of the early twentieth century[35] who described names as *energemata* of what they designated, active bearers of the agency they represented, rather than denominators of some fixed essence.

This whole argument assumes that encounters with our environment are not exclusively or even primarily exercises in gathering evidence that will lead to a conclusion. We noted earlier[36] Wittgenstein's cautions about imagining mental processes, narratives, as it were, for our routine intelligent activity, our response to and continuation of an intelligible series or sequence. If (as we are so often encouraged to believe) what we encounter is, primitively, discrete lumps of sensory data, then everything else is the product of a process – other minds, dimensionality, temporal duration and so on; these non-primitive elements will need to be thought of as somehow the products of that process, deductions we make on the basis of simpler sets of data. But in fact we are faced with a variety of encounters in which it makes no sense at all to think of quanta of material that enable us to come to a *conclusion* about what we are engaged with. Merleau-Ponty invites us to think of standing with a friend, looking together at a landscape, each pointing out to the other feature of what they see: 'Paul's finger, which is pointing out the church tower, is not a finger-for-me that I *think of* as orientated towards a church-tower-for-me, it is Paul's finger which itself shows me the tower that Paul sees, just as conversely, when I make a movement towards some point in the landscape that I can see, I do not imagine that I am producing in Paul, in virtue of some pre-established harmony, inner visions merely analogous to mine: I believe, on the contrary, that my gestures invade Paul's world and guide his gaze.'[37] When I see the finger pointing, I don't *work out* what is going on, making an educated guess that Paul is probably doing what I might do in similar circumstances, both of us acting on the supposition that we may safely conclude that we're using our bodies in the same kind of way. We are not here dealing with material

35 I have in mind particularly the work of Aleksei Losev and Sergei Bulgakov; on these and on the underlying metaphysical ideas implied, see the essays by Antoine Arjakovsky, Rowan Williams and John Milbank which make up Part 1 of Adrian Pabst and Christoph Schneider (eds), *Encounter Between Eastern Orthodoxy and Radical Orthodoxy: Transfiguring the World by the Word* (London: Ashgate, 2009).

36 See above, pp. 68–9.

37 Op. cit., p. 405.

that feeds in to a process. Our presence as communicating beings alongside each other establishes a common world, a common set of possible tasks, challenges, exercises, in which there is for each of us enough that is the same and enough that is different to make exchange possible and meaningful. The pointing gesture is simply read as an instruction within a common framework; I cannot sensibly divorce it from its symbolic freight.

And the I that thinks, observes, gestures and speaks is a *point of convergence* for a field of perception, discovering its locus and boundaries in the sheer fact of contact and continuity, experiencing the meaningful 'instruction' of someone else's gesture/sound delivered from another point of convergence; each 'I' is thus moulded by this as by other elements in the perceptual field. So what happens when a human subject arrives in the world, says Merleau-Ponty, is neither the advent of a mysterious spiritual monad nor the coalescing of a bundle of contingently grouped sensations, but a new set of '*possibilities of situations*'[38] in which the shifting standpoint of the body constantly remakes the perceived world. But this 'remaking' is not a repeated process of putting together discrete precepts, working towards the composition of an integrated scene of ordered and distinct objects, as if our consciousness were engaged in a perpetual jigsaw puzzle. It is, rather, the business of absorbing and responding to the field in which I am located and which is acting *in* me as much as *on* me, feeling my way, resetting my coordinates and, where speech and gesture are concerned, doing so by means of signals which do not need to be examined as possible evidence for the presence of another possibly analogous individual subject but which are purely and simply the vehicles of contact and interaction with other actualities and possibilities in the field. To take another obvious example (not Merleau-Ponty's), when I am aware of 'catching someone's eye', it is impossible to regard the eye as simply a discrete set of sense impressions, another object in my visual field: it is only seen *as* a seeing presence, as including me in a visual field that is not mine. Try to look at even the picture or photograph of an eye without the sense of being looked at: you will discount this sense once you know it is a photograph; but you will have to work against the grain. When eyes meet, we do not go through a process leading to a conclusion ('that organ looks like the eye I see in the

38   Ibid., p. 407.

mirror; it is likely to function in another body in much the same way that it does in mine; there is a good chance that I am in contact with another subject like myself'): we recognize that we are seen, that we are immediately constituted as recipients of intelligent action. Recognizing that the eye we see is a photographed or painted eye is recognizing that this eye belongs in a different situation with different possibilities. It does not cast doubt on what is happening in the ordinary exchange we call 'catching the eye'. And the ensemble of such experiences appears to tell us that to see and understand and speak is to find a place in a field of intelligible embodied pattern, a field always already charged with other kinds of intelligent agency. We are involved in assumptions that what we see has a history, that an eye is how someone looks at us, that an object has three dimensions, that a word spoken to us is a sign of a shared intelligible world; and we have to acknowledge that these are not dispositions we *bring about* by weighing evidence and deciding on a plausible and defensible position. It is the immediate condition of any acting or speaking, it is the 'substance' of life in the world, life as a body.

3

Putting this alongside our earlier discussion of Phoebe Caldwell's reflections on autism, we can connect ideas about the physical 'location' of language with the importance of *trust* in understanding how speech works. People experiencing ASD cope with uncontrollable environmental stimulus by behaving *as if* they were not persuaded that what others take to be the ordinary stuff of the world, including other speakers, could be relied on. The problem for a naive observer of ASD conditions is that people with these conditions apparently have access to all the evidence that other people have, yet seem to refuse to draw the 'normal' conclusion. The work of Caldwell and others explains why this is a seriously unhelpful framework for understanding what is going on; and the more abstract argument we have been developing explains why our relation to the environment is anyway not a matter of assessing evidence and drawing conclusions. What is non-standard or malfunctioning in the ASD case has to do with the lack of a means for absorbing and responding to the environment as part of a shared project – the absence of any confidence that we can make viable selections among the stimuli we are receiving, linked with a difficulty in seeing how this selection works for others. Hence the therapeutic response is, in Caldwell's words, something to do with listening to the way the person with ASD talks to him- or herself; and by echoing this, the helper creates an environment in which making some sense of stimuli appears as a cooperative task, an environment where there are other recognizable sense-makers at work. It is precisely as we diagnose the eccentric workings of language and perception in the ASD instance that we grasp how fundamental trust is to the usual workings of communication. Routinely (as Merleau-Ponty stresses in the passage about looking at the landscape along with a friend), we assume that a word or a gesture is automatically received as significant; the 'trust' entailed is routine, unreflective, not a complex existential decision. What becomes disturbing in any human interaction is when – as in the stories Phoebe Caldwell relates – my significant gesture makes no apparent impact or another's gesture, clearly important for them, cannot be deciphered as significant in my world. Habitual human interaction has moments where gaps of this kind open briefly, but the pain and stress of some encounters with people experiencing ASD arises from the fact that the gap between non-connecting gestures is long-term and apparently unbridgeable.

As we have just noted, it may be misleading even to speak of 'trust' here. It is not that I make a leap of faith in assuming that there is such a thing as shared significance. That could only be true if I began from an individual set of sense experiences named and organized by me which I then venture to make public in the hope that they will correspond to someone else. The truth is more that the naming and organizing is from the start a shared affair. Faced with the classic sceptical question of how I know that the colour I call 'red' is what another speaker calls 'red', we can only say that, if the application of the term is learned and we are able to negotiate its use with apparent success, the shared character of its significance is axiomatic. Yet it is not completely nonsensical to use the language of trust here: we speak to another in the confidence that hitherto unknown collections of sounds will register as I wish them to; we listen in the confidence that the sounds we hear connect us within a shared situation. In such a setting, the incompleteness of our words, discussed in earlier pages, is not a failure or a threatening exposure but an inseparable feature of how we know. we are always going to be in each other's debt for negotiating our way in the world. And in the background is the insistent suggestion that my own knowing/ speaking becomes fully what it can be within the context of an unlimited convergence of points of view, perspectives on the shared environment. The broader our shared situation, the more securely we know and judge; which in turn provides the grounds for being very wary of any strategy, cultural, religious, political, which assumes any perspective to be dispensable: this is an epistemology with discernible political and social implications. And connecting this again to the issues raised by ASD conditions and their treatment, it is clear that a therapist like Phoebe Caldwell begins from the assumption that the person with ASD has a point of view and a capacity to create working symbols, to make sense; the task is to make space enough for this to surface and connect. Pushing a little further: this approach warns us against a faulty and problematic use of ideas of mutual recognition or even 'empathy' as sometimes defined as a basis for ethics.[39] Faced with what we don't recognize or with an apparent lack of recognition, we have to be reminded that the fact of *encountering a recognizable body* presents us with a human point of view: what we encounter is a sense-making organism, in that it is receiving the input of a shared situation. Before we conclude – notice the dangerous word – that a putative human organism (an unborn child, a severely challenged adult, a person with dementia or with a condition that radically isolates them from communication, a person in a so-called vegetative condition) is beyond the community of mutual sense-making, we need to pause and weigh the importance of recognizing not necessarily another speech-user operating just like ourselves but another centre of meaningful experience, another point of view, the focus of another intel- ligible situation – and therefore a contributor in ways I may not easily grasp to my own intelligence.

The human other (and to some extent the sentient other, as this has some evident moral implications for our relation to the animal world) is,

---

39 The problems of an uncritical use of categories such as recognition and empathy are explored with great penetration by James Mumford in his *Ethics at the Beginning of Life: A Phenomenological Critique* (Oxford: Oxford University Press, 2013), especially chapter 4.

as we have already noted, *a point on which relations converge*;[40] this remains true whatever level of linguistic or communicative performance is exhibited by such a subject. And another way of expressing this is to say that any other I encounter is always already 'turned towards' something other than (just) myself as interlocutor or observer. To accept the notion of the body as the centre of a 'situation' and a set of possible situations (in Merleau-Ponty's sense) and to understand the body's life as continuous with the intelligible input of the environment implies that in any encounter we begin from the trust that we are engaged with another perspective that is part of a whole intelligible environment, and thus something I am likely to need in my own developing intelligent life. It is also to accept that the other remains irreducibly other because I can never simply be where the other is, and because the other's relations cannot be mapped exhaustively on to mine. Every imaginable human encounter has these characteristics; and the foundation of an ethical response to the world we inhabit is bound up with this acknowledgement of the other's body as meaningful – meaningful because it is the point of intersection for a specific set of symbolic transactions. However impenetrable they may be (as in the cases mentioned), however hard to recognize or feel our way into, we cannot let go of this assumption that the other is such a 'point of intersection' without being drawn back into the corrosive attitude of regarding the other as material providing (or failing to provide) *evidence* for some conclusion about whether our perceptions can be confirmed by reference to independent witnesses and whether or not a putative independent witness is 'really' an intelligent subject as I am. As the man said, 'The human body is the best picture of the human soul'[41]: which suggests that any adequate account of what is due to the spiritual or moral dignity of human beings has to presume that we take the other's body with complete seriousness as a meaningful presence, never to be reduced to a possession (which, incidentally, raises some fundamental questions for the current discussion around the patenting of human genetic material[42]).

40   C.f. above, p. 112.
41   *Philosophical Investigations*, II.iv, p. 152.
42   See, e.g., D. B. Resnik, 'DNA Patents and Human Dignity', *Journal of Law, Medicine and Ethics*, 29.1, pp. 12–65.

4

If we try to draw these themes together, what emerges is something like this. In a universe in which matter is itself inescapably 'symbolic' – that is, inseparable from the communication of ordered interrelation and operating as part of a global or rather cosmic system of interacting signals – for us to understand any phenomenon is for us to be engaged with and in a shared situation (rather than for us to find appropriate labels for individual component objects, with the ideal of discovering irreducible 'building blocks'). We know what we know as something always already known by another. Our attempts to characterize/represent a situation in speech will therefore be diverse: not chaotic or vague, but equally not reducible to the single authoritative reproduction of some basic structure. To try to be truthful is to try and find a way of speaking that does maximal justice to the diversity and plurality of a situation – so that 'truthful' speech is inevitably committed to metaphor, in order to represent what we could call the overflow of significance that we confront. Each of us as an intelligent linguistic subject stands at a unique intersection of symbolic action, simply in virtue of standing where we physically stand – as bodies. And, if this is so, we should be careful of any scheme of thinking that invites us to measure the acceptability or normalcy of another bodily presence, especially as regards its communicative capacity: that another does not or cannot speak in ways we can digest cannot render them ineligible to count as subjects with meaningful 'points of view'. With some such others we can by careful and compassionate labour (in the spirit of a Phoebe Caldwell) bring ourselves to recognize capacities we had hitherto ignored or misread; with some we cannot. The important point is to resist 'normalizing' what is easily accessible for us in ways that rule others out from the business of human exchange and engagement. And an anthropology of this sort will insist that, whether or not we hear and recognize speech as we usually receive it, the symbolic world of any and every other is something I need to enhance and complete my own. Language does not abolish the all-important distance between bodies; on the contrary, by affirming the always unfinished character of converse or exchange, it acknowledges the non-negotiable diversity of bodies, and gives us a clue to the ethical basis of recognizing the other as never to be *possessed*. As I have argued elsewhere,[43] a philosophical and theological

43 Rowan Williams, 'Do Human Rights Exist?', in *Faith in the Public Square* (London: Bloomsbury, 2012), pp. 149–59.

underpinning for talking about human rights needs to begin from some such account of what bodily difference and distance mean.

But the significance of this discussion for a natural theology lies in the recognition that a world saturated with embodied symbolic communication is one that resists description in the simple terms of mechanical process and one that raises the question of how we are to think of the entire system of the universe as an intelligible *whole* – as 'a' world. To say that it is an intelligible whole is to say that we rightly approach our environment in the expectation of consistency or regularity, wherever and whoever we are, and whatever is before us; and the imagination of a universal consistency, in the light of all the foregoing, requires us to imagine a mind that sees such consistency. Yet the consistency and interdependence of the universe obviously cannot be an object for a single mind among other minds, and it is not at all clear what it could mean to say that it is a possible object for the totality of contingent minds, past, present and future, since every perspective, collective as well as individual, is capable of enlargement or shifted focus. In other words, if there is 'that for which the universe is an intelligible whole', this cannot be characterized as *a* mind among others (only much bigger). William Downes, in his study of *Language and Religion* mentioned earlier, discusses what it means to say that there is something 'absolutely incognizable', absolutely resistant to our knowledge: it is not too difficult to think that for a brain like ours there may be a simple cut-off point for understanding (just as the brain of less well-equipped primates has a cut-off point some way short of what we as humans can cognize); and for any higher form of mental life, the same could in principle apply. 'There would be a reality black hole of "things-in-themselves" for human thought that would get passed upwards in a regress of meta-languages of increasing power'[44] We can avoid the infinite regress by postulating a mind in some important respects *not* like ours which is perfectly cognizant of what not only our minds but any conceivable finite mind will find impenetrable – a mind that 'perfectly represents' what we imperfectly know (even though our imperfect knowing may in many cases rightly be called 'incorrigible'; incorrigibility does not mean we know something 'as it is').[45] What I am suggesting here is similar, though not quite identical, to Downes's argument. It is not so much that there are truths we do not and cannot know about what we perceive, though this is no doubt the case; it is rather that we do not and cannot know what it would be to apprehend the universe as a whole, as 'implicate order', perceiving the full range of possible and actual interdependencies among the events that make up the universe. To imagine that order is – arguably – to imagine the universe as a whole as known, as perceived. This is not exactly a Berkleian view, but it underscores a question that is unavoidable if we take seriously the symbolic character of the material environment we inhabit: to what or in relation to what could the universe as a whole be intelligible? It may be a systematically unanswerable question, but it can be ignored only on the basis of a mechanistic and atomistic picture of the world – a picture which we have seen not to fit with the way we actually behave as linguistic beings or with the ways in which fundamental scientific discourse operates.

Seeing the world as ordered is seeing it as intelligible in its wholeness; and since such a perspective is inaccessible to us, it assumes there is always something 'concealed' from us. Arguably[46] one of the basic implications of seeing the world as in some way 'sacred' is to see it as always hiding something from us, as well as always presenting fresh aspects for understanding and representation; and why we might characterize the systematically secular attitude as one that assumes we should be able to reach and expose any 'hiding places',[47] any aspects of what we encounter that appear to resist conclusive description (even if we can provide *adequate* explanatory description, 'incorrigible' accounts in Downes's phrase, that are perfectly satisfactory as far as they go). Often what the secular perspective is rebelling against is a resort to vagueness and rhetoric about mystery when there are perfectly answerable questions around and we have to beware of laziness, evasiveness or dishonesty. The problem arises only when this entirely proper rebellion goes on to deny that there are other questions that

45 Ibid., p. 188.
46 See, for example, the essay 'Has Secularism Failed?', in Williams, *Faith in the Public Square* (London and New York: Bloomsbury, 2012), pp. 11–22.
47 For a brilliant and disturbing recent defence of the human importance of what is hidden in ourselves to ourselves and others, see Josh Cohen, *The Private Life: Why We Remain in the Dark* (London: Granta, 2013).

can legitimately be asked (indeed, that sometimes insist on being asked); when the search for the most adequate version of a description of what is before us becomes a campaign to rule out in advance those representations that crowd in on the descriptive exercise and suggest connections, implications (with a deliberate allusion to implicate order), not contained in the first-level descriptive/explanatory narrative that is properly the sphere of empirical science. To speak as some do of a need for the 're-enchantment' of a world shrunk and bleached by science is not all that helpful; it does less than justice to the scientific enterprise and can all too easily be read as an appeal for less precision – as if it would be better to stop scientific enquiry at a certain stage of complexity or depth. But what is undoubtedly true is that an account of speech and thought which insisted that what we have been calling the representative response was no more than a sort of leisure activity, an optional extra for those who fancied it, on top of the truly indispensable descriptions of descriptive analysis, would do just as little justice to the plain variety of how we construe what we are engaged with. The shifting and constantly expanding perspectives of historical processes of understanding and representation have no end as far as we are concerned, yet they presuppose a kind of coherence, a unity, that is never itself capable of being represented (let alone described) by us in its wholeness. The theological claim is that such an intelligible unity implies a fundamental informing intelligence. And the Thomist principle that 'the knowledge of God is the cause of things' (*scientia Dei causa rerum*), referred to in an earlier chapter, expresses a comparable belief: things exist with intelligible form because intelligence is what actively structures them.

But – again from a theological point of view – the implication of such convictions is that every finite phenomenon is at some level a carrier of divine significance; it is a symbol not only in the sense that it contributes to an immanent pattern of intelligible exchange and interaction, but as something indicating God or carrying meanings fully or adequately intelligible only when unconditioned intelligence is assumed. One can take this as licence for an approach to the world which looks everywhere for allegories of the divine, ciphers to be decoded: it is an approach found in some sorts of mediaeval literature, not least in texts such as the moralized bestiaries that were written during that period. These have their charm. But it would be more in accord with our cautions about presuming that the world consists of things with fixed boundaries if we were to say that any and every *event* in the world is potentially a communication of infinite intelligence. This does not mean that every event has an edifying theological explanation of the kind typical of bad theodicy ('all suffering has a purpose'); it is more that there is in every situation the possibility for the human intelligence to receive some kind of formation by the infinite intelligent act of God. Our skills in discernment and interpretation – the skills associated with the gift of prophecy in its fully theological sense – are activated so as to produce new levels of understanding of our calling or that of others, even where such understanding is inchoate and conceptually unclear. In briefer and more epigrammatic terms, each situation is a 'word' from God.

This harks back to the early Eastern Christian notion[48] that the world is a system of reasonable and coherent communications reflecting the infinite diversity of ways in which the one divine Word, the eternal self-bestowing of God, can be reflected and participated. If we recognize that every specific act of existing, or currently actual confluence of agencies, is one way in which an eternal act of existing is shared, this reinforces the idea that our linguistic response is a search for transparency to the full range of the active situation in which we are set – and so, ultimately, transparency to the eternal act. And this in turn makes sense of the creative use of language beyond description as a dimension of the attempt to reflect the excess of signifi-cance in what we encounter – what has been described as the way in which the things of the world 'give more than they have.'[49] The work of the artist, in speech and in gesture, is thus not an eccentricity in the human world, but an intensifying of what human beings as such characteristically do. 'The

---

48 Associated above all with St Maximus the Confessor; for a brief but dependable introduction, see Lars Thunberg, *Man and the Cosmos: The Vision of St Maximus the Confessor* (Crestwood, NY: St. Vladimir's Seminary Press, 1985). More recently, see Nikolaos Loudovikos, *Eucharistic Ontology: Maximus the Confessor's Eschatological Ontology of Being as Dialogical Reciprocity* (Brookline, MA: Holy Cross Orthodox Press, 2010), for a complex and far-reaching reading; and a brilliant discussion in C. A. Tsakiridou, *Icons in Time, Persons in Eternity: Orthodox Theology and the Aesthetics of the Christian Image* (London: Ashgate, 2013), Chapter 9.

49 The phrase originates with Jacques Maritain; see his *Creative Intuition in Art and Poetry* (Bollingen Foundation, 1953; Princeton, NJ: Princeton University Press, 1977), p. 127.

"fine arts" are only valid when they see themselves as intensifying this art which is proper to humanity as such', to quote John Milbank.[50] As writers such as David Jones insist,[51] sign-making is pervasive in human discourse: signals or gestures evoke connections that are not obvious and need time to tease out; we cannot leave our superficially clear and definitive perceptions alone, it seems, but elaborate and reconfigure, looking constantly for new relations that make new and enlarged sense of what we perceive. And in the theological perspective, the notion that what we perceive is a facet of eternal activity, unconditioned 'energy', the divine Logos, will further intensify this impulse to imaginative expansion, the quest for more and more relatedness. In verbal art, it can produce a near-chaos of allusion and echo: David Jones is complex enough, but James Joyce, whom Jones admired greatly, makes the point even more clearly. As we shall see in the next chapter, one of the foundational impulses of art is to increase the 'pressure' on habitual discourse or description in order to dismantle the world of fixed concepts and self-enclosed objects. That this pressure sometimes, as in Joyce, results in a plurality of symbolic allusion that is impossible to reduce to argumentative simplicity of any kind is a backhanded compliment to the idea of an 'order', an interlocking unity, which eludes any single perspective.

To pick up another remark by Milbank, what comes into focus in this discussion is the recognition that 'if nature has already "photographically" taken her own picture, she has also already started to "make herself up".'[52] The natural order, in other words, is one that cannot be thought or understood without acknowledging that it has generated its own depiction and representation (in the extended sense of that word which we have been employing), but this generation of a representative activity is also the generation of consciously fictional perspectives – the exploration of possibilities, counterfactuals and imagined worlds. This is, in fact, a much-expanded version of the kind of mental activity that lies behind the 'lion

---

50 John Milbank, 'Scholasticism, Modernism and Modernity', in Rowan Williams, *Grace and Necessity: Reflections on Art and Love', Modern Theology*, 22(4), 651–71 (quotation p. 669).

51 See especially his essay 'Art and Sacrament' in *Epoch and Artist; Selected Writings*, Harman Grisewood (ed.) (London: Faber and Faber, 1959), pp. 143–79.

52 Milbank, art. cit., p. 670.

man' images from the Ice Age which we considered earlier[53]: an abstraction that allows us to see more clearly what is in front of us precisely by moving away from what is 'literally' in front of us. More pointedly, as Milbank observes, when what is in front of us is a pattern of unresolved tension or pain, the exploration of possible imagined alternatives is not necessarily an illegitimate escape but an attempt to penetrate into possibilities of healing that the present situation does not realize but are still in some way intuited as potential in the world we inhabit. It is the search for connections we cannot directly see that might make sense of what is before us, or at least make it bearable. To use Milbank's own framework of discussion, this means that the material world we inhabit as material speakers not only produces makers of its own image but produces makers of alternative worlds: matter, so far from being dead or passive, 'proposes' its own transformation. For the bare fact is that the material world *speaks*. It is, as we have insisted in this chapter, material agents who speak, and this speech is not (as we have seen in several different contexts) a chance decorative addition to mechanical process, but an activity that is implicated in the entire complex of finite agency. If the world is a coherent whole, speech is bound into that coherence: its claims to make present the active form of an event in another medium are not a bit of empty dogmatic optimism. And if part of what speech does is to propose and experiment with representations of what does not exist as an item in the perceived world (from the lion man through to *Macbeth, War and Peace, The Left Hand of Darkness*[54] or *The Matrix*), then the material environment is consistently 'giving out' the possibility of alternative worlds. This is the sense in which we can say that the phenomena of the world 'give more than they have'.

What we speak of as our material environment is not an ensemble of atomized objects defined by supposedly simple and machine-like causal patterns. It invites (the anthropomorphic term is hard to avoid) that particular kind of material following-on that we call language, whose role is indeed partly to chart causal relations but which regularly exceeds this role. The conscious pushing of the boundaries of what we perceive in the exercise

53 Above, pp. 25–6.
54 Ursula Le Guin's celebrated fantasy novel of 1969, set on a planet where all the inhabitants are (biologically) bisexual.

of the imagination is of a piece with all that we think of as the ordinary exercise of speech and significant gesture. And the Coleridgean intuition that imagination is therefore a matter of central theological importance is brought back into focus[55]: the fact that the world ceaselessly prompts new configurations may be a brute fact about experience, or it may point us to an apprehension of unconditioned act, a fundamental energy in response to which all finite agency or movement is constituted as the flow of searching for ('desiring', if we want another anthropomorphism) self-renewing, self-diversifying form. I have argued in earlier chapters that we cannot make any real sense of our linguistic life without reflecting on the diverse ways in which speech opens on to an ever-receding horizon: there are no last words in what human beings say and no point at which we shall have identified the essential structure of the universe exclusively with one descriptive scheme. We cannot think of speaking without recognizing its probing and experimental character. One of the points this chapter has argued is that seeing speech in this light ultimately suggests that we have to suppose something of the same character in the material world as a whole of which our speech is an inextricable part; that the material order can be understood as a 'seeking of form'. The imaginative response to the world we inhabit is, we could say, a collaboration with the energy of that world itself, and can certainly not be reduced to an arbitrary entertainment, the fancy of a bored individual will imposing patterns on passive stuff.

Language insists upon both its limitedness (it is something happening *here*, operating from *this*, not that, perspective, always bound to negotiation with the rest of the material system, always seeking its constantly deferred completion through shared discourse, the perspective of the other) and its unfinished and unfinishable character, its opening on to the horizon of unconditioned active presence. It is therefore, we could say, always under pressure. In the final two chapters of this book, we shall be looking at two ways in which that pressure appears: the disruption of what has seemed to be stable reference through metaphor and other apparently counterintuitive strategies; and the role played by silence both as conscious strategy and as a moment of reverse or frustration. Speakers seem compelled to

---

55 See the recent work of Douglas Hedley for a very sophisticated retrieval of Coleridgean Ideas, especially *Living Forms of the Imagination* (Edinburgh: T. and T. Clark, 2008).

remind themselves and each other of the risks of forgetting that a simply 'descriptive' discourse is bound to be inadequate in all sorts of ways for the actual negotiating of the world; they issue and encode warnings in a range of eccentricities and extremes of speech. We have touched briefly on these already, but need now to spend a little longer on how pressure can be deliberately generated so as to uncover more plainly what language is and is not. This chapter has from time to time noted the importance of *trust* as a feature of our linguistic practice; but it is equally important to signal those elements in our speech which bring us up against misfires of communication, gaps in understanding, challenges to any easy assumptions about how we recognize one another. We began this chapter by reflecting on the experience of people living with ASD and how others respond to them. The orthodox vocabulary we use tells us to speak about such subjects as having 'learning difficulties'. But as we reflect on what we have been discussing here, we might want to echo the words of one theologian who has written with rare and costly insight about communication with those who are mentally and developmentally challenged in various ways: it is *we* who have 'learning difficulties', not simply those we categorize in this way.[56] Our consideration of both the excesses and the gaps in language will underline the importance of acknowledging 'learning difficulties' in our unfolding sense of what language is – and also the importance, to which we have alluded earlier in this discussion, of learning *difficulty* itself as a key to much of this.

---

56 The theologian is Frances Young; her superb recent work, *God's Presence: A Contemporary Recapitulation of Early Christianity* (Cambridge: Cambridge University Press, 2013), touches on the theme at various points (see especially pp. 141–2, 183–4), and looks back to the more extended and more personal treatment in her *Encounter With Mystery: Reflections on L'Arche and Living with Disability* (London: Darton, Longman and Todd, 1997).

5

EXCESSIVE SPEECH: LANGUAGE IN EXTREME SITUATIONS

1

'Paradox is the most extreme kind of metaphor, just as metaphor is the most extreme kind of simile.'[1] This is Margaret Masterman's formula in her paper on 'Metaphysical and Ideographic Language' referred to earlier, and what she notes is that a series of 'descriptions' that violates with increasing recklessness the ordinary canons of consistency may end up saying 'something less preposterously untrue (in the common-sense and scientific senses of "true")' than a single metaphor. In a string of paradoxes, each, so to speak, qualifies the recklessness of each of the others. Logically, though, a form of words that offends against ordinary logical consistency is more startling than a mere assertion that 'x is y'. Paradox is therefore a more pressing problem for a logician than is metaphor; yet it will not do to ignore the fact that paradox is routinely used in our language, and to insist, against the facts of this usage, that any form of words that creates problems for logic has to be illegitimate. Philosophers may well be – as Masterman says[2] – driven to distraction by sloppy appeals to 'poetic logic' or statements about how all language is

1   Masterman, op. cit., p. 295.
2   Ibid., pp. 300ff.

'really' metaphorical. But she argues that it is only by engaging with the problem thus posed that philosophy will escape from a holocaust not only of imaginative literature but also of descriptive linguistics. Tackling the logical issues will allow the philosopher to arrive finally at 'that fully ripened stage of tense despair, out of which alone some unforeseen intellectual leap can come'.[3]

Masterman goes on to set out an example of paradox taken from a scientific rather than literary context: she summarizes a (then recent) paper in cell biology which dismantles the notion of two different kinds of cells, 'organizer cells' and 'ordinary cells' (which were not capable of initiating the processes of specialization associated with organizers), on the grounds that under different circumstances the latter kind of cell could acquire the characteristic action of the former – and could also become pathogenic and transmit its degenerate condition to others. The argument could be summed up, says Masteman, 'by saying that, speaking biochemically, cells both operate causally, and also in such a way as to render meaningless the whole causal conception upon which biochemical theory is based'.[4] Cells are both developmental and pathogenic in action, simultaneously organizers, reproducers and receptors. Experiment displays in them a set of properties that cannot be harmonized. The resolution of the problem is to specify the contexts for the contradictory patterns of behaviour, redescribing one or the other in such a way as to remove the logical parallelism that creates the paradox in the first place (i.e. you redescribe one part of the situation so as to make it clear that the different elements are not *competing* accounts).[5] But this sort of resolution does not, Masterman observes, produce anything very new or interesting for philosophy. If some paradoxes simply point up the desirability of increased descriptive precision, this does not fundamentally challenge our account of how language represents. The interesting cases are those which actually precipitate new levels of understanding as well, and to consider these we shall need a more technical response. And Masterman's proposal is, as we saw earlier, an 'ideographic' language in which, instead of sticking to a subject–predicate based model of

3   Ibid., p. 302.
4   Ibid., p. 304.
5   This is, of course, the classical method of Christology, exemplified *par excellence* in Thomas Aquinas's account in the third part of the *Summa* of the Chalcedonian doctrine of Christ's two natures: there can be no sense in which Divine life and human are competing for the same logical space.

referring (which assumes that the world is composed of discrete units whose successive modifications can be charted in a series of configurations based on non-contradiction within a single framework), works with the model of a *situation*, or a focal event, which can then be qualified by a nest of factors of increasing generality. Paradox, then, is not simply a by-product of insufficient precision in setting out the context in which descriptive claims are made; it triggers a process of reshuffling the conceptual pack, unsettling the simple relations between subject and object as well as subject and predicate. But the point is not that we should then accept a more vague and imprecise account of what is in view; we have to work – in a variety of ways – to discover different and appropriate modes of being precise. Masterman's ideographic schemata point to one way of achieving a different kind of precision. And, as she says, this is the philosopher's way of trying to crystallize what the poet sees instinctively and represents less formally.[6]

To go back for a moment to Masterman's original formulation, we are dealing with 'extreme' forms of utterance. In order to give a satisfactory account of my environment, I begin by saying 'this is like that': to see what's there, you (listening to me) will need to call to mind what's *not* directly there. As I pursue this strategy, I come to the point of saying 'this *is* that': to see what's there, frame it, figure it, as if you saw it in the context, through the lens, of what's not in any straightforward sense there. Push this further and the final stage is, 'To see this clearly, you'll need to imagine drastically different vantage points from which to see, points which you can't in fact occupy simultaneously, and which will deliver flat contradictions if you try to put them together.' What is said becomes more and more expansive in one way: it reckons with more than just this set of perceptions in this moment, and summons up material distant in time and in space in order to configure the here and now more fully. Pushing these strategies of redescription to extreme lengths in this way takes us (paradoxically!) closer to the immediate object. And by the time we have got to the level of paradox, we are really no longer 'describing' in the usual and obvious sense, certainly not cataloguing atomized elements of an object. Our notion of what it is to produce a 'truthful' way of speaking about what's in front of us will have been notably enlarged – not in a way that licenses vagueness

6   Masterman, op. cit., pp. 301–2.

or seeks to come at truth by uttering superficial falsehood, but through beginning to grasp that the truth of this moment is inextricably bound in with a potential infinity of other moments and perspectives. There is a lively debate in the literature as to whether a metaphor is 'literally' an untruth. But the point has been well made by philosophers such as Janet Martin Soskice[7] that when you have a statement whose literal truth would simply be nonsense, it can't be right simply to treat the statement as a falsehood – that is, as a proposition whose truth conditions might be met but as a matter of fact are not. A self-contradictory statement is one whose truth conditions simply cannot be met. The metaphorical 'extremes' of language that are in view here are being used because of what is left out of the formally exact subject–predicate version; they are an attempt not to replace or sideline truth claims but to extend the territory of what we are claiming truthfulness for. It is untidy, and requires both contextual sophistication and what the poet would call negative capability, the willingness to sit with an uncertainty about what might count as 'appropriate' language.[8]

So part of our linguistic practice is to *put pressure* on what we say in order that we may come to see more than our initial account delivers. The context of Masterman's vivid evocation of the 'tense despair' that precedes intellectual advance underlines the fact that we not only *experience* pressure in and on our language, pushing us towards new intellectual patterning, but also *invite* or *construct* it. Developing the implications of an experiment (as in the example Masterman gives from cell biology) in such a way that the underlying models being employed are themselves shown to be inadequate to the problem *as thus phrased* is a familiar affair; we may go on using the routine language, the old ways of configuring phenomena, for most 'normal' purposes, but we are made aware that at the very least the language we use is an heuristic tool, and that we need to specify its context very carefully if it is not to lead us into nonsense. At a more serious level and on a longer timescale, models may dissolve under the strain: increasingly complex

---

7   *Metaphor and Religious Language* (Oxford: Clarendon Press, 1985), pp. 84ff.; the whole of this fifth chapter as well as her chapter 3 provide an excellent orientation on these and related debates.

8   The topic of metaphor continues to generate a large literature; for recent perspectives, see, e.g., the wide-ranging essays in Raymond W. Gibbs, Jr, *The Cambridge Handbook of Metaphor and Thought* (Cambridge: Cambridge University Press, 2008).

refinements of an existing model (epicycles in Ptolemaic astronomy, negative weight for phlogiston, etc.) finally collapse under the weight of elaboration and a new and more economical model appears – though this new model may require a radical reworking of the categories we started with. And, to recall our earlier reference to the work of Mary Hesse and Michael Arbib, we become more wary of speaking as though 'normal' usage were more stable than it actually is. Roy Bhaskar likewise protests about the unhelpful polarization assumed in systems like Rorty's between 'an epistemic absolutism for normal science and an epistemic irrationalism for abnormal science'.[9] He quotes Rorty, claiming that the best we can do is 'manipulate the tensions' in our own era so as to generate the next one; and although this seems to echo Margaret Masterman's reference to tension as a generative moment, the crucial difference is that for Masterman the management of that tension and the breaking through it that we hope will follow is the opposite of a 'manipulation'. It actually, in the medium to long term, delivers a new and demanding model and a fresh set of truth claims. We miss the point here, Bhaskar says, because of 'the over-normalization of normal discourse, ignoring its holes, silences and incommensurabilities, its ambiguities and ambivalences, its open texture and rich potentialities for development, and also the fact that developing traditions are typically characterized by rival or conflicting interpretations'.[10] Advances in understanding come when both theoreticians and experimenters identify the oddity within 'normal' discourse and press its tensions a bit further – not with the aim of removing all tension but in order to find ways of holding it in a larger structure and discovering new tensions at that level which in turn will generate further fruitful crises.

So as we take more risks and propose more innovations in our linguistic practice, we move from the more-or-less illustrative use of a vivid and unusual simile through to increasingly explosive usages that ultimately, as we have seen, invite us to rethink our metaphysical principles, our sense of how intelligible identities are constructed in and for our speaking. Extreme or apparently excessive speech is not an aberration in our speaking. Given that it is (as we have already noted) *difficulty* that drives the sense

9   Roy Bhaskar, *Philosophy and the Idea of Freedom*, p. 28; c.f. note 63 above.
10   Ibid., p. 29.

of a reality to which we are painfully accountable, it is not surprising that making things more difficult is so common, so 'normal', a tool of exploration and discovery. By turning up the temperature in this way, we identify questions that can only be answered when we imagine new contexts, and so new connections, new relationships; we are steadily shifted away from a world of discrete substances in the void, which we talk about in a calculus of propositions. And this is, as Margaret Masterman says, a way for the philosopher to chart what the poet does: a grasp of what is happening in poetry (and in other non-standard kinds of utterance) is important for a grasp of how thought itself moves. If the processes going on in the poet's work are manifestly more than decorative, if they do constitute a way of enhancing truthful acquaintance with our environment, the philosopher is right to point out to the scientist some of the mechanisms involved and to ask how poetic 'tactics' can be transferred.

2

How do those tactics work in poetry itself? What are the self-imposed pressures that generate such 'truthful acquaintance'? As we noted in an earlier chapter, poetry is traditionally characterized by 'non-standard' patterns of rhyme, assonance and stress. In contrast to our habitual speech patterns, poetry organizes sounds in specific and regular ways. Even the loosest forms of free verse work to patterns of some sort, even if only in the division of lines. But what is striking is the sheer complexity of the patterns that different poetic traditions have developed – intricate schemes of internal rhyme even within a single line, the precise counting of stresses and syllables, the systematic use of oblique ways of referring. Anglo-Saxon and Norse poetry makes extensive use of 'kennings', conventionally sanctioned metaphors which give verse something of the character of a riddle – 'the whale's way' for the sea, and so on.[11] Early Greek poetry comparably uses conventional epithets ('rosy-fingered dawn', 'the wine-dark sea'). The poet is under the discipline of *routinely* trying to see one thing through another; the language is marked as poetic by such obliqueness. The difficulty here may

11 See, for example, Arthur Gilchrist Brodeur, *The Art of Beowulf* (Berkeley, CA: University of California Press, 1959).

be minimal: these are ritual moves, familiar to singer and hearer alike. But they act none the less as warning signs that this discourse will be something distinct from the usual exchanges of a culture: it will invite us to set aside for this listening period our assumptions about identity, about the solidity or closure of our perceptions. And the various techniques of rhyming perform another function, perhaps most important for the poet. Finding a rhyme – and ideally finding a rhyme that is not merely conventional – requires a unique moment of holding an idea in suspense while the writer looks for a way of saying it that will echo specific sounds. For the reader/hearer, the resultant echo will leave at least a trace of the sense of an unexpected connection. For the poet him- or herself, it will have been a matter of finding new phrases generated by the pressure of a discipline, meaning that a fresh perspective has been brought to birth. The most relentlessly complex schemes of assonance, like the classical rules of Welsh *cynghanedd*, intensify this as far as it will go, requiring not only rhyme but consonantal groupings and deliberate stress shifts on top of that. Such a technique will increase the possible range of new and unexpected connections

Take as an example a quite well-known Welsh poem, 'Ty Ddewi' ('St David's). In its original form it was Waldo Williams's entry for the Fishguard National Eisteddfod of 1936; it came second in the competition for the Chair – that is, in the category of strict classical composition – and a much revised version is the first poem in Waldo's only published collection.[12] Its first line offers an instance of one of the simpler forms of *cynghanedd*: *Nos Duw am Ynys Dewi*, the assonance of four consonants, n, s, d and w, in the two halves of the line. The literal meaning is 'The night of God on the island of David': 'God', *Duw*, and 'David', *Dewi*, are associated in a fairly obvious way: this is a poem that has something to do with a man of God. But the association of *nos*, 'night' and *ynys*, 'island' is a more challenging one: this place, David's peninsula, is a place where a certain kind of darkness falls: the darkness of God's presence. To be in this place is to be in the night. The stanza continues with an evocation of the water flowing onto the beach as a metaphor for *hiraeth*, the nearest word in Welsh to *eros*: there is a long or slow movement of 'longing' towards the seashore (*traeth*, echoing *hiraeth*),

12 In 1956; see Waldo Williams, *Dail Pren* (Leaves of the Tree), new edn (Llandysul: Gomer Press, 1991), pp. 9–22.

the waves crying in the midst of the stones. And then we are confronted with the idea of a universal longing which finds expression in the language of memory: *Araith y cof yw hiraeth y cyfan* (The eros that belongs to all things is what the memory says), a line where *hiraeth* chimes with *araith* (speech). Language, in other words, chimes with longing; as memory, *cof*, chimes with the totality of things, *y cyfan*. And the stanza ends by juxtaposing the deep slumber of the mountain with the ceaseless *hiraeth* of the ocean. Sleep, remembrance, night – apparent stillness; longing, the unceasing waves on the shore, movement towards a goal of desire. The polarity set up here will shape the whole poem's evocation of local history and the spiritual life it generates. A commentary on the 13 pages of this poem would be an unrealistic project in this context, but the point should be clear. The search for assonance produces a very strong form of the analogical vision that allows us to see one thing through another – all the stronger because it arises from the accident of similarities in sound. And of course there can be play with diverse kinds of similarity, as when the consonantal pattern of the first line is repeated much later on in the poem,[13] further complicating the resonances of that opening phrase: *Mae anwes dawel am Ynys Dewi* (there is a still embrace around David's island) or 'stillness hugs David's island to itself'. So, indirectly, the 'night' of the first line of the whole poem is linked, by the repeated assonance, to the intimate *anwes* (fondling, caressing).

This is indeed language under pressure deployed as a means of exploration, invoking associations which may be random in one way, yet generate a steady level of unsettling alternative or supplementary meanings in the margin of the simple lexical sense. It is true that there is a kind of magical thinking in some cultures that sees verbal assonance or association as indicative of a specific affiliation of some sort – a linguistic version of homeopathy, we might say. But what is going on in this tightly disciplined poetry is rather different. It is, at the first level, an invitation to see one thing through the 'lens' of an unexpected other. But then, at a deeper level, it is a reminder that we are always seeing 'through the other', that we never see anything in its own isolated terms, and that we cannot rule in advance which 'others' are acceptable and which unacceptable in the business of extending and enlarging our perception. The entirely accidental chime

13 Ibid., p. 18.

of *araith* and *hiraeth* in Welsh, like the less pronounced chime of (say) 'longing' and 'language' in English, doesn't indicate either an etymological common ground or a mystical essential bond. It simply tells us that we never know what we might need, what we might be glad of, in understanding any one element in our environment. Pile on the pressure and you force yourself to see freshly. There may be genuinely absurd homophonic patterns; but the challenge of a good poem in such a classical form is precisely to find patterns of this kind that are surprising but not simply arbitrary. Symbolist poetry, especially French symbolist poetry, often plays deliberately with the near-absurd in order to create sound-patterns; and this is routinely taken as bound up with a strong commitment to the 'randomness' of verbal signifiers.[14] But without embarking on the fairly formidable task of tracking the metaphysics of Symbolist verse, we can at least say that the effect is not simply to dissolve 'proper' reference, but is also a kind of appeal to some imagined plenitude of linguistic response to the environment. Nothing we say, no mode of representation, is going to be final; and so we cannot but guess, in more or less disciplined and coherent ways, as to what will or may fill out what has been said.

The simplest poetic forms have the same purpose at their heart – the complicating of what seems normal in order to uncover what 'normal' perception screens out. The search for a rhyme is perhaps the simplest of all. Christina Rossetti's biographer[15] records how, as a young woman, she produced a substantial and surreal –and rather disturbing – poem in an exchange of *bouts rimes* (i.e. having been provided with a series of rhymed end-words only). Victorian versifiers such as W. S. Gilbert took great delight in inventing rhymes for what look like impossible words (lovers of *The Pirates of Penzance* will recall the Major-General's song). The counting of syllables restricts what can be said; and writers of *haiku* know what sharpness of perception can be induced by both the restriction in the

14 Steiner, *After Babel*, pp. 190–8, discusses this in relation to James Joyce as well as the Symbolists, noting the political character of some styles of refusing ordinary referential usage, supposedly corrupted by the abuse of language in the service of power and violence (see especially pp. 193–4).

15 Jan Marsh, *Christina Rossetti: A Writer's Life* (London: Jonathan Cape, 1994), pp. 104–5; whether we interpret them, as Marsh suggests, as evidence of personal trauma remains speculative.

number of syllables and the expectation of no more than a single moment of perceived 'focus' as the starting-point, the single sound or instant of movement. I spoke just now of 'complicating' the normal; it would be just as true to say, though, that techniques like that of the *haiku* also simplify the normal. The 'more' that there is to say is, paradoxically, represented in some circumstances by seeing and saying *less*. What has been buried in normal perception and description has to be set free from overloaded or indulgent habits of speech (we shall be returning to this in the final chapter). But just as much as with the technical adventures of Welsh metre or traditional rhyme, the point is to make us see what we otherwise don't; and the poet of whatever background or tradition assumes that there will always be more to discover than what we think we see.

Pause for a moment to reflect on this, and it should be clear how odd it is. Why should we assume that our language can discover anything simply by playing games with itself? But, as we have seen throughout this book, we cannot assume that our speech is either a leisure activity with no connection to its environment or a handy means of cataloguing ready-made objects; it is something shaped by the fact of the body's participation in the 'action' of the world. And if it is at some level shaped in this way, its own ways of shaping the environment through representation will show the traces of what has been received from that environment. Listening hard to what we say prompts new levels of understanding – new ways of 'going on' from what is before us. And when we press harder on what we say and deliberately try to coax more from it, we recognize that our 'normal' conscious minds are habituated to screening out aspects of what is before us or directing our attention only to what sits comfortably with a narrowish range of perception. Just as in conversation we implicitly ask each other for a different – even if only slightly different – 'take' on the environment we share, so with extreme, poetic, metaphorical, ritualized and formalized speech, we converse with ourselves, with our unexamined perceptions, our half-conscious associations of sounds and sense alike, and are ready to be surprised by what associations may arise. Poetic practitioners will often speak about the experience, in the composition of poetry, of listening, of being taken aback by what is heard and then said. And the poetry that results may set out to reconstruct perception as if things were indeed being seen anew. Craig Raine's celebrated 'Martian' poems are a witty, challenging re-viewing of what is familiar: what would *this* look like if really seen for the first time, seen by an extraterrestrial? If we really were trying to find words for something strange? It is a particularly marked instance of what poetry in general seeks to do. And at its root is an instinct that, because language is connected in opaque and sometimes untraceable ways with what it talks about, it will generate new perspectives when we are not looking, so to speak – when we are not preoccupied with reinforcing habitual and normal idioms and practices.

However, the point can be broadened out from poetry to include many sorts of fiction, many varieties of visual art and, of course, music. Fiction – in its modern European sense – is a curious cultural development, heavily involved in the mythologies of the 'modern' self and its formation over time. But whether we think about 'realistic' novels or more experimental examples – whether we think of *Anna Karenina* or *Ulysses* – some of the same factors apply. Here is a narrative asking for recognition – but also making a particular mode of telling about human experience a discovery, an encounter with the unexpected. Realistic fiction does this by obliging us to see what we thought we knew as if for the first time: the abiding fascination and power of Tolstoy is often in his observation of minute detail so familiar that we usually ignore it – the distracted thoughts and half-conscious habits that accompany our actions, especially in what we imagine to be our most concentrated or elevated moments. 'Experimental' fiction does it by making language play with uncontrollable allusions and echoes, as in Joyce, or with radical diversities of narrative viewpoint and refusals of narrative closure (John Fowles), or distortions or reversals of temporal order (even to the point of running the story backwards, as in Martin Amis's *Time's Arrow*). Dickens in *Bleak House* presents two narrative voices, one of which refuses the linear movement and associated moral consolation of the other. Bakhtin's account of the 'polyphonic' nature of Dostoevsky's fiction is well-known:[16] voices constantly undercut, amplify, contradict and challenge one another, as if to make it clear that the novel is not, after all, the creation of

16 Mikhail Bakhtin, *Problems of Dostoevsky's Poetics*, ed. and trans. Caryl Emerson (Minneapolis, MN and London: University of Minnesota Press, 1984); see also Rowan Williams, *Dostoevsky: Language, Faith and Fiction* (London: Continuum, 2008), especially chapters 1 and 3.

a new and self-sufficient 'world', if what that means is a coherently finished picture of interacting subjects, but the exposure of the unresolved undercurrents of the environment we know. And – in case we should suppose that only the tragic is an authentic fictional form[17] – there is also a dimension of fictional narrative which imagines possibilities of positive change that our 'normal' perceptions routinely encourage us to ignore, hope that cannot simply be brought out of the simply given. If ultimate convergence, healing, consolation, is apparently impossible to imagine, that's why it is necessary to imagine it. Or, to avoid merely annoying paradox: if we cannot rationally predict or organize or guarantee some sort of reconciliation and healing, we have no choice but to approach it through fiction – not as a means of evading or denying an unpalatable present but as a form of acknowledging resources that are there in or for our present world, but to which we do not yet have straightforward access.

Thus the deceptively simple process of telling a story may become another sort of pressure on language to disclose unnoticed wounds or unimagined possibilities or both. With our ordinary visual perception, we cannot help recognizing, once we reflect on what is physically happening, the possible plurality of stances already implicit in our routine seeing; in a comparable way, certain kinds of fiction – like *Bleak House*, or, in a quite different way, Ian McEwan's *Atonement* – remind us that our narratives of ourselves and others are impossible to reduce to a single line, a single point of view. Modern literary criticism has made us familiar with the notion that even the single authoritative/authorial voice is not necessarily to be trusted as a 'view from nowhere', and has taught us to listen for the voices that such a narrative suppresses or distorts (whether consciously or not). The recognition of irony in a narrative tells us that what we initially and instinctively see is not to be taken for granted; and irony is one of the longest-established modes of 'pressurizing' our speech and persuading us to be careful about settling down with atomistic ideas of true correspondence. Irony is one of those phenomena which illustrate vividly the complexity of

---

17 See John Milbank, art. cit., and on the perils of an uncritical identification of the tragic with the authentic, c.f. 'A Critique of the Theology of Right' in Milbank, *The Word Made Strange: Theology, Language, Culture* (Oxford: Blackwell, 1997), pp. 7–35, especially pp. 18–24.

'truthful representation' – as Kierkegaard knew very well.[18] Good fiction presents 'character' not as something fixed and transparent, but as invitingly complex, sometimes apparently paradoxical, shifting over time and shifting in relation to diverse points of view. It is a verbal performance which undermines superficial certainties – whether the certainty that we know what a person will do or the certainty that any person can simply and successfully decide for themselves to change their 'destiny'. Its representations play with our ideas about freedom and necessity: Thomas Hardy will insist on a karma-like outworking of people's choices, through the medium of what at first seem random events; Tolstoy on the other hand will declare that he is surprised by the decisions his characters make. Fiction embraces both sorts of 'play', since both are modes of representing dimensions of human development and transaction that we are frequently educated in ignoring.

A life represented in the way Hardy represents Henchard in *The Mayor of Casterbridge* is made strange to us in the sense that we are going to find it difficult to believe that 'fate' can work so inexorably in a biography, through malign coincidence. A life represented as Tolstoy represents Anna Karenina is made strange in the sense that we both follow and are bewildered by her choices. The common point is the *making strange*: the 'excess' either of overdetermined actions or of underdetermined ones, the 'excess' of an invocation of fate or an invocation of random liberty, is the way in which this particular fictional form of saying more than we have to discloses dimensions that our habitual and pre-reflective ways of grasping human agency and personal history do not nurture. Jonathan Lear, in his admirable Tanner Lectures on irony, speaks of Socratic irony as a means of conveying 'the difficulty of becoming human';[19] irony tells us that knowing who we are, and what we should and could be moving into, paradoxically involves a moment of radical scepticism about what we know. 'Part of what

18 For a recent discussion, see K. Brian Soderquist, 'Irony', in John Lippitt and George Pattison (eds), *The Oxford Handbook of Kierkegaard* (Oxford: Oxford University Press, 2013), pp. 344–64, especially pp. 350–2, on the 'expression of the inexpressible' and the refusal of univocal discourse.

19 Jonathan Lear, *A Case for Irony* (Cambridge, MA: Harvard University Press, 2011), chapter 1 *passim*, especially pp. 1–16; note also pp. 37–9 for a perceptive challenge to Rorty's definition of irony as a tactic to defer commitment – whereas Kierkegaard's irony is about deepening commitment and refusing trivial versions of it.

it is to be, say, courageous is to recognise that one's practical understanding of courage is susceptible to ironic disruption. Part of what it is to be courageous is courageously to face the fact that living courageously will inevitably entangle one in practices and pretences and possible acts all of which are susceptible to the question, what does *any of that* have to do with *courage*? Ironic existence is the ability to live well with that insight.'[20] So a properly difficult narrative performance, however exactly it is realized, takes us through a process of relearning our way with ourselves as well as with other subjects. We need to be repeatedly reintroduced to the fact that we must acknowledge what we do not know and cannot do. Just as, in the theatre – to go back for a moment to Cavell's account of what happens when we watch a drama on stage[21] – we are summoned to be imaginatively present in situations we cannot affect and can only contemplate, so we are faced in the serious novel with fictional transactions energized by motivations we may be able to see more readily than the fictional characters can, yet are unable to interact, clarify, warn. And this means that what is represented for us is precisely the typical gaps in human self-awareness: the extreme narrations of lives dominated by fate and lives disrupted by random action display in sharply contrasted ways the character of our ignorance. To *recognize* fictional representations of human agents is to recognize the ignorance we share with them and the terrible fallibility of *self*-representation. Our own inability to warn or clarify uncovers the difficulty of hearing warning or clarification from where we stand as readers. Learning to become human is hard and can be done only in a steady awareness of the difficulty, an awareness that slowly constructs our own self-portraiture.

3

This element of 'relearning our way' in becoming human takes us back to the fundamental theme of why things are made strange in the work of the imagination. The environment we encounter and inhabit is more than it seems; sometimes it takes extreme and excessive speech to prompt this acknowledgement, and the deliberate 'making extreme' of our language

20   Ibid., p. 37.
21   Above, pp. 84, 93.

is a tool of discovery. So far we have mentioned the techniques of poetry and the ironies of fiction; we might equally point to those narratives that deliberately fracture the language itself – not only *Ulysses* but *Finnegans Wake*; or, a bit less dramatically, Anthony Burgess's *A Clockwork Orange* or (the most brilliantly sustained fiction to be written entirely in an imagined dialect of apocalyptically fractured English) Russell Hoban's *Riddley Walker*, where extreme human situations (compulsive and sadistic violence or post-apocalyptic desolation) are signalled by means of specially constructed languages or dialects.

Hoban's dystopia, a post-nuclear Kent that has reverted to a 'Dark Age' culture, shot through with half-remembered fragments of the old civilization, is extraordinarily effective in making us look and listen for our own familiar landscapes of thought and speech and physical neighbourhood in the chaotic and decayed but also startlingly poetic language of a new barbarism. Walker Percy's comments[22] on mistakes and mishearings and accidental puns as generative moments in speech are illustrated here in the most marked fashion. In Hoban's world, the 'Eusa Story'[23] is the one narrative people have in common: it is the ritual recital of how the nuclear catastrophe came about, telling how 'Eusa' is persuaded by 'Mr Clevver' to try and stop wars between people by making the '1Big 1'. To make the One Big One, Eusa must find 'the Littl Shynin Man the Addom he runs in the wud'. Eusa, 'a noing man', pursues the Addom by going into the 'hart of the stoan', into the smallest space imaginable, the forests of dancing interrelatedness within things, where at last he sees the Littl Shynin Man with arms outstretched between the antlers of a stag (the pun on 'hart' for a deer and 'heart' has already been flagged early in the book[24]). 'Eusa sed to the Littl Man, Yu mus be the Addom then. The Littl Man sed, I mus be wut I mus be.' Eusa pulls the Littl Man in two, and the catastrophe begins. Disentangling the allusions here is quite a task. The story of St Eustace,

---

22 Above, pp. 54–5, 60–1.

23 Russell Hoban, *Riddley Walker* (London: Jonathan Cape, 1980; Picador, 1982) (references to the latter), pp. 28–34.

24 Ibid., p. 2: 'There is the Hart of the Wud in the *Eusa Story* that wer a stag every 1 knows that. There is the hart of the wood meaning the veryes deap of it thats a nother thing. There is the hart of the wood where they bern the chard coal thats a nother thing agen innit.'

converted by encountering while hunting a stag with a crucifix between its horns, provides the structure – a story depicted in one of Canterbury Cathedral's mediaeval wall paintings, part of the Kentish folk memory of Hoban's world. But Eusa is also the USA and the atomic research programme where knowing is 'no-ing', denying self and world; the Littl Shynin Man is the atom that is to be split, the Adam whose primordial self-betrayal ruins the world, perhaps the 'wodwoose' of folklore, the wild man in the woods, and ultimately the God who meets Moses in the Burning Bush and declares, 'I am that I am'.

As the story moves towards its horribly ironic and poignant climax (the reinvention of gunpowder and the beginning of another cycle of violence and disaster) the complexity of reference deepens, the language draws in more and more echoes and puns ('many cools' and 'party cools' for the molecules and particles discovered in the search for the Addom, the Puter Leat – computer elite – who made the fatal decisions, and so on). Hoban's idiolect is one of modern English literature's most sophisticated experiments in extreme language, making things strange to prompt a new level of recognition; the narrative deploys almost unreadably involved degrees of irony, working not just through narrative development but through the very texture of the language, through the absurd, suggestive, poetic distortions of words ('Addom', 'pirntowt' – printout – for 'thought' or 'concluded'; not to mention the Ardship of Cambry, heir of the hardship that Eusa brought about by tearing apart the Littl Shynin Man). The central image of the narrative, the tearing apart of the Addom, is clearly identified with the tearing apart of the human mind itself: the Littl Man says to Eusa, 'the 1 as tears the other a part has got to put some thing to gether nor you aint done that ... 2 peaces is what Iwl be in til you get your head back'.[25] The 'Chaynjis' that are released by the splitting of the Addom have to be lived through now before Eusa can recover the 'idear' of himself.[26] There is no one 'peace' for the divided mind/imagination. So this broken language and chaotic imagination, this splitting and recombining and turning on itself that our speech displays, is part of the process of discovering if we have an

25 Ibid., p. 47.
26 Ibid., p. 34: 'Eusa sed, Wut is the idear uv me? The Littl Man sed, That we doan no til yuv gon thru aul yur Chaynjis.'

idea of who or what we are. It comes from a violent disruption and it is always in danger of slipping back into violent disruption; but the business of speaking, putting together these echoes and wordplays, and the shamanic experience of the 'connection men' who utter oracles from time to time, all this is constantly on the edge of some breakthrough into meaning and self-knowledge. It is our 'clevverness' that has made us difficult, alien, to ourselves, but there is no way to transparency except through the words. Facing and negotiating the difficulty through what we say is our only path forward; so we leave Hoban's hero at the end of the book travelling with his Punch and Judy show, trying to hold up to his audiences a picture of the terrible things in the heart of human beings: 'Why wil he [Punch] all ways kil the babby if he can? Parbly I wont never know its jus on me to think on it.'[27]

In a related vein, though totally different in execution, Alan Garner's extraordinary novel *Boneland* imagines a prehistoric mind – close to those of the Ice Age artists mentioned earlier – in the very act of 'representation', sustaining the world itself through ritual action, the painting of the cave wall, the dances and songs that mark the changes of the stars: 'If the dancer did not dance and sing and make new the Bull on the sky wall, the Stone Spirit would not send eagles'; the 'eagles' flying out from the stone on the horizon feed the stars and guarantee the return of the sun after midwinter.[28] The only adequate way of reading this is to watch the midwinter sky and 'read' it afresh in the language of this mythology, a real seeing for the first time. And the description later on of the creation of a flint blade makes the same intense demands on the reader, obliging us to guess and feel our way through an unfamiliar process imagined in unfamiliar words. 'He turned the last piece. It was no bigger than two hands. The brown ran through all the weight that he had brought; but ended here. In this one fist there was no flaw. He took the white and black, and tapped. The bone answered, and it was another song, deep where he could not see. He took the yellow and grey. He tapped. He took the white and black again and worked down into the bone ... Something lay within. It was close, though he could not see. He

27 Ibid., p. 214: the Punch and Judy show is one of the surviving rituals of Riddley Walker's society and a deliberate vehicle of cultural and political transmission.
28 Alan Garner, *Boneland* (London: Fourth Estate, 2012), pp. 14–16.

came upon it as he would a hare.'[29] What is remarkable about this writing is that it invites us to sense not only a physical process but a *relation* with the material and the whole environment that is profoundly strange – so that we are 'de-skilled' by the writing, obliged to stumble forward in a new territory.

To be brought to such a point is to find ourselves forced to think fundamentally about the nature of representation; to be confronted with a world that is symbolically charged, with whose complexity we are always catching up. Garner's representing of representation does two things. It shows us a speaking consciousness engaged with a world that is assumed to be saturated with meanings beyond the pragmatic and technical – or which sees the pragmatic and technical as always already within a symbolic economy. And it puts us in the position of speaking consciousnesses deprived for the moment of the words we would normally have available. We might conceivably be able to 'translate' Garner's account into an acceptable twenty-first century story of watching the stars or testing various kinds of rock for their suitability for making flint knives. But we should first have to follow, silently, the material process and learn the ways in which it divided up a world we divide rather differently. We should have to see it through another pair of eyes, in such a way that we could not afterwards see it simply as we did before. We do not become prehistoric thinkers, inhabiting this new world of perception as Garner's character is presented as inhabiting it, but are made to experience the 'difficulty' of the world, its complex resistance to exhaustive description, at a new level. And, to add a final layer of ironic refinement to the narrative, we literally meet 'ourselves' as strangers in the story, when (in a significantly less harsh reworking of a well-known treatment of the same theme in William Golding's *The Inheritors*[30]) the central figure in the prehistoric episodes of the book first encounters *homo sapiens* in the shape of three women, to his eyes indistinguishable from one another. 'Their mouths made sounds. They were not words but chopped noise ... They were women but they were not people. They were three but they were only one.'[31] Yet despite an initial reaction of mutual fear and incomprehension between the Neanderthal and the new

29 Ibid., p. 66.
30 *The Inheritors* (London: Faber, 1955), chapters 7–9.
31 Garner, op. cit., p. 105.

people, there is an eventual meeting of spirits as the shaman of the new people telepathically 'hears' the story of the Neanderthal: 'It is a true Story,' said the other.'[32] The strangeness of what the reader now recognizes as the Neanderthal mind is not a completely alien thing; not more or less difficult and alien than our own buried ancestry.

Exposure to new kinds of difficulty is the theme that is central to this part of our discussion. Thus far, we have focused a good deal on the new kinds of difficulty in responding to our environment that fiction and poetry open up. But we also noted earlier how these imaginative disciplines make our own humanity 'difficult'. Seeing ourselves as puzzling, Jonathan Lear notes, is part of mature self-understanding, and imagining that we have arrived at a satisfactory level of self-understanding is a fairly reliable indicator of the lack of it. Fiction and drama offer a particular kind of mirror – not one that simply shows us a single clear image of ourselves but one that tells us 'it is possible for you to be seen like this': in that sense it is not unlike a dream, if it is true that 'in a dream, the dreamer plays all the parts', since we are invited to find ourselves behind the faces of others. The difficulty of strained language, the difficulty of unfamiliar metaphor, the difficulty of recognizing what we know in what we thought we did not know, all of these have to do with the central difficulties of attending to the strangeness of another speaker and attending to the 'idea' of who I am, to borrow Hoban's word. The search for different and better sorts of precision, which we noted as basic to Margaret Masterman's discussions of metaphor and paradox, is tightly connected with the attempt to 'locate' myself as a speaker – that is, in terms of Masterman's own proposal, to qualify our situation as comprehensively as possible. An exercise like Hoban's novel helps us to imagine what it might be to speak out of a dramatically fractured context, seeking to make sense of a half-understood corporate story at the same time as seeking an identity, a *persona*, a coherent speaking presence for oneself. The extreme conditions in which Riddley Walker lives hold up a mirror that exaggerates but does not distort aspects of our present world; the sometimes apparently wild 'connections' invoked by the constant wordplay defamiliarize history and landscape and much of English vocabulary itself, and introduce us to possible crossings-over of meaning that are deeply unsettling – the

32   Ibid., p. 112.

splitting of the atom, the fall of Adam, the cross of Christ. Alan Garner's Watcher similarly unsettles our understanding of how we are present in our world: here we are asked to feel our way into a humanity that is both more passive to the environment (having to learn its rhythms and patterns with a gruelling patience and attentiveness) and more active (being responsible through our ritual action for the passage of the seasons and the return of the sun). Both writers are virtuosi of irony in Jonathan Lear's sense, showing in language what it is to have to re-learn *how we are* in the world by acknowledging something of what it is to inhabit another's disrupted perception and/or to have our own perception disrupted.

4

However, this prompts the question about how extreme language, used in varying degrees in such a range of literary conventions, moves us in the direction of theological questions. Religious ritual is of course a familiar context for more or less defamiliarizing strategies, dramatic redescriptions of who we are and what we do, probably the most dramatic being the language of eucharistic practice – 'eating flesh and drinking blood'. But, while that is in itself an intriguing area for reflection,[33] our interest here is in what if anything is shown or suggested by practice outside the specifically ritual environment. We have seen in this chapter so far a spectrum of the ways language behaves under pressure, all of them taking it for granted that pressurized language *delivers* something. If we are seeking to locate ourselves, to find a place to speak from, we need a map of our environment – that is, of our habitual relations to other speakers and to the stuff that language deals with. That map is not constructed simply by a physical account of what has brought me to this point and what measurable processes I am involved in. I cannot – as we have observed earlier in this book – speak as if there were no such processes, let alone as if there were no physical constraints on my situation, but I shall not be able to decide what to say for or about myself on the basis even of all the available information

---

33 For a splendidly imaginative reflection on this, see Angel F. Mendez Montoya, *The Theology of Food: Eating and the Eucharist* (Oxford: Wiley/Blackwell, 2009), especially chapters 3 and 4.

concerning my environment. What I say is significantly bound up with what is said to me. And the tactics of disruption and pressure we have been looking at here are means of allowing myself to hear more being 'said' to me than I habitually acknowledge. The more I pick up, register, learn to deal with, the more I have to say for/about myself. The 'idea' of myself matures and I learn the skills of speaking from a location – quite paradoxical skills in that they involve recognizing when I can say nothing, or, perhaps, when saying nothing is seriously a moment of maturing in skill.

And this in turn inescapably carries with it the point we have noted earlier in different contexts: understanding in this way how we locate ourselves and how we shape our stance[34] in the light of what is said to us is to approach the environment as in some sense pregnant with intelligence. Our exploration in words of who we are or might be or should be treats our utterances as significant deposits from an encounter with an environment that is always already symbolic, communicative. What this chapter has been tracing is the ways in which this attunement to the symbolic is extended in a remarkable act of *faith in language*, an act of faith which assumes that words can be persuaded to say more than they initially seem to mean, whether by the elaborations of metaphor, the pressures of rhythm or assonance, or the breaking down of 'normal' speech in paradox and in fractured idiolect (as in Hoban). What I earlier[35] called the restlessness of language, its playful and profoundly serious reflections on itself, the way it 'makes jokes in its sleep', to borrow Iris Murdoch's vivid phrase,[36] is the token of this constantly regenerating act of faith that the sheer connectedness of sounds will enlarge

---

34 I borrow the word from Daniel Dennett: it is the word he chooses to designate a fundamental point of departure for the analysis of conscious processes where we could have no conclusive evidence that would compel us to adopt one approach rather than another (a 'design' stance rather than an 'intentional' stance, roughly a third-person-friendly rather than a first-person-friendly reading of the phenomena). I do not here take a view on the complex question of what precise status to give the notion of a 'stance' in his thought. Don Ross's remark about the need to avoid taking the word 'as simply a loose synonym of "perspective" or "attitude"' (in Introduction: The Dennettian Stance, Don Ross, Andrew Brook and David Thomspon (eds), *Dennett's Philosophy: A Comprehensive Assessment* (Cambridge, MA: MIT Press, 2000), pp. 1–26, quotation from p. 20) is a helpful steer.

35 Above, p. 54.

36 Iris Murdoch, *The Black Prince* (London: Chatto and Windus, 1973), p. 81.

what we understand: as if some fundamental significant utterance were being everywhere echoed.

This is the kind of sub-poetic language that can exasperate, of course; it may call up echoes of the Hindu idea of the primordial syllable echoing in the cavern of being, but this does not make much of an argument in itself. What is perhaps a little more of an argument is simply to spell out the implications of regarding our environment as carrying, symbolizing, intelligence; because, if intelligence, then intelligibility – that is, communicability to intelligent subjects. If intelligence is fundamental in our apprehension of our environment, if, as has been argued, the notion of 'mindless' materiality is a confusion, then we are indeed in an important sense 'addressed' by what we encounter; and what we encounter includes the words that are shaped out of encounters. Once spoken, they become themselves data of an environment, and thus potentially symbolic in their new embodiment of their subject matter. To put it in rather archaic terms, the form of what is encountered informs the new material vehicle of speech; and the indeterminate life of what is encountered is carried through in the ambiguities and crossings-over of what is said. 'Extreme' utterance presupposes that only when the fullest imaginable range of allusion and cross-reference has been explored do we begin to be capable of 'precision', because only then do we see what it actually means for some agency within our experience to come into speech. And, as noted already, seeing what such understanding means is inseparable from seeing the self more completely. If human art, verbal or visual (or indeed musical), makes us strange to ourselves, this is a part of growing into a more resourceful or resilient selfhood, able, in Jonathan Lear's terms, to 'live with the insight' that our stability or virtue always stands under scrutiny and is always to be suspected of not being what we should like it to be. And a focal aspect of living with that ironic perspective – so this chapter has suggested – is living in the awareness of never being the originator of speech but always the respondent; we are always at a disadvantage in our speaking in the sense that we do not ever 'possess' the first utterance that begins the exchange, and are aware of shaping our speaking selves always in answer to what we have never completely or definitively laid hold of. We continue to test out whether we have heard adequately by reflecting, re-making what is received; our linguistic extremism is simply this process at its most challenging and adventurous.

However, it is not surprising in this context that we turn to 'linguistic extremism' when we actually try to speak of God. Given that God is never a candidate for description as a member of the field of objects I encounter, how do I presume to represent God? What I am seeking to represent is not an item in any list; it is a particular aspect of every perception, the aspect that gives to any specific perception its provisionality, its openness to being represented afresh. William Downes, in the monograph referred to earlier, treats religious utterances as 'placeholders' for the belief or intuition that there is actually a maximal range of perceptible aspects in a thing or situation, a final and comprehensive plurality-in-unity that makes up the 'real' life of something.[37] But this means in practice that when we invoke a God's-eye perspective as our final horizon on the world, we are, in that very act, acknowledging the always receding horizon of our knowing; we are recognizing that representation for us has no end, because we cannot occupy the entire range of possible perspectives from which something can be seen. And, whatever God knows, it is not the ensemble of finite perspectives but something of another order.

Thus we cannot represent the whole way in which agencies or 'presences' in the world interlock; if we could, it would be another object. We cannot represent what God knows/sees/indwells as intelligence. The fact of 'representation' in our language points us towards a dimension that systematically eludes final expression. Yet we attempt to use words and sentences about God that we claim are not simply arbitrary; we engage in something at least analogous to representation. But lest we imagine that we are doing exactly what we do in other sorts of representing, we shall be well advised to expect our language about God to be in many ways eccentric, and indeed to explore and develop its eccentricities to avoid misunderstanding. Odd as it sounds, our (quasi-) representing of God is least off the mark when we are furthest from anything that looks like a fully coherent schema. Which is not an excuse for slackness, but an implicit plea for our words about God to be – as it were – carefully calculated shocks. This is simply to repeat Aquinas's point early in the *Summa* (a point originally articulated in Pseudo-Dionysius) that the 'crudest' metaphors for God are often the most successful, just

---

37 Downes, *Language and Religion*, chapters 4 and 6.5.

because no-one could mistake them for accurate depictions.[38] We do not try, in seeking to speak truthfully of God, to find words or images that will reproduce or imitate the divine; we specify a 'situation' or possible range of situations through a dramatic metaphor (God as a rock – to stand on or shelter under; God as a fire – to purge, to destroy, to give light) and so on. And to take the principle further, we can speak, as does Jesus in the gospel parables, through calling up a sequence of events, reactions and relations as a sort of complex metaphor. What is God like? 'There was a man who had two sons ...' 'A certain man went down from Jerusalem to Jericho ...' 'The Kingdom of Heaven is like treasure hidden in a field ...' God is represented by a whole narrative; to enter into this story and discover where you as a hearer fit and what role it is possible for you to adopt imaginatively, is to become able to offer a representation that claims truthfulness but not – in the usual sense – verisimilitude. If we think of some of the parables – the Unjust Steward and the Unjust Judge are the obvious examples – it seems that 'carefully calculated shocks' were an aspect of Jesus' own speaking about God. 'We have sections in our Dogmatic Theologies entitled "God as Shepherd", "God as King", or "God as Judge", exploiting the safe analogies. There are no sections entitled "God as magistrate who ought to be struck off the bench." It is an embarrassment to have to preach on such a parable ... And it appears that at least one fundamental purpose of the parables is to lead us precisely to such embarrassment.'[39] There are in scripture, of course, even more difficult and extreme metaphorical complexes – Ezekiel 23, for example, with its deeply ambiguous picture of God adopting and abandoning the child prostitutes Oholah and Oholibah, symbolic of the two Jewish kingdoms. No denying the embarrassment there; but, as with the gospel parables, we are dealing with presentations to be absorbed or apprehended as and *only* as they prompt ways of 'going on', new modes of

---

38 *Summa theologiae* I.ix ad 3 (referring back to Dionysius's *Celestial Hierarchy* 2): 'It is obvious [in the case of simple material metaphors] that these things are not being predicated in their ordinary strict sense (*secundum proprietatem*) of God – which might be doubtful if divine matters were being described under the forms of more elevated material realities.'

39 Roger White, 'MacKinnon and the parables', Kenneth Surin (ed.), *Christ, Ethics and Tragedy: Essays in Honour of Donald MacKinnon* (Cambridge: Cambridge University Press, 1989), pp. 49–70 (quotation from p. 56).

action that will somehow be more transparent to the divine love and intelligence. And the very 'embarrassment' of such extreme or inappropriate
analogies is part of what does this prompting. Understanding God – or 'the
Kingdom', the state of truthful seeing and appropriate action that is made
possible in the presence or through the action of Jesus – is very definitely
a matter of 'knowing how to go on' once we have encountered ourselves
anew in the context of hearing these parables. But an inescapable aspect of
this, it seems, is something like embarrassment – the sense of sharp incon-
gruity between where we want to 'get to' in representing the sacred and the
absurdity or moral murkiness of what we find ourselves saying and hearing
at stages along the way. And – just to avoid any confusion – this does not
imply that there is no place for anything but the simplest metaphors or the
most dramatic narratives in the attempt to speak of God. All it does is to
underline the function of these apparently simple elements in weaning us
away from what has been called 'philosophical anthropomorphism' – from
the idea that we are somehow being more representationally accurate in
calling God the Being of all beings or the Ultimately Significant than when
we call God Rock, Shepherd, or even (as in the parable) Unjust Judge.

5

'Extremity' in language works by pushing habitual or conventional speech
out of shape – by insisting on developing certain sorts of pattern (rhyme,
assonance, metre), by coupling what is not normally coupled (metaphor,
paradox), by undermining surface meanings (irony) or by forcing us to
relearn speaking or perceiving (fractured and chaotic language, alienating
or puzzling description). And I have not (because of my incompetence in
this area) elaborated on the uses of extremity of a somewhat different kind
in scientific discourse: a few minutes spent reading an introductory article
on string theory will make the point. Extremity is the most developed and
ambitious –and problematic – form of representation; in trying to characterize it, it is hard to avoid the terminology of violence, piling pressure
on words, twisting words from their usual habitat, assaulting habitual
perception and so on. Yet the assumption is that something about habitual
perception and the speech that goes with it is so inadequate or distorted
that a degree of shock to the system or embarrassment (to revert to what

was said about the parables) is a necessary aspect of becoming acquainted with the truth.

Talking introduces us to ourselves; 'extreme' talking introduces us to what we might not immediately welcome but delivers us from a merely complacent or defensive representing of ourselves to ourselves. We touched earlier on the question of trust in our language – the confidence that language under stress produces meaningful outcomes and viable insights. But to think about how we are introduced to ourselves in the way we have outlined is to express the trust that language under stress also delivers something like therapy for the speaking consciousness. Through metaphor and irony in particular, it dismantles constructs of the linguistic self that are evasive, self-reinforcing and so on. As has been argued more than once,[40] the idea of self-knowledge, let alone that of a 'true self', can suggest a mythological picture of some untouched interiority that needs to be rescued from the compromises of life in the world, including the world of language. This is none too helpful; but the belief that there are forms of speech that dissolve certain kinds of satisfying fictions about ourselves is a belief that there are other forms of speech that make possible a more serious or less 'defended' or more comprehensive engagement with the environment, a habit of *truthfulness* in a fairly generous sense of the word. And this is perhaps the best content we can give to the notion of an 'authentic' self-knowledge: a particularly steady and self-critical habit of speech, constantly informed by the extremities we have been discussing. If we are allowed a paradox here, the violence done to unexamined habits of speech is a condition of challenging and reducing the violence done by a lack of self-awareness, in our individual and corporate relations – though that is a longer matter to spell out than is possible here. The capacity to meet oneself as a stranger, which we have identified in various forms of extreme speech, is precisely a capacity to expose oneself to scrutiny, not to take oneself for granted; and this is a crucial component in anything that could be called a reconciled or

---

40 Cavell, *The Claim of Reason*, pp. 378–93 has some treatment of this – explaining why, in one sense, we cannot *not* know ourselves (pp. 389–90). See also Rowan Williams, '"Know Thyself": What Sort of an Injunction?', in Michael McGhee (ed.), *Philosophy, Religion and the Spiritual Life* (Royal Institute of Philosophy Supplement: 32) (Cambridge: Cambridge University Press, 1992), pp. 211–27.

interdependent human ecology. And to act as though language itself could in some measure free us from delusion is something that might well cause us to stop and reflect. We are trusting our speech to deliver us precisely from the traps of speech, from the 'easy speeches' of G. K. Chesterton's hymn;[41] it is an odd confidence, at least as odd as those other features of our language that we have examined in these pages, implying that our speech is at once the ailment and the medicine (Derrida on the dual sense of *pharmakon* is in the wings here[42]). If we recall Russell Hoban's myth of Fall and recovery, the violently split consciousness that splits the Addom in the name of violent triumph over the other can now only run on through the 'Chaynjis', the branching complexities of knowledge, psychological, scientific, aesthetic, if it is ever to find its 'idear'. 'Yu let thay Chaynjis owt & now yuv got to go thru them.'[43]

However, it is a confidence that makes rough sense against the background we have so far sketched. We act and speak as if our language carried resources beyond its immediate referential vocabulary; as if in some elusive sense it embodied the action of the things it spoke of. And if we are in the habit of treating our words as vehicles of an energy beyond them – let alone vehicles of an ultimate creative energy, as in the Greek theological world – it is not too surprising if we also implicitly treat them as capable of disclosing futures we had not consciously imagined. The violence we do to our words when we try to shock ourselves out of idle and selfish thinking/ speaking/seeing arises from the sense that we have 'always already' done violence to a more integrated perception through the normal ways in which we construct ourselves in language, and need to be jolted back – or forwards – into another mode of action; another mode which may exhibit a de-centring of the defensive or aggressive subject and thus a different kind of implied relation with the environment. If 'extreme' language can

41 'O God of earth and altar', no. 562 in *The English Hymnal* (1906): 'From all the easy speeches / That comfort cruel men ...'

42 Jacques Derrida, 'Plato's Pharmacy', in *Disseminations* (London: Athlone Press, 1983), pp. 61–172, on the ambiguity of the Greek word as meaning both 'poison' and 'medicine'. Plato's *Phaedrus* speaks of writing as *pharmakon* – in the context of presenting writing as toxic for speech. Derrida famously presents a more nuanced account in which writing is always necessarily both poison and remedy.

43 Hoban, *Riddley Walker*, p. 34.

locate us differently in our world, undercutting our sense of being a finished subject with a clear agenda of need and desire, ironizing our claims to self-awareness and repeatedly persuading us to begin again in learning what it is to speak and to represent, it is a necessary tool of human maturity. It is the single-minded concern with description as a means of comprehension and control that is more likely to generate a violent *practice* – a point clearly signalled in Iain McGilchrist's reflections on brain function. This ought to make it clear that not any and every sort of 'extremism' is defensible in this connection: we are thinking about the extreme used as a sort of 'skilful means' to shock us out of complacency and dispossess or displace the lazy or domineering or over-ambitious ego, about metaphorical violence used to undermine the roots of actual and destructive violence (Shakespeare would have had a view on this, one suspects).

In an earlier chapter,[44] we looked at the experience of the autistic subject, and at how it is important, in any therapeutic intervention or accompaniment, to try and listen to how such a person talks to themselves – what are the rhythms and patterns that are developed to cope with an unmanageable environment? The theory is that autistic behaviour arises from a condition in which the brain is overstimulated by data that it cannot organize or process as others do; and the sometimes extreme and violent actions with which an autistic person may respond to the environment are to do with this anxiety over the lack of control. Such behaviour is capable of modification if the subject can recognize 'outside' something of the sense he or she makes 'inside'; if they can see themselves or hear themselves as if in another shape. In the light of our more recent discussion, we could say that the same fear and anxiety about controlling the level of stimulus coming in is part of what motivates the consuming passion to describe exhaustively and rationally – but with something of the same effect of isolating the subject and fostering panic reactions when models and predictions can't cope. What this chapter has sought to suggest is that the work of 'extreme' language is both to break open this isolation and anxiety and to offer the possibility of *recognition* in and through the reality of what is at first felt as strange. It has the same sort of effect as the painstaking echoing of the autistic person's pattern-making that gradually brings them into something

44 Chapter 4.

like a linguistic exchange, even where no words are involved. If, in the extremities of art and certain kinds of science, we are able to recognize ourselves, we recognize that our purely descriptive capacity, our ability to construct detailed models replicating the constitutive elements and casual patterns of the environment, is something that exists in a wider context of interaction with what is presented to us, a context in which we are constantly looking for appropriate ways not of describing but of absorbing, transmitting, re-embodying what we receive. We see ourselves as more than we thought, more than we had thought *of*. But it is also worth underlining that this clarity about what 'extremism' in language serves gives us some critical purchase: not any and every kind of 'extremism' in speech is equally constructive in this respect. What we are concerned with is the sort of linguistic extremity whose effect is to dispossess us in some way, to open us to a truth that is changing us and never leaves us in complacent possession of the power we think we have.

All this begins to point to what we shall be discussing in the next and final chapter, the ways in which we are brought to silence. Remember Cavell's account of what is involved in watching a play on stage: in order to experience the drama as drama, we must suspend all power of action and intervention; we must be silent as the drama unfolds. But he goes on to argue[45] that, in being thus brought up against my limits as I witness a narrative developing quite outside my scope for intervention, I discover my real identity with others – the common human truth that there are limits to both what we can understand and what we can do, the truth of our *isolation,* our separateness. The suspension of my identity as agent and participant is a necessary moment of reconnection with something that is *prior* to me-as-agent. It is the moment in which I grasp the real impenetrability of one self to another, and so it is how I genuinely face their otherness, the fact that I cannot suffer what they suffer and so must respond to that suffering as something different from a mere extension of my own. 'If ... I am in awe before the fact that I cannot do and suffer what it is another's to do or suffer, then I confirm the fact of our separateness. And that is the unity of our condition.'[46] Cavell, as we have seen, speaks with evident

45 Cavell, *Disowning Knowledge*, pp. 108–10.
46 Ibid., p. 110.

embarrassment about wanting but not quite being able to cast this in terms of connecting with 'Being'; as if 'Being' itself were in effect the irreducible mutual otherness of speakers, the complex of inexhaustible potential for relatedness. It is an embarrassment that arises from a proper reticence in this context: if what we are talking about is a suspension of the capacity to act, this involves the act of speaking itself, and perhaps especially the act of speaking about metaphysics. Is it the case that we 'discover solidarity' in silence as well as in other kinds of suspended action? Of course, an essential aspect of our chosen powerlessness in the theatre is that we don't speak: we can't warn, inform, console. We cannot release our tension or manage our anxiety as we normally do by talking, and so are left with the feedback of our emotions, including our fear. Silence obliges us to confront vulnerability and finitude – and thus is involved with all the various challenging and inviting aspects of language we have been considering thus far. It is there in the acknowledgement of indeterminacy; there are no conclusive words for a genuinely open future. It is part of the incompleteness of any linguistic project. It is implicit in the acknowledgement of our bodiliness, the fact that we do not speak from a safe distance above and beyond the flesh but in the whole of our physical presence, whether we are 'literally' speaking or not. And it is a condition of the renewal of speech: we cannot handle the radical reshaping of our speech without listening, hearing what we do not usually let ourselves hear, silencing the habitual chatter and buzz of egotistical self-reflection. In the next chapter, I'll be attempting to trace how our understanding of silence in 'ordinary' contexts begins to move us into this territory, where a silence that is framed, faced and thought enables something to emerge that is not simply the product of this chatter and buzz.

6

Saying the Unsayable:
Where Silence Happens

1

'Gentlemen of the Jury, there are many kinds of silence. Consider
first the silence of a man when he is dead. Let us say we go into the
room where he is lying ... and we listen. What do we hear? (*He listens
intently*) Silence. What does it betoken, this silence? Nothing. This
is silence pure and simple. But consider another case. Suppose I
were to draw a dagger from my sleeve and make to kill the prisoner
with it; and suppose their lordships there, instead of crying out for
me to stop or crying for help to stop me, maintained their silence.
That would *betoken*. It would betoken a willingness that I should do
it ... So silence can, according to the circumstances, speak.'[1]

Thomas Cromwell's speech, from the climactic trial scene in
Robert Bolt's play *A Man for All Seasons*, vividly expresses the recognition that silence is not pure absence (one might well question his
assumption that the silence of a room where a dead man is lying
'betokens' nothing; but Thomas Cromwell is probably not a very
reliable guide to such subtleties). We can mean something by *not*
doing or saying; withdrawing from speech allows something to be
communicated. But, in Cromwell's phrase, this is 'according to the

---

1   Robert Bolt, *A Man For All Seasons* (London: Samuel French, 1960), p. 82.

circumstances'. We cannot imagine an 'unframed' or pure silence: we can only imagine the silence in which *we* are not hearing anything, not hearing what we might expect to hear – that is, it will have to do with what has shaped our expectations, our history and fantasy and so forth. Silence for us is always the gap that occurs *here*, in this specific place between words or images. Pictorially, it is like the gap between the two winged creatures in the Jewish Temple which denoted the unrepresentable but not absent God. In the context of the argument of this book, thinking about silence is thinking about how we might be said to represent something by what I have called 'framing' silence. For some contemporary writers, of course, this is to ask absolutely the wrong question.[2] For them, the point about silence is that it undercuts representation itself; it repudiates language in the name of what is timeless and imageless. In a way that echoes some of the themes touched on earlier in this book, it sets two sharply contrasted levels of reality against each other. On the one hand is a linguistic world that is defined either by contests and negotiations over power or by play and improvisation; on the other, the world of the white margin, the absence, the anti-linguistic that simply exposes the illusions or corruptions of language.[3] Language may be ideology and manipulation; or it may be playful improvisation. Over against both, silence is both emancipatory and serious. But this is a danger-ously absolute and even romantic notion of silence. To talk about silence, I would argue, is always to talk about *what specifically* we are not hearing; or what we decide not to listen to in order to hear differently; or what specifi-cally we find we cannot say. Silence 'betokens' in the context of speech and image; which is not to deny or diminish the radical challenge silence can pose to speech, only to warn against a loose and even sentimental discourse about it which ignores the basic question of how silence actually and particularly criticizes and modifies speech and thus itself 'says' something.

There is no shortage of examples to provoke reflection. John Cage's famous 4' 33" is a measured space of non-deliberate sound, the deliberate withholding of music in the usual sense so as to insist on another sort of

---

2   I have in mind particularly the work of Mark C. Taylor; see, for example, *Tears* (Albany, NY: State University of New York Press, 1990).

3   Taylor, ibid., chapter 12, offers a very subtle account of this.

listening.[4] It is not exactly silence in the absolute sense, sheer absence of sound – any more than someone meditating 'silently' is absolutely silent; it is a space in which otherwise unheard sounds emerge and are attended to. In this particular context, with the expectation of hearing music, we are obliged to hear something else and to become aware of the absence of music. Or, again, we might think of the silence of the therapist in the psychoanalytic or psychotherapeutic encounter: the therapist/analyst is trained in a rigorous withholding of comment or reaction, so that a different sort of speech is drawn out of the analysand – a speech increasingly free from the pressure to shape and interact with the speech of another speaker, whether a competitor or a judge, who needs to be engaged or impressed or wooed or resisted.[5] Or, silence can be felt to be the only possible response to a particular context of corrupted and facile speech: Cordelia, invited to declare how much she loves her father, expresses her despairing impotence in her aside, 'What shall Cordelia do? Love, and be silent.' Speaking would be to engage with a demand that should never have been made – and when she does speak, she cannot find words to justify her silence in terms Lear might understand; she is doubly 'silenced', by her own unwillingness to say anything, and by her father's response of incomprehension when she tries to articulate that unwillingness. But the point in relation to the present argument is that her silence is significant as a protest against the language she is being forced to speak: it is not that her silence as such is somehow a token of 'transcendent' meaning.[6] It gains significance only from what it specifically denies.

Another example: consider the silence at the end of the performance of a play or a piece of music: performers and audiences will be familiar

4   For an illuminating brief comment, see Sara Maitland, *A Book of Silence* (London: Granta, 2008), pp. 197–8.

5   See Michael Parsons, *The Dove that Returns, the Dove that Vanishes: Paradox and Creativity in Psychoanalysis* (London: Routledge, 2000), pp. 179–81; and c.f. David Michael Levin, *The Listening Self: Personal Growth, Social Change and the Closure of Metaphysics* (London: Routledge, 1989), pp. 79, 232–3.

6   Sara Maitland, op. cit., p. 28, quotes a letter from Janet Batsleer objecting to the valuation of silence as such; and there is in the background here a powerful feminist critique of 'enjoined' or enforced silence. See, for example, Susan Griffin, *Pornography and Silence; Culture's Revenge Against Nature* (New York: Harper, and London: The Women's Press, 1981), pp. 201–49. 'We must choose between beauty and silence' (p. 249).

with the brief but pregnant moment before applause is 'allowed' to break out. The longer such a silence lasts, the longer may be the subsequent applause; but we can see what it might mean to say that the moment of silence is what the performance has worked for, displacing the habits of an audience, the compulsion of the group to act or intervene (remember again Stanley Cavell's model of the drama as insisting that we suspend our urge to intervene). This silence is precisely what the performance has made possible, or indeed made imperative; it is significant because of what has been said or done. And to turn to the most challenging and – painfully – the most hackneyed example: the often-quoted axiom about the impossibility of poetry after the Holocaust[7] tells us, similarly, that it is *this* utterly concrete historical atrocity that makes us silent *here*. Being silent here and now, like this, is something that – rather than being simply an eruption of timeless quiet or non-sound – poses a question as to how this silence has been generated: how it is sensed and read as obliged or even 'commanded', how it has been coaxed, earned, imposed. It directs us back into the process that generated it and invites us to see something there that escapes whatever categories seemed most appropriate for talking in that specific context. It invites us to recognize how and where we have encountered what is not speakable. It does not simply *cancel* what has been said (or indeed sung); it 'loosens the texture' of this preceding activity, telling us that there is something we have not captured (and are not likely to), whether in the excess of atrocity (the Holocaust) or the excess of joy or beauty (the end of the concert).

In a teasing and very suggestive piece written for a symposium entitled 'Apology for Quietism', published in the periodical *Common Knowledge*,[8] the Russian/American philosopher and critic Mikhail Epstein proposed that we needed a symbol to indicate that, within a text, we were invoking the presence of the margin. He proposed a blank space between quotation marks (" "). 'This sign', he writes, 'transforms the environment of the text into one of its components, a new sign that functions among other textual

---

7   Or, more strictly, the 'barbarity' of writing poetry after Auschwitz, in the original formulation of Theodor Adorno.

8   Mikhail Epstein, " ", *Common Knowledge* 16.3 (2010). *Apology for Quietism: A Sotto Voce Symposium*, pp. 367–403.

signs.'[9] Space is being made within the text for what is not being said. And in contrast to particular words for the non-conditioned environment that makes particular utterance possible (words such as 'absolute'), this is not an utterance with a home in any one language. It 'enacts' the non-conditioned environment within the text by being itself as blank as the margin. It is[10] the equivalent of a pause. All forms of discourse need at some point, in some way, to 'present' the conditions within which they operate; yet they cannot make those conditions into signs like others. Any such presentation has to be 'sequestered from representation'.[11] Thus the sign " " both exposes and conceals;[12] and it has the effect of 'marginalizing the centre, centralizing the periphery, voicing the mute, uncovering and advancing suppressed layers of culture'.[13] Because it escapes any definitive translation into more conventional signs – there is no one word that will render it adequately for all contexts – it brings us up against the unavoidable defeat of any aspirations to an all-sufficient and universal language, and so disrupts 'textuality as such'.[14] Thus it puts in question all particular ideological interests, all claims to final and definitive power exercised through words, so transforming our relationship with what we say and what we think, and what we think we say.

All this is persuasively said. The only hesitations I have are to do with the implied contrast between presenting and representing – a contrast that relies on understanding representation only or primarily as imitation, reproduction and so on, an understanding I have been challenging throughout this book; and also with the lack of focus in the argument on *where* exactly this paradoxical sign comes to be located in a text and why. It cannot be introduced just anywhere in an utterance; there must be something that 'calls for' it. And, if so, it is indeed a calling into question of any and all ideological ambition, but is also a historically situated challenge. As I have suggested, it is a silence that has an identifiable significance as calling into question this particular utterance at this moment. And this is a particularly important aspect of how we are to understand silence. If we value silence

9   Ibid., p. 371
10 Ibid., p. 376.
11 Ibid.
12 Ibid., p. 383.
13 Ibid., p. 402.
14 Ibid., p. 399.

or absence as such, as absolute absence, we risk implying that *wherever* silence occurs it is a manifestation of an otherness pregnant with depth and critical force. But what about the silence of those who *have been* silenced, whose presence has been denied? It is not hard to understand the vehement protest quoted by Sara Maitland from one of her friends: 'There is no silence without the act of silencing, some one having been shut up ... Silence is oppression and speech, language, spoken or written, is freedom ... All silence is waiting to be broken.'[15] And a former Gifford lecturer, in his comprehensive and imaginative overview of the meanings of silence in Christian history, lays out with detail and precision some of the ways in which silence has been at best ambivalent in large tracts of that history. It has been a strategy for survival for various minorities, ethnic, credal and sexual, for people whose lives or security would be at risk if they spoke truthfully about themselves. And it has been a strategy for denial in respect of the memories and the reality of child abuse, slavery, anti-Semitism, and all other kinds of violence towards those silenced or self-silencing minorities, a strategy for an institution afraid of hearing the truth about its past (and present).[16]

These corrosive forms of silence are not, he says, unique to Christians: 'they are products of how human beings construct the world around them and negotiate their way through the embarrassments and opportunities created by our search for power and control, over others and over ourselves'.[17] But it is uncomfortably true that a religious culture which seems to value silence as such may be able to find something edifying in corrupt and corrupting silences; as if the retreat into an absence of words were itself healing or absolving. Any such retreat serves only those whose abuse of power (whose abuse of *speech*) needs to be named, spoken out. To 'find one's voice' is universally seen as a mark of emancipation, because the denial of this is so manifestly a privation not only of mutual relationship but of the fundamental ability of human speakers to affect their world, to confer as well as to receive meaning. But this also makes sense of the way in which a self-chosen silence in certain circumstances can be so radical a

15 Op. cit., p. 28.
16 Diarmaid MacCulloch, *Silence: A Christian History* (London: Penguin Books, 2013).
17 Ibid., p. 235.

self-denying gesture. Stories of early Christian monks (and similar stories of Buddhist sages) accepting in silence, as a form of ascetic self-denial, accusations of rape or violence (until events vindicate them);[18] the refusal of Margaret Clitherow to plead when accused, under Elizabeth I's draconian anti-recusant laws, of harbouring Catholic priests (effectively condemning her to death);[19] the silence of Paul Scott's tragic Indian protagonist, Hari Kumar, in *The Raj Quartet* when charged with raping the white woman with whom he has been tentatively establishing a relationship, because she has told him to 'say nothing' – all these are instances of self-chosen silence bringing scandal and suffering that is accepted as somehow imperative, even desirable or perhaps reparative; instances of giving meaning to the experience of injustice. Yet the fact that silence like this *can* be meaningful in virtue of a speaker's free choice does not make any and every sort of silencing good or justifiable. The examples mentioned are instances of silence acquiring meaning from particular things not said – from a refusal to compromise or endanger another, or to engage in burnishing a self-image. They are not instances of a univocal breaking through of some kind of sacred absence.

Where silence comes in is all-important; so that we cannot in fact discuss it without the closest attention to the speech it interrupts or refuses. Its 'betokening' is about some dimension of what has been or might be said or done, and it points, just like the examples of 'extreme' speech in the previous chapter, to excess of world over word. We have reflected at several moments on the central importance of *difficulty* in the experience of speaking subjects, and on the inescapable unfinishedness of speech: the way in which silence 'comes in' should be something to do with admitting the most formidable level of difficulty (which is why silence as evasion or denial is such a monstrosity). If were we *just* to say that language was insupportably compromised and inadequate to truth-telling, and that pure silence was the alternative place to seek truth or transparency, we should

18 The story is originally associated with the name of Macarius the Great; see *The Sayings of the Desert Fathers: The Alphabetical Collection*, trans. Benedicta Ward, SLG (London: Mowbray, 1975), p. 105.
19 She was executed in 1586 and canonized in 1970. Maintaining silence under a potentially capital accusation was punishable by death.

risk losing sight of the fact that it is speech that points into silence and is itself altered by it. To pick up again a point touched on earlier in this book,[20] D. Z. Phillips, in a controversial passage in one of his early works, protested against the idea that 'language itself' could be thought of as inadequate. He was not suggesting that our language should recognize no limits, but arguing against the rather loosely phrased commonplace that words cannot not express the transcendence of the divine or the myste-riousness of life beyond the grave, so that we need to get rid of language in order to perceive or encounter truth. In response to criticism, he later explained that he was simply pointing to the fact that it is *language* that presents mystery, language is where mystery occurs: 'Language is not a screen which hides God from us. On the contrary, the idea of God *in* the language we have been explaining, is the idea of a hidden God.'[21] To use an example Phillips is fond of, if I say 'I can't tell you how grateful I am', I am telling you something about my gratitude: I am not claiming that my gratitude is inherently mysterious or transcendent, accessible only in radical abstention from all speech; just that it is of an order which makes it difficult to articulate it in any specific formulation without slipping into cliché and staleness. *This* is the difficulty which I am now naming. The fact that language cannot and does not offer simple and exact reproductions of its subject matter, credible 'imitations', we might say, of the world, does not mean that it is somehow not fit for purpose.

But for Phillips's point to be completely clear, we need a more flexible account of what we mean by representation, and – something Phillips does not quite provide – a clearer picture of language not as a system for reproducing impressions but as a system of variegated material responses to its environment – some of which responses are gestures towards that excess of environmental stimulus over conventional representation which we have discussed throughout this book. Thus there is not some super-linguistic order of speech or being in which something other and better than language will be available as a medium of knowing or encountering. The incompleteness of speech is not a failure exactly. Nor is my gratitude something defying language: we are simply showing that *this* is one way in

20 Above, p. 109.
21 Phillips, *Faith After Foundationalism*, p. 289.

which language copes with *this* sort of difficulty, by naming the bare fact that it is difficult. And this naming of the difficulty is what may motivate us to look at the story behind an effusive expression of thanks: why is there something about this which resists conventional forms and clichés? Which takes us back to the silence at the end of a play or concert. If this is prolonged a second or two beyond the conventional pause, we may – in due course – be prompted to go back and revisit what it was in the performance that resisted the obvious and expected response.

This is the sort of silence which Epstein describes as both exposing and concealing.[22] He quotes Alain Badiou on how 'evil' is a matter of forcing the naming of the unnameable. In a slightly different context, some have reflected on the difficulty if not impossibility of 'representing pain well', when there is heavy pressure towards inappropriate representation – to explain or to avoid or to focus unhealthily on the suffering going on: a theological conundrum which we have become rather more alert to in recent decades. In the sense that such forcing is a mark of seeking decisively to domesticate the world we inhabit, to express control, it can indeed be seen as fundamentally inhuman. If we say (if we *say*) that we must stop talking here, we are not saying that there are things that cannot be talked about, but identifying how we talk about them – i.e. by indirection, by allowing the pause of inarticulacy, by gesturing to the difficulty, perhaps ultimately by simply saying nothing. To pursue Epstein's analogy, we enlarge the margin and shrink the text; we extend the gap between the quotation marks. But the fact of the text or the commas is essential in making sense of what is going on here. We are not seeking a silence that will deliver us from the specificity of the world we inhabit but one that obliges an ever-deeper attention to it. And in this light we can see how certain disciplines of self-silencing, as in meditation, can intelligibly be developed. Particular ways of speaking or of monitoring physical processes become pathways into a mental stillness that is not numbness or 'absence of mind' but enhanced awareness. I referred earlier to the *koan* in some varieties of Buddhist practice – a question that is 'resolved' only when the meditator, having sat with the words for a long period, acknowledges that no answer is the right one: the response that matters is letting yourself be projected beyond

22 Epstein, art. cit., p. 303.

dualities of here and there, subject and object.[23] This acknowledgement
allows a way of seeing what comes into consciousness in terms other than
the habitual relating of objects to our needs and personalities. The process
is to some extent paralleled in early Christian literature, where we read of
the imperative to develop a non-passionate attitude to the world, seeing it
in relation to God, not ourselves.[24] The passions, the reactive forces at work
in the self, aggressive and/or acquisitive, have to be stilled so that what is
seen is seen free from the self-related images or fantasies we bring to it. This
is what it means to understand silence as liberating – freeing the world from
the agenda of the self, freeing the self from the compulsion to mastery of
the environment. It reveals, in the sense of exhibiting depth; it conceals,
in the sense of marking where supposedly straightforward description and
analysis cannot go. By refraining from trying to 'name the unnameable', it
acknowledges something about the inherent character of our speech – its
incompleteness, its time-and-matter-bound nature, its participation in an
environment it does not control from some safe epistemological distance.
By making space within speech for the 'unnameable', it names it in the only
way possible, as that which surrounds and underlies and makes possible
what is said. Speech and action have their 'precondition in the other', says
Epstein:[25] the " " sign 'cites' the precondition of our being,[26] but without
either reducing it to the terms of the text or locating it in a total otherness
that can only be evoked as the absence of all that we understand as meaning.
Silence is a place or a dimension in the world of language that is evoked,
achieved and 'cited', presented in the framed pause; the drastic dualism
which would suggest we should simply oppose language and radical absence
has the effect of making silence inhuman. And it is perhaps such a lack of
frame that makes some people who are condemned to literal and unbroken

23 See, for example, the lucid summary in John Crook, *World Crisis and Buddhist
    Humanism. End Games: Collapse or Renewal of Civilisation* (New Delhi: New Age
    Books, 2009), pp. 110–20.
24 Key texts from Evagrius of Pontus can be found in *The Philokalia. The Complete Text
    Compiled by St Nikodimos of the Holy Mountain and St Makarios of Corinth*, trans.
    G. E. H. Palmer, Philip Sherrard and Kallistos Ware, vol. 1 (London: Faber and Faber,
    1979), pp. 40, 42–3.
25 Art. cit., p. 381.
26 Ibid., p. 382.

silence around them lose their minds, hallucinate voices and images, descend into torpor or delirium.[27]

Philip Davis, in a wonderful essay on the nature of reading, analyses how imaginative writing creates a 'holding space' – 'a focal space, a field, which represents [notice the word] the nameless dilemma, in order to create what we might call a holding-ground for investigation and contemplation'.[28] Whether in literal silence, in the crafted pause, or in the gap of transition between one stanza and the next in a poem, what is in view is a means of challenging and extending 'the normal fields of consciousness', making our awareness and our speech 'porous'.[29] And this can be a deeply un-reassuring, alarming matter. Davis refers to Russell Hoban's fantasy, *Fremder*,[30] in which we are introduced to a future world in which it is possible to 'teleport' human individuals by the almost instantaneous dismantling and reassembling of their molecular structure; the anxiety for someone who has experienced the 'flicker' effect accompanying this process is whether there is real continuity between one state and another – which is a strictly unanswerable question, since to answer it would require 'objective' access to both the pre- and the post-teleportation state. Electronic brain-imaging is able to offer the teleported subject a picture of what is going on, but what it depicts is an intermediate moment which suggests primal terror – a look into 'the black cosmic origin of things'. The observer 'feels the particles of his self move apart a little letting in the dark';[31] the more we look at the dark, the more we sense the terror. But, at the same time, it is in this darkness, where the raw condition of the self is displayed in its imageless potential, that the elements of the activities of thinking and representing are being generated. The dark gap indicates all that makes thought possible and indicates also the impossibility of thought adequately thinking its own origin. Which is not to say that we cannot think into and out of this darkness or that it is simply absence or formlessness – because it is what makes form happen. The stillness

27 Sara Maitland, op. cit., chapter 3, gives a good overview of some of the more disturbing effects of prolonged silence especially combined with isolation.

28 Philip Davis, *Reading and the Reader* (Oxford: Oxford University Press, 2013), p. 12.

29 Ibid., p. 21.

30 *Fremder* (London: Jonathan Cape, 1996).

31 *Reading and the Reader*, p. 22.

between words and acts, the gap where other energies than the conscious arise, is what actually keeps speech and thought moving. When we stop thinking/speaking/imaging, there is not so much a void as a plenitude; to recognize this is to recognize the strangeness of silence within speech as 'saying' something that cannot be brought to words in the ordinary sense, representing what is not to be represented.

2

Human communication exists in the context of a communicative, meaningful environment which cannot be exhaustively mapped or articulated but can in some sense be 'represented', though not by any simple addition to the sum total of representable objects. This has been the model advanced throughout these pages. And silence above all – in the form of something like Epstein's blank space of citation – refers what is said to a hinterland of significance: we are always saying more than we entirely grasp, certainly more than we can securely 'ground'; the peculiarities of language which this book has attempted to explore are ways of indicating the scope of this hinterland a little more, in the full recognition of the fact that we are not thereby advancing towards a full, limitless, perspective-neutral account of the meanings we inhabit. The word 'inhabit' is crucial here. We occupy a meaningful space which is available to us prior to any specific human attempt, individual or corporate, at charting meaning; or, to put it more simply, we are involved in relations of communication before we realize it (or realize them). Behind and within our speech is what makes speech possible – the white margin, yes, but a white margin that shapes and is shaped by *these* specific utterances or meaningful acts.[32] Language is therefore not some kind of 'fallen', distorting medium or activity: it is finite and historical but not intrinsically corrupt; capable of truthtelling in the sense of representing what is not itself, or not the contents of some demat-erialized mind, but telling the truth often by indirection, by the admission of difficulty and limitation, and by its own scrutiny of its workings and its learning.

32 C.f. Epstein, art. cit., pp. 369–72 on the interweaving of text and margin – though I think there is more to be said on how the text *shapes* the margin.

Silence in the sense we have just been exploring is thus the point on which all the features of language we have looked at in this book finally converge. The non-determinate character of our speech means that there is always a possibility of silence: if stimulus does not specify response, there will always be diverse possibilities of utterance and representation – including those which embody hesitation, gaps in the surface, paradox and development over time, as opposed to a single definitive act of naming. There is a gap of silence, at least potentially, between the prompt from an environment and the unique verbal acknowledgement and following of it that will emerge. The unfinished character of language means that we are always aware of what has not *yet* been said, even if we have no way of knowing what exactly it will be: and so once again a gap opens up within what we are saying between any particular utterance at any one time and the actuality to which the utterance witnesses or with which it seeks to be aligned – because there will always be another perspective to be admitted, a perspective not yet voiced and heard. The admission of this gap and the waiting for what has not yet been said may manifest literally in silence, or may simply be a perennial question mark, a habit of ironic acknowledgement of the margins. Language as an embodied activity implies that not only gesture and noise but sheer physical presence is in some way communicative: the silent physicality of a body – or an object – in certain circumstances is meaningful (that is, it establishes intelligible connection with what is not the individual ego).

This is worth spelling out at a little more length. Both images and physical spaces can act in this way, although it takes a fair amount of countercultural energy to do justice to this, given our preoccupation with what is meant to be verbally definitive. But the wordless deployment of physical signs may be the most adequate (or least inadequate) testimony to the most intractably difficult of circumstances. Visitors to the Yad Vashem museum in Jerusalem regularly say that the physical layout of the building is an integral part of the experience of being introduced to the horror of the *Shoah*   the irregular pathways through it, the single candle reflected in a complex of mirrors to become an incalculably repeated signifier, and much more. To take a couple of simpler but related examples, the placing of a single bowl or flower in an empty room, or the way in which the architecture of an old fashioned Catholic church leads the eye towards the tabernacle where the Sacrament is reserved (a powerful instance of a non-verbal sign) likewise work on the assumption that what I have called intelligible connection happens when the normal verbal carriers are deliberately removed. David Jasper, in an intriguing study of the body and the sacred,[33] notes how the religious icon realizes a kind of silence because it acts as a threshold rather than a depiction. And he goes on to interpret early Christian asceticism as an essay in making the body itself a meaning-charged presence. 'They [the early Christian monks] sought absolute participation in the body of the Godhead at its deepest depths of humanity, at a point so far beyond the bearable, in the absolute desert, that its own deepest being met God as truly total absence wherein alone is Total Presence. In this utterly profane moment there can be no severance of spirit from body, for the body, in all its physicality now is nothing but spirit.'[34] Allowing for some discomfort at the way in which Jasper's rhetoric indulges the idea of a *cancelling* of word and image rather than their relocation or radical opening up in the way I've been suggesting, there is a significant insight here about how the ascetical body, having abandoned its 'normal' means of imposing intelligibility on its environment, becomes intensely charged as a sign – 'speaks' in a unique fashion.

And of course, finally, the phenomenon of language under pressure – in metaphor, rhythm, rhyme, in all the various forms of 'making strange' that we examined in the last chapter – once more creates a distance between what is spoken of and what is said, the distance into which silence insinuates itself. Not that this posits a gulf between word and world which it would take some metaphysical miracle to cross: the point is rather that the way in which the environment is present in speech is likely to be paradoxical and baffling, so that we can't understand it without suspending our habitual words, and allowing others to emerge out of that suspension. The gap opens between what *has* been said and what is not yet said, what might be said, what particular things might very deliberately *not* be said. The silence in between is not quite, therefore, a 'total absence' but the witness to a plurality of meanings that cannot be mastered – a presence, if

33 *The Sacred Body: Asceticism in Religion, Literature, Art and Culture* (Waco, TX: Baylor University Press, 2009), p. 30.
34 Ibid., p. 45.

we want to use this language, that is so densely interconnected and variously representable that every specific utterance is going to be under question. As was suggested sketchily in the preceding chapter, the element of pressing or probing the language we use so as to generate fresh levels of meaning, fresh ways of seeing, implies a deep and provocative trust that intelligibility will emerge (rather than simply being deliberately created by sense-making speakers) if we allow enough space for it. To propose a metaphorical idiom or structure in speaking of a familiar object, stripping it of its familiarity, is to claim that its meaning (what it communicates intelligibly) is more than the familiar account permits us to see. As and when we allow it to become a puzzle to us, something prompting further listening and further speaking, we acknowledge implicitly a dimension of meaning not straightforwardly dependent upon us as observers and speakers. We acknowledge the object's *life* over and above us, its presence to what is not us. I have argued in another context[35] that one of the central elements of any view of the world that takes account of the 'sacred' is one in which we accept that we are speaking of/relating to a world which is already related to something other than ourselves. What lives within our visual field also lives in other fields – and we live in its field also.

This is where the entire discussion of the oddities of language in which we have been engaged poses for us most clearly the question of whether we can think with adequate imaginative reach about language without some reference to the sacred in this sense, to what is intrinsically demanding of unqualified, 'unselfing' attention. If our language is systematically indeterminate, incomplete, embodied, developed through paradox, metaphor and formal structure, and interwoven with a silence that opens up further possibilities of speech, it is a reality which consistently indicates a 'hinterland'; as if it is always following on, or always responding, living in the wake of or in the shadow of intelligible relations whose full scale is still obscure to us. To put it a little more sharply: these aspects of language seem to show that we live in an environment where intelligible communication is ubiquitous – where there is 'sense' before we *make* sense. Nothing will establish beyond debate that this is not illusory, of course; but the fact of experienced difficulty in finding what to say, a simple fact to which we have returned

35 See the essay, 'Has Secularism Failed?', in *Faith in the Public Square*, pp. 11–22.

regularly, obstinately challenges any denial that our language is in some way *answerable* for the sense it makes, the sense we decide to make.

And if we put this in slightly different terms, perhaps we can see how it has faint parallels with certain kinds of theistic argument. How might such parallels work? Well, what has been argued is that any particular utterance, any meaningful representation (in the broad sense we have been using), is necessarily partial, even when presented in terms of general truthfulness; it may be truthful but still capable of supplementary or alternative representation (there is no level of representation to which all others can be reduced). From one point of view, this would seem to mandate what William Downes calls a 'philosophy of uncertainty': 'the species-mind can't tell in advance what can be naturalized and what cannot, or even to what degree a conceptual domain containing mysteries can be clarified, philosophically or even poetically, over centuries of enquiry',[36] and so we must refuse various tempting varieties of closure – reverential abstention from questioning in the face of 'mystery', conviction that all apparent mysteries are just linguistic/conceptual malfunctions capable of being straightened out in due course with better mental equipment, incurious acceptance of the unresolved as just 'brute fact'.[37] *But*, from another point of view, there is an insistent implication that, wherever you happen to start thinking from, there is meaning 'elsewhere'; and this suggests at the very least an 'order' of intelligibility, a coherent pattern of mind, that pervades the contingent objects of perception and speech – a universal pattern or structure of intelligible/intelligent life of the sort Hegel posits and traces. In such a framework, truthful thinking would always be a pattern of dispossession or displacement, an ascetical exercise that foregoes the ambitions of final mastery or absorption of the object so as to allow our perception and response to be adequately shaped by what is extra-mentally there. And beyond this recognition of what truthfulness involves is the further question that might be put from the point of view of a traditional believer: is not this something like, 'what all understand to be meant by "God"', as Aquinas would put it? If the intelligent/intelligible life we find being 'gestured towards' in this argument is properly active independently of all

36 Downes, *Language and Religion*, p. 260.
37 Ibid., pp. 262–3.

particular relations of knowing and representing, if it is that upon which the very idea of intelligible communication depends, it is clearly something whose reality must be in the ontological neighbourhood of an unconditioned source of being – what is understood by 'God'.

Thus expressed, this is an echo of Aquinas's arguments from contingency and necessity. And the relation between natural and revealed theology becomes a little clearer if we think carefully about the way in which this has just been framed. If reflection on language leads in a certain direction, it still needs an interlocutor to put the question that takes the argument to another level. If this discourse is insisting upon a 'pattern of intelligent/intelligible life', and if faith in revealed religion involves a belief in the sharing of intelligible structure from outside the system of finite concepts and objects, is there a convergence we can recognize? That is the basic question of these chapters. If we are led to speak about human speech as located against the background of an active but imageless depth which is intelligible in the sense that what it makes possible is intelligence, yet not intelligible in the sense that it cannot be reduced to an item in the mind, the believer in revelation may reasonably observe that the God alleged to speak in revelation is quite well characterized by such formulations – active and mind-like, not representable as an agent among others. As in the case of Aquinas's arguments, we cannot claim anything resembling a wholly watertight argument: the substance of the argument is not at all about reasoning conclusively that a certain entity is bound to exist – the kind of argument that Kant dismantles. It is more a matter of posing the question, 'If this is how we "track" the distinctive patterns of intelligible talk (whether talk about the interconnection of agents in the world or talk about our own talking), is there a match with what religious believers claim about God?' This does not of itself mandate religious belief, let alone create a 'religious' attitude (adoration, humility, joy, penitence ...), but it brings us to the kind of potentially fruitful halting point that was sketched in our first chapter. We press a particular kind of discourse to its furthest point and confront the question of whether at the end we are simply left with a problem wholly resistant to resolution, or whether we might be prompted to shift the level of the discourse. Examining our speech may bring us to the point where we recognize that language cannot describe or contain the conditions of its own possibility – and that this incapacity is precisely the source of its energy, its movement, its capacity for correction, innovation and imagination. Language behaves as if it were always 'in the wake' of meaning, rather than owning and controlling it. And we have the alternatives of regarding this as a brute fact about our linguistic being or treating it as something which indicates what we have called a hinterland of meaning that is imperfectly accessible to finite speakers/thinkers.

3

However, to do justice to this latter possibility, we have, of course, to be seriously careful about the sort of claims we make for any kind of talking *about* what it is that language is 'after'. To repeat the point: we cannot represent this as an item within the sum total of things to be talked about, and if we seek to represent it at all, it must be by other and potentially eccentric strategies. But the whole of our argument thus far has been to detach the idea of representation from depiction, description, imitation and so on, and to underline the fact that *any* representation at all, not only representations of the unconditioned, may spill over into what a strictly descriptive approach to speech might see as 'eccentric' linguistic behaviour. This simply is the character of our speech's relation to its environment. If we are serious about our gesturing towards what it is that language is 'in the wake of' – the intelligible environment we can recognize as intelligible but cannot master – we shall need a repertoire of styles and idioms that undercut the possibility of understanding our speech as attempting straightforward description. A huge amount (ironically) has been written about 'negative' or 'apophatic' theology in this connection. To borrow the language used by Ian Ramsey in his work on religious language (rather neglected in recent discussion, and unfairly so),[38] we develop a tension between 'models' and 'qualifiers' – i.e. between words that have a currency in routine accounts of action in the world, and expressions that qualify such words so as to make it clear that they cannot be 'exact currency for God'.[39] But (as has been said especially by some Eastern Christian writers) this variety of negative theology can sound, if we're not careful,

38 *Religious Language* (London: SCM Press, 1957).
39 Ibid., p. 53.

like a conceptual game whose outcome is simply a kind of definitional fastidiousness: as if we were just saying 'not quite' about various predications concerning infinite agency. Modern Eastern Christian thought has argued that negative theology has to be a more radical business[40]: it is about the ultimate silencing of *both* terms of the model-and-qualifier tension, and the resignation of the mind or subject to sheer attentive receptivity. It is the abandonment of all aspiration to definitive 'experience' of God as God, whether through a supposed positive sense of God's presence or the felt lack of that specific sense.[41] There is no 'object' there to experience in the same way we experience the contents of the world, but this also means that a sense of God's absence is not like the sense of a missing element in our inventory of the world. Knowing God, in plain terms, is not to be identified with a state of religious ecstasy; and not knowing God is not to be identified with a feeling of abandonment or spiritual desolation. Ultimately, what matters is neither a positive nor a negative affective state, but a developing understanding of how our thinking and feeling become 'de-centred', dispossessed of controllable material.

So the language of negative theology is not merely the refining of strategies for showing that such and such a phrase cannot be 'exact currency' for infinite agency: this is a helpful corrective, certainly, but a means rather than an end. In the first chapter, we looked at the way in which the *koan* operated in some kinds of Buddhist discipline, as a means not of 'qualifying' what was said but of shifting the entire set of expectations within a scheme of discourse, blocking off certain ways of hearing what is said and opening others. So, if we are looking for language that has this effect, we are looking or listening for language that focuses our minds on the need to be receptive if we are to be in touch with the truth in this context: if we are seeking a representation for unconditional action, the only way in which we can avoid distortion is ultimately to look for what is also a representation of our own incapacity to contain or describe. Richard Hooker famously wrote

---

40 The classical discussion remains Vladimir Lossky, *The Mystical Theology of the Eastern Church* (London: James Clarke, 1957); see also Rowan Williams, 'Lossky, the *Via Negativa* and the Foundations of Theology', in *Wrestling With Angels*, pp. 1–24.

41 Denys Turner, *The Darkness of God: Negativity in Christian Mysticism* (Cambridge: Cambridge University Press, 1995), p. 264.

at the beginning of his *Lawes of Ecclesiastical Politie* (I.ii.2), 'Dangerous it were for the feeble brain of man to wade far into the doings of the Most High; whom although to know be life, and joy to make mention of his name; yet our soundest knowledge is to know that we know him not as indeed he is, neither can know him; and our safest eloquence concerning him is our silence ... He is above, and we upon earth; therefore it behoveth our words to be wary and few.'[42] Yet the actual sparseness of what we say, or indeed what we show in image or action, is only one vehicle for this representing of incapacity; some of the kinds of 'excess' looked at in the preceding chapter have the same effect. Displaying language under the stress of repetition, sustained paradox, metaphorical extravagance or oddity is also a way of representing what language cannot do as well as what it can. As we noted earlier, it was not for nothing that Meister Eckhart called God *omninominabile* – nameable in every way – as well as *innominabile* – not nameable at all.[43] Against this background, the test of anything claiming to be authentic representation of God must be whether what results is some sort of dispossession, some deepened capacity for receptive stillness. '*Every true sacred sign effaces itself*', writes Maggie Ross in a notable meditation on silence in the liturgy[44]: that is, the sign of the sacred or unconditioned is one that refuses to absorb our gaze, our attention, in itself but undercuts itself, questions and relativizes itself, not as an intellectual riddle or an invitation to uncommitted curiosity but as a way of bringing us into a different kind of awareness.

This points us back to some of what has been said earlier about speech and the body. Representing the unconditional happens (as David Jasper intimates) through the silent body – not the *silenced* body that speaks of someone else's dominance, someone else's bid to own the body and dictate

---

42 *The Works of ... Mr Richard Hooker*, John Keble (ed.) (Oxford: Oxford University Press, 1841), vol. 1, p. 201.

43 Above, p. 65; the theme appears particularly in Eckhart's *expositio libri Exodi* and the eighth of his Latin sermons. On this, see Vladimir Lossky, *Theologie negative et connais- sance de Dieu chez maitre Eckhart* (Paris: Vrin, 1960), chapters 1 and 2, especially pp. 41ff., and Bernard McGinn, *The Mystical Thought of Meister Eckhart, the Man From Whom God Hid Nothing* (New York: Herder and Herder, 2001), pp. 99–100.

44 *Writing the Icon of the Heart: In Silence Beholding* (Eugene, OR: Cascade Books, 2013), p. 46.

its meanings, but the silence of bodily presence consciously entered upon, the intention to allow something to emerge that is more than the speaking mind's 'normal' content. Similarly the body engaged in ritual movement and gesture represents a dispossessed mind to the extent that it sets aside the usual model of moving so as simply to enact one's individual projects and meanings. Music, which engages the body in a unique form of concentration and communication, has the same function of displacing individual agendas and easily formulated meanings. In all these ways, literal silence and/or immobility, ritual gesture and musical performance, the body can become a token, a representation, of that which is never thinkable as an object. And religious language that facilitates silence and accompanies ritual or music is bound in to the reality of the displaced or dispossessed body; it too shares in the distinctive and elusive representational work of silence or stillness.

Against this background, it becomes possible to see how a religious tradition that refers to or rests upon claims to revelation need not necessarily be appealing to a simple model of divine utterance – an otherworldly agent providing otherwise inaccessible information. The point might be explored with reference to a variety of families of religious practice, but its application in the Christian context is especially clear. Revelation here begins precisely with a phenomenon in the material world, a *body*: the body of Jesus of Nazareth, which is an active and speaking body, then a helpless and suffering body, then a dead body, then a body that is both significantly absent and at the same time believed to be present in very diverse modes – as the community itself, as the food the community ritually shares, as the proclaimed narrative and instruction derived from the record of the literal flesh-and-blood body. The story of Jesus' body represents the unrepresentable God by tracing a movement towards silence and motionlessness within the human world: its climax is not a triumphant theophany but a death and its complex aftermath (the resurrection is not a theophany in the sense of some sort of public manifestation of triumph). It works with the existing expectations of divine manifestation, but then fleshes them out by telling a story of how divine power and liberty are 'emptied out' in the life of this body. And whatever else St Paul does with the history of Jesus, this dimension is strongly maintained and affirmed. In both the first and the second letters to the Church at Corinth, we see the same movement being traced: the inexplicable or humiliating failure, void, loss of control that is seen in the death of Jesus establishes the key in which the believer – and especially the believing teacher or pastor – has to live (and die).[45] The 'apostolic' representation of God becomes, like Jesus' own representation of God, a matter of finding significance in silence or in speech that is in some way broken and awkward, not in a fantasy of ideal articulacy. Paul famously congratulates himself on his lack of physical presence and fluency, so that there should be no confusion between his 'performance' and God's agency (I Cor. 2.1-5). Much later, St John of the Cross, writing in sixteenth-century Spain about the most acute stages of dispossession in the life of the spirit, describes the crucified Jesus as 'at the moment of his death ... reduced to nothing in his soul, with no comfort and no alleviation' and goes on, 'And so in this he performed the greatest work of his entire life, with all its miracles and great deeds, in earth or in heaven; and that was to reconcile and unite the human race with God through grace.[46] The emptying of merely created will, purpose, sensation, hope and so on allows something to be manifest and effective that is not part of the sequence of created cause and effect. Hence – for John of the Cross – the essential importance of the fact that in prayer and discipleship the believer at some point meets the most intractable frustration, the 'non-experience'[47] that moves us out of our usual expectations, ideas and pictures of ourselves as well as of God. The entry into the 'dark night of the spirit', in John's scheme, is the beginning of a new freedom for us to represent the God whom Jesus decisively represents in his own displacement and dispossession.

Here, though, as in the more general context of thinking about silence, it is important to avoid easy misreadings. If we understand Jesus' being 'reduced to nothing' in his death as a valorization of imposed passivity in itself, let alone a symbol that sanctions the silencing of anyone or gives us leave to ignore such silencing, that is a serious distortion. John of the Cross's conviction about both the cross of Jesus and the inner emptying of the

---

45 The most relevant passages are in 2 Cor. 2–6.
46 *Subida del Monte Carmelo (Ascent of Mount Carmel)* II.7 (tr. RW); *The Complete Works of St John of the Cross*, trans. E. Allison Peers (London: Burns and Oates, 1934), p. 92, for an older translation.
47 The use of the term and many other insights in this area I owe to Martha Reeves.

believer assumes that these are what we could call *achieved* silences: they are silences with a history behind them of free decision and of pre-occupation with a vision that is most actively desired. And their effect is thus also to challenge any specific bids to power over the body and language of any other person: there can be no theological ground for a desire to control or exploit another if the goal of the healed or renewed human identity is so radical a challenge to our obsession with power. Likewise – and the foregoing remarks are relevant to this too – there is not, as we observed earlier, a blanket valuation of silence in and of itself, as a timeless and absolute margin alongside speech or significant gesture: if significant silence in this context is 'achieved', its history matters: it is the silence that emerges out of *this* set of transactions, these specific frustrations. 'As a non-sign it gains signification from other signs which surround it and in which it is embedded. In other words, it signifies by other signs.'[48] Silence is significant because of where and how it comes in, and so is arrived at by a variety of 'strategies'; those strategies are themselves meaningless without the silence they induce, but the silence is equally meaningless without the time taken to arrive at it, the particular narrative of its achievement – and the meaningful speech/action thus generated. 'It is not a question of silence *or* speech, but rather that the transfiguring energy given in silence is expanded and integrated by making us attempt interpretation through speech, while in the same moment insights that arise from speech deepen and expand again into the silence.[49] And this is the fullest and most decisive answer to those who – understandably and rightly – object to the moral cloudiness of valuing silence in itself. Of course there is silence that is corrupt, abusive, oppressive; and we know it as such by tracing how it came to be. The silence that emerges because of a steady refusal of the uncritical agenda of the ego is something other.

---

48   Oliver Davies, 'Soundings: Towards a Theological Poetics of Silence', in Oliver Davies and Denys Turner (eds), *Silence and the Word: Negative Theology and Incarnation* (Cambridge: Cambridge University Press, 2002), pp. 201–22 (quotation from p. 222).
49   Maggie Ross, op. cit., p. 89.

SAYING THE UNSAYABLE: WHERE SILENCE HAPPENS   179

4

'Our safest eloquence ... is our silence'; yes, but it is eloquent because of what it has stopped saying, because it is a silence fashioned and framed by the enterprise of speaking our way into the most extreme difficulty. In some ways of using the *koan*, much is made of the need to go on offering verbal reflection or interpretation until exhausted; it will not do to take refuge in silence too easily and too soon. Throughout this book, we have been examining, not exactly the points at which language 'breaks down', but the aspects of language that simply lead us towards a point of *aporia*, as the Greeks would say: not exactly a brick wall, but the moment where we have to pause, acknowledging the issues or perspectives that cannot be dealt with within the framework we started with. And this does not mean that there is in any straightforward way an alternative or 'higher' register in which such questions are resolved; simply that the framework we start with is irresistibly oriented towards an articulation of its own limits, whatever its initial promise may have seemed to be. The way human beings use language – or enjoy or inhabit or just experience language – is a subject full of oddities and potential frustrations if what you are looking for is an account of an orderly behavioural pattern, let alone a causal sequence. The argument of this book has been, in effect, that taking seriously the various open-ended aspects of our speech identified here is a way of rethinking how we come to refer to the unconditioned activity which, in the conviction of religious believers, surrounds all that we are and all that we say. But it has been equally part of the argument that this requires the closest attention to what we say and to how its limits are displayed, not some cavalier dismissal of argument and labour. And in this following-through of the nature of our difficulties and our eccentricities, we have identified at least one aspect in which this account of language converges not only with a general language of the sacred but specifically with the Christian model of an *embodied* sacred whose sacredness is inseparable from its silence or marginality. What points of convergence could be identified with the themes of other religious traditions I have not explored, though there could no doubt be such explorations: my goal has been not to claim that the Christian narrative alone can be shown to do justice to the oddities of human speech, but that the oddity of this doctrinal claim both casts light on and is itself illuminated by the sort of account of how we talk that has been offered here. If there are gaps in our speech that, by bracketing the struggle for control or ultimate reduction, show what it is that happens when the ego is dispossessed, even for a moment, then the 'gap' in the world of struggle and aspiration to power represented by the silence or impotence of what might be thought to be power without limit takes on a further dimension of significance.

And this takes us back to the questions posed at the start of this book, about the relation of 'natural' and 'revealed' theology. A 'natural' theology need not be an exercise in trying to replace revelation, to forestall the action of God. It may be a way of tracking that action through the impress left upon our speech and action, as upon other aspects of our world; and thus it may be, as Hauerwas's Gifford Lectures proposed,[50] a form of 'faithful witness'. And as we learn so to track it – to track the insistence in language of what is alien and uncontained – we may develop an enhanced capacity to recognize at least what is being claimed in this particular discourse of revelation that is Christian theology. A natural theology does not deliver either a theory or a vision of the sacred; it identifies where our thinking and speaking about our thinking and speaking come to the point where we either acknowledge an inescapable halting-point or begin to re-work the style of our questions. If the latter, this will not simply take away the blockages, let alone offer answers to unsolved puzzles, but it will frame the difficulty simply as *what we might expect to encounter if the universe were as the believer claims*. Revelation does not fill a gap, but shows why the gap is there, not resolving difficulty but offering a perspective in which difficulty is what makes sense and what we must become accustomed to. I use the word 'difficulty' here where it is tempting to use 'mystery'; but the trouble with 'mystery' is that it has become irredeemably bound up for too many people with an evasion of questions that could perfectly well be answered, with avoidable vagueness. Living with difficulty is living in the awareness of an incompleteness that never ceases to pose questions and to generate

50 Hauerwas, *With the Grain of the Universe*, especially pp. 209–15 and 224ff. on witness as what makes believers intelligible to themselves as well as others (because it clarifies what difference it makes that God exists); pp. 231–40 on faith and reason, arguing that intellectual witness entails the location of philosophical argument firmly within the horizon determined by faith, and that this is paradoxically the only secure defence of a 'reason' that has any claim to universality.

both unexpected new strategies and unexpected new frustrations – never ceases, in fact, to generate speech. 'Living with mystery' can perhaps too readily suggest settling for a more passive stance. If the argument so far has any substance, then it is only in confronting difficulty that we become intelligently receptive to the actuality of what resists final capture in speech; the resistance must be experienced in its full toughness. Hence, once again, the importance of how silence is achieved or arrived at ('earned'? Not quite; it is hardly a reward). And it is against this background that the silent/silenced God spoken of in connection with the image of crucified dispossession can come to be seen as actively self-revealing.

A natural theology is thus an exercise in locating and mapping difficulty. It is clearly distinct from the mapping of unsolved problems; these are by definition problems that belong in the ongoing sequence of questions within a particular discourse. The difficulty we are interested in here is more to do with a sense of restlessness around the discourse itself at the level at which we have been engaging in it; and as such it may generate a new discourse with new sequences of problems – or it may finally push us to a point where we can only gesture towards a discourse that we have no clear way of developing in the ordinary way. The difficulties that are of interest to a theologian will be those that bring us to that point of 'gesturing'; to those kinds of representation that go outside the categories of imitation and reproduction. The theologian will have an eye for kinds of discourse that set up unmanageable paradoxes, either in the sciences or in the humanities; discourses that insist on irony – on some irreducible disjunction between what is said and what is true but – in one way or another – unsayable. And the point of connection with theology is certainly not an offer by theology to dissolve the paradoxes and ironies or to name the unnameable; it is that theology will regard these sorts of speech as central to the enterprise of language-using, rather than marginal, and will have a framework in which what is present but unsayable is understood as pervasive and generative. The claims of Christian doctrine are to do with pointing as clearly as possible to the focal irony of the unconditioned reality communicating itself not only in conditioned form but in the ultimate conditionedness of death – a dead body – and matter – eucharistic food – and written reported speech – scripture; speaking in forms that seem inherently not to have what we normally understand by the power of speech, the power to reply or continue.

Kierkegaard, the supreme theological commentator on irony,[51] sees the freedom opened up in ironic consciousness (I am not identical with, bound by, what I say) as subversive of any sustainable sense of self *unless* it is incorporated into a conviction of being in the active presence of God: the search for reconciliation with God is a search for something to which I am constantly related, throughout all that happens to me materially, something that allows me to orientate my words and acts in regard to what is beyond them all and which thus makes it possible to 'locate' them all, as with a literal orienteering point. In the absence of this, irony ironizes itself out of existence: there is no speaker left. If it is acknowledged, there is always, spoken or unspoken, a dialogical element in our existence which anchors us in some kind of continuity. We can connect this to our earlier examination of aspects of Richard Rorty's understanding of language and truth.[52] Rorty's radical disjunction between what we (think we) say and what we are actually doing in saying anything carries (I argued) a serious moral problem in that it may license someone to deny intelligent attention to what another says; it may allow one speaker to dismantle the seriousness and reality of another's intention or what they understand to be their agenda or their grounds for holding and defending a belief. There is no point 'between' us to which we are equally accountable. I am not identical with what I say, and the 'true' causes of my utterance may be completely inaccessible to my present knowledge; likewise with the person who speaks to me. But this means that there is no basis for any act of epistemic trust between speakers. We are taken back to some sort of naked contest for control rather than a form of common labour. And irony itself loses any meaning if there is nothing but such a contest: irony is significant as and when we are aware of the gap between what is said and what is the case, and this requires us to be aware in some elusive way of what our saying fails to lay hold of: it must suppose a 'presence'. Without this, I have no claim on the trust or even the tolerance of another speaker, any more than they have a claim on mine. But if I do have some concept of a reality with which I must be 'reconciled' (a loaded word, of course), a reality with which I need to be aligned if I am to live appropriately and sustainably in my environment,

51 Above, pp. 137–8.
52 Above, pp. 37 9.

then what is exchanged in speech becomes an exchange between speakers who each occupy lastingly different places *in relation to* something that is not identical to any of them. And thus an intelligible notion of *selfhood* emerges as the specific location in history and geography of such and such a set of unrepeatable perspectives, needing the distinctness and difference of other such sets for its survival and flourishing, and equally being necessary to those others in the same way. The silence between us as speakers which indicates what is not yet exhausted even by the fullest or most fluent combination of our perceptions is the guarantor of selfhood. Irony, comedy and tragedy all alike make sense only on such a foundation. Failure and error are empty terms without this unexhausted invitation that lies between speakers and is regularly signalled by silence. The 'breakdown of communication', the conversation punctuated by Pinteresque gaps, is one of the surest signs of a discourse that is taking 'selfhood' seriously; we could perhaps go so far as saying that it is these silences that give content to the idea of the soul – the unrepeatable perspective on things that every speaker embodies and every other speaker needs in order to speak and to live as a subject.

5

And if that is where our argument leads, we can say that our natural theology is not only a way of indicating where language about God 'comes in', but a way of suggesting where language about the speaking self comes in also. It is worth remembering that it is not simply God's existence that is at issue in our culture, but the existence and survival of a certain kind of *humanity*. Throughout this book, we have assumed that particular uses and styles of language are – if not strictly uniquely, since we cannot know this absolutely for certain – distinctively human: bound in to the phenomena of exchange, exploration, uncertainty, trust, error, excess and so forth. Versions of humanity and of human language which, deliberately or not, work towards excising some of the difficulties involved in this are ultimately hostile to that account of humanity which sees it as basically *accountable*, engaged in growth, risk and love; shaping itself in relation to what is given. What we say about the processes of language and specifically about what I have been calling representation is a way into constructing an anthropology as well as a theology, a picture of the human; as we have seen at earlier stages of this book, there are versions of human self-description which in effect make it impossible to understand at all what is going on in the language we actually use – and thus make it, if not impossible, at least unintelligible that we ourselves should speak. And this is not an easily sustainable position.

This means that the most comprehensive and thickly textured account we can give of what is recognizably human is deeply implicated in concerns about 'the sacred' – about what is not yet said, what is not sayable, what precedes our understanding and both confirms and challenges specific acts of understanding. Such an account does not deliver a 'proof of God's existence'; what it does is to map the territory of human speech in a way that enables us to see that what is affirmed in the language of specific religious ritual and reflection – in the language of 'revelation', if you will – *goes with the grain* of what matters most and is most distinctive in anything claiming to be an adequate picture of our human speaking. As noted above, a merely senti-mental and impressionistic appeal to 'mystery' is not enough; we have to follow through the range of ways in which language incorporates dangerous levels of trust, the possibilities of radical error and the strange phenomenon of putting itself under pressure in order to discover things not yet seen or said. And, ultimately, what the various languages of revelation propose or imply is that our most fully aware and deliberate and freely accepted silences, when the speaker's agenda is most manifestly suspended, are moments where truthfulness is most evident, where there is the most potent and appro-priate act of 'representation'. And because this is a representation of what we cannot ever in principle control or contain, we can say also that this is where the sacred appears – in whatever paradoxical sense we give to the word 'appears' here. For those who accept the Christian revelation, this paradox is articulated with special clarity in the focal image of the bearer of ultimate revelation silenced and immobilized: a place where there is a convergence of two journeys of dispossession, divine and human. Spelling this out, narrating or imaging those 'journeys', is what theology does, in a variety of modes.[53]

---

53 On the essentially 'kenotic' character of theology, its necessary focus on self-dispossession, see Williams on Lossky, above, note 40; see also Andrew Louth, *Discerning the Mystery: An Essay on the Nature of Theology* (Oxford: Clarendon Press, 1983), chapter 6, and Oliver Davies, *A Theology of Compassion* (London: SCM Press, 2001), especially chapters 10 and 12.

The preparatory exercises for theology which these chapters sketch may not compel anyone to a theological sequel. What they intend is only to 'hold' for a moment (reverting to the language used in the first chapter) a perception of our language which allows us to see something of where those limits appear which both energize and disturb what we say; to put some flesh on the notion of our intelligence being ordered or oriented to the unknown; and finally to suggest that sharing and owning this perception helps us grasp how conviction about the sacred as free and active in a way distantly analogous to our own intelligent action – the conviction implied by a belief in revelation – belongs with the most significant things we can say about our very human identity.

APPENDIX: ON REPRESENTATION

The word 'representation', as we have noted, has a very wide range of applications, and it may be helpful to add a few remarks about some of the varieties of its use, particularly those which have shaped the sense given to it in the preceding pages. It has a significant role in aesthetics, in political philosophy and in philosophy of mind, and any reader will need to be careful not to assume that the use of the word by, say, Nelson Goodman in his important work on the nature of art,[1] bears any close relation to discussions of 'representational properties' in philosophical discussions of consciousness such as those of Daniel Dennett or David Chalmers.[2] And, just to complicate matters, there is also the fact that English translators of Hegel have regularly rendered his *Vorstellung* as 'representation'.

To begin at the beginning: discussions about the alleged 'representational properties' of the human mind are about whether the activity of consciousness could be exhaustively characterized in terms of 'phenomenal' properties (what it is like to be experiencing a specific mental state here and now) or whether we need also to speak of 'intentionality' (the relation between what I am experiencing and what is true of things other than myself). If the latter is true, there is work to be done in assessing whether a particular

---

1 Nelson Goodman, *Languages of Art: An Approach to a Theory of Symbols* (Indianapolis, IN and Cambridge, MA: Hackett Publishing Company, 1976).
2 Dennett, *The Conscious Mind: In Search of a Fundamental Theory* (Oxford: Oxford University Press, 1996); Chalmers, *The Character of Consciousness* (Oxford: Oxford University Press, 2010).

intentional content is in fact related to a state of affairs outside the mind
– whether it satisfies the conditions required to *represent* something.
Representing may take a number of forms, from visual presentation to
descriptions of function or analyses of the contents of a phenomenon; but
in every case there is some state of the world in virtue of which this state of
the mind is or is not an accurate representation. The mind may as a matter
of fact be representing its environment without any conscious sense of
doing so; that is, our minds may have representational properties without
corresponding phenomenal ones – we may have unconscious 'background'
beliefs which do not figure in an account at this or that moment of what
it is like to be us, what we are experiencing. But, conversely, phenomenal
properties – what it 'feels like' to be conscious at this moment – can
plausibly be said to entail representational properties: we can't be aware of
ourselves or our mental state without implicit claims about more than the
state of our minds. This means that what is going on in producing the state
of mind we experience is a causal process: we assume that this or that aspect
of how it currently feels to be me is caused by properties of the environment
in which I find myself.

This is a very rough summary of the exposition offered by David
Chalmers in his most recent work[3]: and he concludes by arguing, in effect,
that neither the representational nor the phenomenal can be reduced to the
other. We cannot hold that the phenomenal aspect is devoid of intentionality, that mental states simply are what they are independently of external
causes for their content; nor can we hold that there can be intentional relatedness wholly without awareness of what it is like at a particular moment
to be me (we recognize that there are such things as unconscious beliefs
precisely because we are habitually aware of conscious ones). 'Intentional
content appears to be part and parcel of phenomenology: it is part of the
essential nature of phenomenology that it is directed outward at a world. If
so, we cannot reduce intentionality to something more fundamental.'[4] This
means that what it is like to be me at such and such a point is essentially
informed and conditioned by causal systems which 'register' features of the
environment in my experience. The risk is that this pushes too much to

3   Ibid., chapter 11.
4   Ibid., p. 371.

the margin the active element of consciousness – that is, that by stressing the causal connection between the world and the representative properties of the mind we lose the first-person perspective itself, the experience of the perceiving 'I' which structures and connects causal stimuli. As Raymond Tallis observes in an astringent review of Chalmers,[5] we need a clearer rebuttal of a view Chalmers is obviously not attracted by, the view that treats conscious goings-on as functional transactions, the processing of determinate input into determinate output.[6] Even the most apparently straightforwardly 'caused' material perceptions are 'dense, layered and multifaceted; *located* in ... intentional objects'.[7] To take the hoariest philosophical example, the red patch I see is always the redness of an object that is culturally and linguistically presented to me, an object which I locate and explore in and through the sense I have of being aware. Chalmers is not denying this; but Tallis is right to question whether the rigorous 'representational/phenomenal' dualism with which he begins is the best vehicle for avoiding functionalist and reductive language.

The point for our present purpose, however, is that if consciousness is indeed irreducibly a matter of both the intentional and the self-aware, we need (as Tallis hints) a broader notion of 'informing' and 'information' than the notion of a plain transmission and reception of signals. In the chapters of this book, I have been taking 'representation' to mean broadly what Tallis, I think, means by 'presentation': the object that is my face in the mirror is a representation, but my perceiving of it is a making present to myself of what is there.[8] I have, in fact, used 'representation' to mean the widest possible category of 'mental goings-on' that can be seen as *appropriating* the stimuli of an environment as part of a continuing conscious life – or, in the more metaphysically ambitious language I have sketched, as fusing the agency or energy of this particular bit of the environment with my own agency, allowing the external stimulus to shape my action, yet also shaping the stimulus in particular ways as I make it my own. Hence

5   *Reflections of a Metaphysical Flaneur and Other Essays* (Durham, NH: Acumen Publishing, 2013), pp. 93–125.
6   Ibid., pp. 117–20.
7   Ibid., p. 120.
8   Ibid., p. 118.

I would argue for a fairly generous use of 'representation': if what we are talking about is the active presence of an environment within, or even 'as', the active presence that is my conscious life, it helps to have a word which marks the transition between two kinds of presence in the world, presence as simple agency and presence as agency understood and appropriated by intelligence (and if I am right overall, the former is always moving towards the latter). In the sense I am proposing, representation includes what I have called 'description', cataloguing elements in what is perceived, diagrammatic and mathematical reductions (the latter itself being currently a matter of some philosophical interest), various kinds of imitation and more. But it is important to insist that it has a meaning not reducible to description alone. Downes's book on religion and language gives a fivefold analysis of what counts as representation in language[9] which moves from any utterance cast in intelligible linguistic form through the breakdown of this into logical form, the incorporation of that logical form into particular context-related claims, the formation of 'fully-propositional' claims whose criteria of satisfaction are fully specified, and finally propositional forms whose satisfaction of truth-conditions is radically incomplete or unclear (we cannot be completely sure what would establish them as true), yet which are not nonsense, which communicate intelligible content and which have 'sufficient logical character' to make them useable and defensible. Downes has some interesting things to say about traditional religious claims in this connection, but for the moment we shall keep the focus on his general thesis. The main point is that 'representation' here denotes a range of levels at which we refer truthfully or appropriately and *effectively* to our environment, and that this range importantly includes modes of speech which cannot instantly be mapped on to schemes of point-by-point correspondence (with each element appearing in speech having a determinate state-of-affairs in virtue of which the speech counts as accurate). The implication of this, of course, is that speaking truthfully needs to be an activity that relates to complex perceptions ('dense, layered and multi-faceted' in Tallis's words), not simply to some supposed world of elementary facts, synthesized for convenience into larger compounds. To refer back

9   *Language and Religion*, pp. 129ff.

to McGilchrist's discussion of perception,[10] it must relate to right-brain modes of knowing in which wholes are more than the sums of parts. Thus, in regard to Downes's analysis, I should want to say that the last-named of his stages of representation is a bit more common than his discussion might imply: the varieties of 'enrichment' that can supplement well-formed 'fully propositional' statements are to be identified in many kinds of discourse; and it is these that therefore exemplify the widest possible meaning for the activity of representing.

Nelson Goodman's aesthetic theory is primarily concerned with representation as a category in visual art, and at moments he therefore understandably uses 'description' to designate the sort of rendering of an object that is *furthest* from being an imitation or reproduction – whereas I have suggested that description, imitation and reproduction have something essential in common, in that they seek to provide itemized versions of an original. But because he wishes to argue that representation is precisely *not* bound to reproduction or imitation, to subsume description under representation is a helpful tactic to wean us away from an uncritical notion of representation. Representation cannot be 'an idiosyncratic physical process like mirroring';[11] it is always involved in symbolic systems. 'Realism' is an unhelpful category in aesthetics because symbolic conventions vary so radically.[12] And representation is what it is in virtue of relations between the symbols that constitute it, in such a way that what may seem contingent aspects of it are in fact significant – in a way that is not true of 'diagrammatic' rendering.[13] A representation is such not because it reproduces an object's appearance but because it constitutes itself a complex of internally related elements recognizable in a symbolically literate culture as rendering something other than itself in a new form. But Goodman ends his immensely innovative and sophisticated discussion by observing that this does not by any means leave us with a notion of art that is divorced from questions of truth: we may more easily use the language of 'aptness' or 'appropriateness' than truth where art is concerned, but that does not

10 Above, pp. 27 ff.
11 Goodman, op. cit., p. 43.
12 Ibid., pp. 34ff.
13 Ibid., pp. 226–31.

mean that we don't expect art to engage with the environment we actually experience, fitting or failing to fit it. And 'fitness' is something that both confirms and changes what we know of the world around.[14]

I mention Goodman's account primarily to avoid possible confusion; here is a philosopher operating a distinction between description and representation which works rather differently from what I have proposed in this book, and the parallels and differences need to be flagged. But Goodman's work is important also in reinforcing the broad sense of representation argued here, representation as a form of potentially truthful (or 'apt' or whatever) denotation embedded in a symbol system which does not attempt to find simple substitutes for the elements of reality but looks for something like analogical patterning in the elements of a different medium. One of the things which this has significantly in common with what I have been outlining is thus that representation is not something which comes *between* a reality and its apprehension by a subject – a sort of obstacle to or substitute for the real thing. Rather than seeking to stand in for what's 'really' there, a representation is the 'thereness' of the object in relation to the perceiver. And this gives us a perspective from which to think about the complicated legacy of representation-words in the Hegelian tradition. Because Hegel uses a word commonly translated as 'representation' (*Vorstellung*) to denote thinking that has not yet attained to properly conceptual status, the temptation is to read Hegel as if he were saying that mature thinking moves on from 'representing' to something else. But, as many Hegel interpreters have argued over the last few decades, we need to tread very carefully here. *Vorstellung* is literally a setting-before; it is 'a consciousness of something that one has before oneself as something objective'.[15] Thinking that makes use of *Vorstellung* is thus not 'absolute' thinking – that is, the thinking of thinking itself; it uses specific images drawn from the experience of the contingent facts of the world's existence so as to identify and clarify a content which has yet to be allowed to emerge in thought in its proper guise – 'a mode of consciousness which is freeing

14   Ibid., pp. 263–5.
15   Hegel, *Lectures on the Philosophy of Religion. One Volume Edition: The Lectures of 1827*, Peter C. Hodgson (ed.) (Berkeley, CA: University of California Press, 1988), p.144.

itself, as it were, from the merely sensible in order to reach the universal'.[16] It is a stage further on from the *Darstellung* of art, which invites us to know our act of knowing in the immediate and sensuous images it offers without inviting us to the more obviously analogical move of religion, in which sensuous references are being deployed as tokens of non-sensuous process.

Even granted this clarification, though, we should be cautious about supposing that Hegel is simply and consistently seeking to banish both artists and dogmaticians. As Nicholas Adams's monograph[17] and other recent studies[18] argue forcefully, we misread Hegel if we think of him as telling us a story about how thinking gets better by stages. Thinking our thinking is, *as such*, 'absolute' thinking, thinking which recognizes that it has no object but itself. But this is not to claim that the paradigm of genuine thinking is a sort of unimaginable abstraction, because the act of thinking is always in fact the thinking of this or that. Indeed, Hegel is profoundly hostile to the idea that 'real' thinking is subjectivity turned upon itself alone; it is, rather, the thinking of what is entailed in its own relatedness, in the fusion of interior and exterior, subject and object (which makes even the formula 'thinking which recognizes that it has no object but itself' highly misleading because it still implies that there is a definable subject over against the world, or that the subject is faced with some sort of competition for its attention between its own reality and the objects of its activity). It 'overcomes' the order of representation in the sense not that it supplants it but that it shows it is not exhausted by it and is the only thing that finally gives intelligibility to it. John Walker shows[19] how we need to understand Hegel as identifying those aspects of modernity which make the representation of concrete, determinate or particular situations and sets of precepts problematic; we have lost our innocence about appearances and so are pushed in the direction of philosophies which focus on the fragmentary and compromised character of representation and the alienated and 'stranded' aspects of subjectivity. But, precisely because of

16 Charles Taylor, *Hegel* (Cambridge: Cambridge University Press, 1975), p. 480.

17 See Chapter 1, note 52.

18 E.g. John Walker's stimulating essay on 'Art, Religion and the Modernity of Hegel', in Stephen Houlgate (ed.), *Hegel and the Arts* (Evanston, IL: Northwestern University Press, 2007), pp. 271–95.

19 Ibid., pp. 287ff.

this, what we need is a philosophy that is not content to settle for a standoff between fragmentary percepts, a world without given form, and a homeless or centreless self: *thinking* the difference between representation and substance is thinking 'into' the reality of being humanly conscious, being a person. We become human in the act of finding a place to stand within the irreducibly difficult and mobile interweaving of diverse presentations of what is there for our minds, grasping that to know something in the world is not to arrive at a final structural scheme for it but to inhabit a process of discovery in which there is always more otherness to encounter, the otherness of new perspective and new requirements for 'negotiation'. The difference of representation and substance is not the difference between what is ambiguous or misleading and what is real: 'it is a difference that must be philosophically comprehended precisely because it can never be existentially removed.'[20]

The importance of this is in relation to the twofold danger from which Hegel (interpreted in this way) delivers us. We may be lured into a pure postmodern dualism (see above) of compromised speech and silent, formless, non-historical interiority, or into a pre-critical revival of would-be simple representation, representation without mediation (what we see is real; what we are persuaded to see by the prevailing forms of cultural power is real; what is 'seen' by any cultural other is unreal and dangerous) – which is what has been understood to be the essence of fascism in its various forms (from naked and violent hegemonies right through to the totalizing voices of populist culture).[21] And to go back to our basic question about representation, we need to read Hegel in something like this way. *Darstellung* and *Vorstellung* (let's say, roughly, 'imaginative deployment of sensuous depiction' and 'analogical objectification') are not some sort of primitive and embarrassing version of human thinking that sophistication and self-awareness must leave behind (as if Hegel were a sort of James Frazer figure, telling us a story of the emancipation of 'reasonable' thought from magic and cult). They are quite simply the matter, the actuality, of thinking. What needs to happen is not that they should be forced into retirement in the face of better qualified candidates, but that we should learn to recognize the

20 Ibid., p. 290.
21 Nigel Tubbs, *Education in Hegel* (London: Continuum, 2008), p.74.

implication of our thinking selves in the work of imagination and analogy. When we think with images, either in art or in religion, we are genuinely *thinking*: that's to say, we are coming more and more fully to 'inhabit' our humanity, to see ourselves and question ourselves and ultimately to grasp the convergence of human agency towards a reconciled future in which the narrative of my own growth into 'absolute' knowing is inseparably fused with the narrative of every possible or actual human subject. This may or may not be an intelligible or possible future,[22] but it cannot be reduced to a vacuous hope for a future that is 'rational' *as opposed to* imaginative or religious, a future of unmediated universal reasonableness. Hegel's universalism is of another order, involving the distinctive labour of recognizing the self in the other.

But that is another and larger story. Our present point is to do with what he is and is not saying about 'representation'. *Vorstellung* is not some kind of second-best or a barrier between mind and reality: it is the moment in which (i) one's self-presence is fused with the intelligible presence of a material other and (ii) this fusion is already grasped as in some way a vehicle for self-understanding, for thought's recognition of itself (which is not necessarily the case for *Darstellung* alone in Hegel's scheme). Mind does not have to detach itself from the particularity of this moment to discover some more abstract or immaterial truth which will replace it. So the act of representing, so far from being a flight, as we might say, from substance to substitute, is an act which simultaneously recognizes the other, the 'object', as thoroughly bound in to the life of the subject, and recognizes the self, the 'subject', as invested in the object – so that conventional categories of inner and outer, mind and matter, are suspended and transformed ('sublated', in the usual idiom of English versions of Hegel). To shift the vocabulary a little, we could say that representation *performs* what it refers to: it enacts the mutual investment of subject and object. It is not a matter of creating a new object which might stand in for the immediate datum of perception; rather it claims that for any element in the environment in which we live, there is

22 See Adams, op. cit., p. 111 on the problems of moving so cavalierly from the analysis of our logic to a renewed social order; but note his remark that Hegel, as a Christian, saw a 'perpetually available alternative to our damaged life; even if we constantly refuse it, it always remains a possibility.'

an irreducible (and central or focal) dimension of its reality which is *its life in speaking and thinking*. What confronts us has something in common with a musical score: we treat it as an ordered set of instructions that will shape an ordered act that translates what is 'there' into a series of actions, words, gestures which may superficially have no resemblance at all to it.

So I am taking Hegel's language about representation – a vast topic in itself, whose surface I have barely scratched here – as consistent, in significant respects, with the usage proposed in this book. *Vorstellung* is a moment in the self's recognition of itself as already materially situated, already 'spoken to' (receiving intelligible form into itself). Representing is performing or enacting a form of being in a new mode; it presupposes that subject and object are not two items standing alongside each other needing to be connected by publicly agreed tokens of reference, but two phases in a complex life. Representing does indeed carry information, but a representative form does not exist simply as a vehicle for a set of propositions. Hence the fact that representations of one set of data may be significantly diverse yet aspire to truthfulness or adequacy or 'aptness'. And approaching the question in this way allows us also an important flexibility in thinking of a representation's adequacy to the possible emotional content of a situation; figural varieties of visual art (importantly including photography[23]) seek to challenge stereotypical images and stock or sentimental responses and thus to induce a more adequate – in the sense of a less restricted or predictable – reception of what is perceived. In consequence, they are habitually caught up in self-critical questions about how far an image may seek to *control* rather than simply facilitate a response, and so become entangled in the seductions of representations pretending to be unmediated presence.[24] What matters is that it is possible to argue about the emotional directiveness of a work and the ambiguities of seeking emotional control in the context of a commitment to representational adequacy. A sentimental or propagandistic work identifies itself as one which reduces rather than enhancing possibilities of response by implicitly claiming one emotional position as the 'obvious' or 'natural' one. But equally to idealize some fiction

23 A point I owe to Sangduck Kim of New College, Edinburgh, in his seminar response to the Gifford Lectures.
24 See above, note 23.

of an emotion-free image has precisely the same difficulty. Discernments around these matters are the flesh and blood of proper critical argument.

I am aware that 'representation' has an important *political* sense which would again require a longer discussion than is possible here. But the last paragraph points towards where connections might be made with what we have been considering. There are those who, following Rousseau, assume that the essence of political action is the confluence of unmediated or unrepresented agency on the part of citizens. But this can have dangerous implications: there is little or nothing here to prevent majoritarian tyranny. A mature democracy is more than decision-making by plebiscite majorities, because there will always be perspectives that are not 'represented' in the outcome of such a process – the very young, the minorities of diverse kinds, the variously disabled or disenfranchised whose voice is not audible but whose interests are inseparably bound to those of the majority in so far as they constitute with them the actual political/social community. If that is the case, representation or mediation is inevitable: the individual political agent has to confront the question of how citizens speak for each other and for non-citizens – how the interest of the other or the stranger *informs* and is *performed* by any one civic agent, and how the interest of any one civic agent (because it is ultimately invested in the interest of all) requires mediation that is negotiated through channels other than the direct expression of wants: through legality, in plain English – the mediated processes of a society seeking to accord equal respect to every member and thus challenging or restraining the individual's 'unmediated' account of his or her needs. To represent someone in a complex and legally ordered political process is not to reproduce an unexamined version of their interests: politics properly conceived is a business in which such versions are tested, negotiated and modified so as to become genuinely political concerns rather than an agglomeration of individual wants. This is a substantial question asking for more discussion, but it is worth noting where some of the issues involved link up with apparently very different concerns about speech and understanding.

This painfully brief and jejune survey of some of the debates around the meanings of representation is intended simply to indicate that, although the senses given to the word in modern philosophy are diverse, there is a convergent set of issues connected with it   the difference between representing and imitating or substituting, the character of mediation as what enables us to recognize our act in the other and the other's act in us, and the need to understand truth as more than the correspondence of formal elements in a structure. We have looked at the technicalities of contemporary discussions of the properties of consciousness, at the need to locate claims about representation within a coherent system of symbolization, at what Hegel does and does not say and (fleetingly) at the parallel but equally absorbing debates about the meaning of representation in politics. As a long footnote to the main argument of my text, it may help to suggest some of the unfinished business which might emerge from that text: the tasks of filling out the basic notion of a relation to our surrounding reality which is both serious in its claim to (defensible levels of) adequacy and critical of unfeasibly narrow models of what counts as truthful presentation. To defend a view which seeks to do justice to both the constrained and the creative in our speaking about and apprehending of the world is, I believe, an imperative in a culture where one or the other seems in constant danger of being forgotten, in shapeless ideas of liberty and autonomy or in mechanical notions of what counts as 'real' or 'hard' knowledge. And the job of theology is surely to join in the struggle against the dehumanizing prospects of both these distortions.

INDEX